Revealed

Revealed

Spiritual Reality in a Makeover World

Linda Clare and Kristen Johnson Ingram

Revell
Grand Rapids, Michigan

© 2005 by Linda Clare and Kristen Johnson Ingram

Published by Fleming H. Revell
a division of Baker Publishing Group
P.O. Box 6287, Grand Rapids, MI 49516-6287

Printed in the United States of America

Library of Congress Cataloging-in-Publication Data
Clare, Linda, 1952-
　　Revealed : spiritual reality in a makeover world / Linda Clare and Kristen
Johnson Ingram.
　　　　p.　　cm.
　　Includes bibliographical references.
　　ISBN 0-8007-5935-4 (pbk.)
　　1. Feminist theology. I. Ingram, Kristen Johnson. II. Title.
BT83.55.C55　2005
248.8′.43—dc22　　　　　　　　　　　　　　　　　　2005013381

For women who have waited
all their lives for this book.

Contents

Contents

Welcome to a Spiritual Spa

An Introduction

Your Spa Day

A Call to Transformation

If you're lucky, you've experienced a day of rejuvenation now and then. You pamper yourself—refresh your skin, hair, and nails; enjoy a catered lunch. Maybe you indulge in a complete body wrap at the spa or relax your mind with soothing music and peaceful surroundings. Yet you sense there's something missing. Something deeper and lasting . . .

In today's makeover-crazed world, change looks easy, at least on TV. Try a new outfit, hairdo, or manicure, and voilà! You're a new person.

Maybe.

More likely, down deep, you and God know the same old troubles lurk. You're overwhelmed, harried, frenzied. Plain worn out. You worry about your appearance, your status, finances, relationships. What you really long for is total transformation.

This book is your guide to a spiritual makeover, but not in an atmosphere of self-indulgence or faux chic. God's idea of transformation targets you as a whole person, in a setting more like a quiet retreat than a noisy salon.

Revealed will guide you through this retreat. The structure allows you to go on your own, in the company of a friend, or with your small group. Each chapter begins with our dialogue as authors and friends asking hard questions about what it means to be a modern woman of Christ. Following are reflective stories from our lives and other women's. Near the beginning and end of each chapter you'll find a salon led by Kris

15

for reflecting upon Scripture and the issues women of Bible times confronted—the passages that show how transformation happens (or not). Along the way of this retreat, you'll experience personal inspirations and poems by additional gifted and insightful women to help you in your physical, emotional, and spiritual life. Prepare to:

- Call out your own beauty in the Salon.
- Balance daily life in the Workout Area.
- Rest with God in the Wind-Chime Atrium.
- Relax your schedule in the Aromatherapy Alcove.
- Cleanse in the Mud-Bath Room.
- Consider your community at the Massage Table.
- Contemplate relationships next to God's Reflecting Pool.
- Nourish yourself with God's grace at a Luncheon.
- Experience healing in the Hot Springs.
- Fire-walk with God on the Lawn.

Revealed, you'll find, is a journey, in which real women talk about real issues. The stories show the cost of transformation. Each woman's willingness to engage in the questions will reassure you that you are not alone. Our yearnings are shared; God knows every one. He is there with us, and he will be our guide.

We hope you'll emerge a new you—both to others and yourself. As those makeover shows and the apostle Paul often taught, the big reveal celebrates putting on the new self.

You can experience transformation. In fact, you are welcome. God invites you right now. Walk with us.

1
Check-In

Dare to Transform

Life loves to be taken by the lapel and told, "I'm with you, kid. Let's go!"

Maya Angelou

Beyond Faux

Kris: Okay, just what is this spiritual reality that we're talking about?

Linda: To me, it's total transformation, something like a spiritual makeover.

Kris: Everyone seems to want a makeover these days. It's all over TV, in all the magazines. But what we see there is usually an outer change: a coat of paint, new light fixtures, a haircut, an updated wardrobe. When you talk about spiritual makeover, who changes? Me? God? And how? Is it from the outside in or the inside out?

Linda: Maybe it can be both, inside-out and outside-in. God's always worked in all kinds of ways.

Kris: True. I change from the outside when I start a spiritual practice, such as prayer or meditation or fasting. And one can change from inside when making new decisions that transform everyday life.

Linda: But exactly what do you mean by *transform*?

Kris: Transfiguration, really—as when Jesus was suddenly changed on the mountain before three disciples' eyes. Who changed? Did Jesus suddenly become the Christ, talking to Moses and Elijah and wearing dazzling white clothes? Or were the disciples able for the first time to see him as he always really was? Either way, I want to be so transfigured so that my *real* self, the ideal that God created, shines out of me.

Linda: That *real person* you mention—how is she different? That's worth exploring more. The real person is the woman we're looking for, a woman who's tired of hiding behind a mask of niceness.

Kris: What do you mean, the real person won't be nice anymore?

Linda: I'm talking about living in grace and being authentic instead of being dishonest for the sake of politeness or how others might feel. For example, if I behave according to my real feelings, I might be grumpy, angry, or sad, and I can either cover up those true feelings and thoughts with a mask of nice politeness, or I can acknowledge that I'm flawed but God loves me anyway. I'm then at least being honest.

Kris: Oh, nonsense. Too many women like you won't even admit there's a perfect Linda, a God-created woman, inside you. You see yourselves as flawed and unfit and unlovable to everyone except *maybe* God, and even then, you think God has you on probation.

Linda: Stop it. I'm not ready.

Kris: Imagine if we could look at that more closely, help one another realize that what's inside is beautiful and sacred.

Linda: Mmmm. That's the point, isn't it, to find the connection with one another and God in faith? But we're not talking about "anything goes," or uncivilized behavior, are we? We're talking about going beyond the clichés and ideas that we've read about in too many Christian books, heard from pulpits, or bought into and mimicked, then told one another in small groups. We want to find real examples, real women who face today's challenges and still look for a deeper life with God. We're after revealing how a direct relationship with God brings out beauty and releases you into a new spiritual freedom instead of relying on automatic Christian responses to social and personal situations. It sounds risky, yes, to be truthful instead of shallow and saccharine.

Kris: But *truthful* isn't synonymous with *unpleasant*. The real truth is beautiful. Jesus is alive and wants you and me to be alive. I think he was transfigured and shining all the time, and that the disciples were changed for a moment so they could see who and what he was and is. And that's what I want God to do for me: Transform me. Reveal me to myself and to the world. Make me fit for the kingdom.

Linda: Maybe I'm more ready than I thought . . .

One Size Doesn't Fit All

I love being comfortable. So, when one of the first verses I read as a new, born-again believer was Colossians 3:9–10, where we're told to "put on the new self" (NIV), the idea appealed to me. I thought it would be easy to lay aside my ugly, tattered life like the tight clothing I loathe. I was ready to don a brand-new self, preferably without gaping holes or confining waistbands. I thought spiritual change would be easy, like walking into a salon and coming out looking fabulous.

I didn't realize that becoming a Christian isn't a one-size-fits-all endeavor. This wasn't good news for someone who had so many problems: marriage to an alcoholic, chronic health issues, an infant son to raise without the support system of family, which was far away. I was trying to do it all but failing miserably. Desperate for comfort, wanting only to fall into the arms of Jesus and experience sudden perfection, I was baffled. Where was the transformation of Jesus I'd been promised?

Transformation was the main reason I was attracted to Christianity. To experience rebirth sounded like a second chance to me, a new opportunity to trade in the old me for a brand-new version.

If "re-birthdays" count, I had mine in 1979. I came to God after I had checked out every other possible solution. For two years I'd chased down tarot-card readers and astrologers, aura healers and cults that proclaimed the inner Christ. With my new husband I tilted tables and conjured spirits via Ouija boards. We prayed to Jesus. And Buddha. And a bunch of other inner gods whose names I've forgotten. I had a collection of books about metaphysics and wore baggy clothing. With the rest of the cult members my husband and I sang "Love Is the Only Power," but I was lonely. I wasn't sure why, but I suspected that my loved ones didn't see the cult as the answer. Worst of all, I still felt like the same old miserable person I was before.

Most of my old friends stopped calling me, and my co-workers at the little art supply store gave me funny looks if I mentioned my newfound "religious" views. Even my mother, who'd hauled me to sunrise services once a year on Easter Sunday, begged me to give up the cult. It was a crazy time, all right. I came away not believing much of anything except the raw facts: the cult was full of losers like me, and my spouse was a raging alcoholic.

So I turned to pop-psychology books. I learned about games people play and that my inner child was begging to get out. When that didn't help, I went to Al-Anon. Nothing wrong with those things . . . except that I sensed a bottomless void inside myself, the one they say is God-shaped. Still I was afraid to go near any church, especially the Protestant church of my Easter Sundays. I was afraid that in surrendering to Christianity, I'd be transformed, but not by God. In particular I worried that the saintly and the sanctified would demand a makeover. They'd find my shattered life so full of omissions that they'd see right through the façade I had by then so carefully built.

For five years I hid the craziness brought on by my husband's alcoholism. I told my family and friends little white lies: he was working late, or he was out of town. I knew the situation was pathetic and dangerous, but I couldn't bear to let anyone know the truth.

Then one day my husband landed in the local jail for driving while intoxicated. In an instant I saw Jesus holding out his hands to me. I decided to give God a try, for which my sister and mom were relieved and very thankful. I told everyone who would listen about my new born-again status. Overnight I became an avid Bible reader. I attended church three times a week and twice on Sunday. I even got baptized in San Diego's Mission Bay. Yet deep inside, I had a hidden agenda: to become a "good" Christian others could look up to or at least think was "walking the walk."

With a lot of effort and some adjustments to my book collection and wardrobe, I'd be able to conquer sin myself and unfurl my own banner of victory in Jesus, right? What could be more pure?

I didn't know it at the time, but what I really longed for was approval and a place to hide from family problems. The women in my nondenominational church provided me with guidance and biblical instruction, friendship and role models. I learned to cook and to quilt. I started Scotch-taping Bible verses on the bathroom mirror, above the toilet, over the kitchen sink. With my husband's disease getting worse by the day, I sat in the pew (or on the folding chair in the high-school gym), sang "maranatha" songs, and volunteered in the church nursery with my saintly sisters. As soon as I learned enough Scripture and attended enough Bible study, I reasoned, surely the ladies would think of me as a good Christian.

Those women weren't phonies. Their attitudes were genuine: they sought to please God and their spouses. It's just that I was striving to put on a self that didn't fit me. Instead of transformed, I felt downright miserable.

An unnamed longing filled me. My college education was dismissed as "humanism." Most of the women in my circle read the Bible and little else. Other literature, including masterpieces by authors such as Tolstoy and Hemingway, were suspect. The women even exposed the children to "Christian Mother Goose" because the original verses were too gruesome and worldly. The intellectual stimulation I craved didn't fit into the model of Proverbs 31—yet another area where I failed to be good enough.

Meanwhile, my husband grew more distant and came home drunk more often. The more I tried to smile, the more I found myself sobbing at church. I kept a wad of tissues in my purse at all times, because as soon as Jesus came near, whether in prayer or in song, I immediately fell apart. I told the women who saw me leave I had a nervous stomach, but I always slid back into my seat with smudged mascara and a red nose.

I tried so hard to project the image of a solid, upstanding Christian woman. I stopped wearing baggy clothes and dressed as well as I could. Although I couldn't afford manicures or hair salons, I made up for it with my smile. I volunteered, baked casseroles, and made baby quilts. But after several years of intense worship and study, the only leadership role the other church women wanted me for was to help toddlers scribble with fat crayons and to sing "Jesus Loves Me" with the children.

I'd failed the test and was not going to become a good Christian, no matter what I did. I wasn't even sure I was qualified to call myself a real Christian, period. I stopped going to all but Sunday morning services and was too tired and discouraged to volunteer. All I wanted was to become invisible, just fade away.

By the next fall I'd separated from my husband. I had two sons by that time and wasn't sure Jesus loved any of us. The ladies in my Bible study probably wondered what had happened to me. I never told them I was leaving; I just took the kids to Mom's house in another state. After all, they thought my husband simply traveled in his job and that's why he didn't come to church. That's what I'd told them. I couldn't let them know the real story or the real me. To them, to God, even to myself, I was stuffed into a role that wasn't my size.

Living that way, I felt as squeezed as if I had wriggled into a pair of too-tight panty hose. I was suffocating. There were so many things to remember, things that didn't come naturally to me. I couldn't keep my Scripture references straight—I kept getting Job and Jonah mixed up. I thought my Christian image counted most, and it took an enormous amount of energy to maintain it. My "quest for excellence" approach to Christian living somehow had become tangled with my cultural values and my desperate need for love and acceptance.

And I hurt inside, an empty pain I couldn't quite describe. Longing for a deeper experience with God, I was dying to break free of the "shoulds" and "oughts" that weighed me down. As long as I was more interested in what others thought of me than I was about what God thought, I could never be real, much less good. A phony. For too many years I stayed away from church altogether, afraid I could never measure up.

But God had other plans. What had started out as a spiritual transformation had fizzled on the altar of self-improvement. I wanted to be a good Christian woman for all the wrong reasons, and, instead of putting on a new self, I just wore bigger holes in the old me. It was as if Jesus's admonition about pouring new wine into old skins was written just for me.

When those holes got too large to mend, I finally surrendered, but not without a battle. Troubles with my sons, unexpected health problems, and other frayed places in my messy life kept me clinging to fear and doubt. Once again I wondered if God cared at all about me, about my family, about anybody.

Then one day I was getting dressed in a casual and roomy outfit for the cold winter's day. The fleecy sweater and warm trousers fit my mood and my comfort zone. "Put on the new self," I heard myself say. I smiled and took a deep breath. I noticed how much happier I was when I wore clothes that didn't bind or constrict.

Perhaps it was my crazy, ripped-up "good Christian" ideas that had fueled my fear and loneliness. Maybe there was more to being good than squeezing myself into a one-size-fits-all lifestyle. Maybe God did care after all.

I was skeptical at first, but I agreed to join a Bible study group for the first time in years. The other women were patient and watched as I changed my mind about God's love. We each picked a Scripture to study and I complained, but eventually I began to experience a revival of my faith. Only then did I see God peering at me through the thin excuses I'd used to avoid my spiritual side.

In my tight little world, the pressure became unbearable. I floundered around for years, until God graciously helped my husband into recovery and instructed me (over and over) to forget trying to do everything "right." God keeps nudging me, whispering that there is so much more. God extends a welcoming hand to all those who seek the tranquility, comfort, and challenge of change. In God's spa I've found a depth of love that is so enormous I can't understand it, and with that love, a loving God.

When I first started writing this book, I didn't realize how much it would cost me. Some of my early drafts brimmed with hurt, anger, or tired Christian ideas I've read in many other places. Then Kristen said she felt God was saying, "Dare."

Dare to be real? Dare to be changed? As I wrote, I began to experience the transformations about which I wrote. And they were costly. New dimensions forced me out of a predictable Christianity, into a real relationship with God. I'm not saying my relationship wasn't real before, but now my changes are something like eating well-seasoned food after years of eating cardboard.

My spiritual hunger has awakened, but the meal doesn't come cheap. In exchange for new dimensions, God insists on owning everything I am. And I have to pony up every single day. So as much as I'm able, I dare to crawl each day toward God.

These days, every time I get into my comfy clothes I know I am being transformed. Along with you, I can be who I am and sit at the feet of Jesus, and we don't need to look or act a certain way to do it. The words "put on the new self" take on new meaning for me now. God wants you and me to experience the "big reveal," but only if we're willing to shed our flimsy images and clothe ourselves with God through Jesus Christ. With a love so complete, can we afford to settle for anything less?

Reflection

Let's choose today to quench our thirst for the "good life" we think others lead by acknowledging the good that already exists in our lives. We can then offer the universe the gift of our grateful hearts.
Sarah Ban Breathnach

Kristen Johnson Ingram

Mirror, Mirror

Mirror, Mirror on the wall, who is fairest of them all?

Snow White

What kind of mirror do you use? You might dress in front of a full-length glass on your closet door, or perhaps you have to share the bathroom mirror on hurried mornings. Maybe you comb your hair before an ornate gold-framed one over your dresser. Whatever your mirror, how important its placement is in your house and how long you stand in front of your reflection may tell you a lot about yourself.

When I was growing up, I used a looking glass in a bird's-eye maple frame, a mirror made before the Civil War. Although the glass had aged with cloudy and spotted corners, I thought the mottled surface was interesting and I could see even more than I wanted of myself in the clear part at the center.

My nose was too small, my hair too fine. I tended to have circles under my eyes. I made facial masques out of egg whites and honey and rubbed my teeth with a cut lemon to whiten them. Like most young girls, I spent a lot of time alternately loving and hating my hair (I usually hated it in the morning before school) and trying different shades of lipstick. I spent more and more time pinning my hair up or twisting it into French braids, trying to find my best "look." And like most of my friends, I had no idea who I was, so my mirror became the place I looked for my identity.

We all did it. Young girls try themselves on the way they hold clothes up to themselves in stores. Society egged us on, reminding us that what mattered was what showed. Of course, I never had a safety pin in my underwear because—as most girls of my generation learned—I might be in an accident and the nurses would see the pin and be scandalized. Cosmetic companies filled magazines with their ads, and quasi-cartoons depicted husbands who avoided their wives because the women didn't use the right deodorant or douche powder or hand lotion. *Beauty* and *femininity* were the watchwords: a woman's job was to be beautiful and make her husband happy.

So my friends and I grew up polishing our outer selves, and I believed I was that self. We worked hard to be pretty and we did what was right, but for the wrong reasons: we were our parents' and the school's mirrors. Our grades reflected on our parents, so we nice Christian girls usually made straight As. Although I have a painful spinal curve, I stood ramrod straight to honor my parents and ancestors. I practiced breathing with a Los Angeles telephone book on my stomach and plucked my eyebrows to match those I saw in the movies, so I'd be a credit to my school, my parents, God, and anyone else who had a claim on me.

But we girls also expressed restlessness and a longing for something more, whatever that was, and we struggled with what Scripture said. We especially stumbled over Peter's insistence that "your beauty should not come from outward adornment, such as braided hair and the wearing of gold jewelry and fine clothes. Instead, it should be that of your inner self, the unfading beauty of a gentle and quiet spirit, which is of great worth in God's sight. For this is the way the holy women of the past who put their hope in God used to make themselves beautiful" (1 Pet. 3:3–5 NIV).

Hoo, boy. Now we were in trouble. The world and the fashionable women at church were whispering into one of our ears, and the Bible yelled in the other. I wasn't sure whether I should wear high heels and makeup or copy my Mennonite friends, with their modest demeanor and covered and uncut hair. I didn't know whether I could wear cool clothes and two pairs of earrings and still get that quiet and gentle spirit. Could having such a spirit automatically preclude glamour, or would I have to wash my face with tar soap and wear a shapeless Mother Hubbard?

My old mirror got too discolored to use, so I bought a new cherrywood dresser. And I kept telling God I didn't like my face without some makeup: I had a rosy rash on my cheeks, and my Scandinavian eyelashes were so pale that I looked expressionless. I loved the beads I once bought in Istanbul and the earrings my husband had given me for my last birthday. So I prayed and studied and wondered.

And then I saw through the looking glass.

While preparing to lead a retreat, I read about the ancient tabernacle and found the words: "He [Moses] made the basin of bronze with its stand of bronze, from the mirrors of the women who served at the entrance to the tent of meeting" (Exod. 38:8).

Oh. *Oh!* Here was truth at last. The women of the exodus loved God so much they not only served at the door of the tabernacle, but they let God change them from beauty-seeking to beautiful. They gave their mirrors. Their *mirrors*.

This has nothing to do with mascara or no mascara; it has something to do with the spirit you bring to God. I could wear six pairs of earrings and still be within the will of God so long as I laid my vanity before the throne and boasted not of my beauty but, like Saint Paul, boasted of Christ.

A mirror is dangerous if all you adorn yourself with are braids and jewels and Estée Lauder foundation cream, if you spend too much time trying to look good, even to yourself. Because that's vanity. But God is only a sigh away, waiting to transform that vanity. And us.

Reflection

The best and most beautiful things in the world cannot be seen, nor touched . . . but are felt in the heart.

Helen Keller

Kathleen Ruckman

The Gem Within

Crystals grew inside rock like arithmetic flowers. They lengthened and spread, added plane to plane in an awed and perfect obedience to an absolute geometry that even stones—maybe only the stones—understood.

Annie Dillard

I spotted the geode in the science museum. I had often admired rocks with hidden treasures, such as a purple amethyst in its glory or agate thunder eggs cracked open to reveal what looks like the ocean, an orange sunset, and even a tiny bird flying overhead. From the back, the bumpy gray-brown rock might be something I'd trip over on a hike; but its inner splendor amazed me. Dazzling white, its crystal planes kept me in awe. There it was a gem, hidden in nature until broken open to reveal its beauty.

I am like that hard, lumpy rock. I walk in darkness until I am cracked open, and the light shines on me. The light reflects the gem, outward and upward. But I have to be cut open, and my heart exposed, for true transformation to take place.

Transformation of the deepest kind came when I was eleven years old. Some would say I was just a shy, young girl, who grew up in a steel-mill town, who didn't need conversion. But regardless of age or circumstance, I needed a Savior who would start my ultimate transformation.

Most of the people in my hometown of Johnstown, Pennsylvania, were Slovak and had immigrated to start a small congregation in the valley, near the steel mill. The little white church, dusted with pink from the iron ore, stood out among tall row houses. During sermons I often heard the whistle of trains pulling coal and steel. I'd glance at my grandmother singing in Slovak, her babushka wrapped around her sweet face. The saints there possessed a gem deep inside their hearts, so it wasn't hard for me to want that same treasure. I knew those saints had struggled to come to America. I also knew that the greatest possessions in their crates and trunks, on their way to Ellis Island, were their Slovak Bibles.

Each year, my siblings, cousins, and I stayed for one week at the church's camp meeting in Ohio, where people sang simultaneously in Slovak and in English, and where I heard the gospel preached.

One night in July, the pastor gave a message and invited anyone who wanted to pray to come to the altar. Just eleven years old, I felt drawn to go forward, and as the Slovak pastor from our home church prayed with me in broken English, I was transformed.

A desire to read the Bible almost burned in my heart the next morning. I began with Genesis and read as often as I could. I found the Bible to be inexhaustible in its wisdom, and I began to apply that wisdom to my everyday life. Its promises stirred me and began to chisel the rock inside me—and I found that God's truth transforms.

I began to see where I needed to be chiseled and carved, and what needed to be cut out or polished. The Stonecutter gently began his work in me and I discovered that when God's light shines, I can reflect more, like a prism, whose refractions dance on the wall. Alone, encased in rock, I could never have experienced what life was meant to be.

After my confrontation with God at the altar that night, I began to pray constantly. I remember walking to school as a little girl and thanking God for the blue sky and flowers on the trees. Prayer became like breathing, since God was as close as my next breath.

Since transformation is active, I'm still being changed as I pray, commune with God, and listen for his voice, sometimes even in bursts of thankfulness and praise. Prayer transforms me by taking my mind off my troubles and the selfishness that tries to creep in.

Scripture promises me that I am like a royal diadem in God's crown. Could I really be one of his crown jewels? That fact makes suffering bearable, because hardships are not worthy to compare to the glory we will see some day.

The sparkling geometry of the designs in that white crystal geode reminds me that my Creator is also making something beautiful out of me. And I will be finally transformed on the day when I see him face-to-face.

According to the apostle Paul, "It is the God who commanded light to shine out of darkness, who has shone in our hearts to give the light of the knowledge of the glory of God in the face of Jesus Christ. But we have this treasure in earthen vessels, that the excellence of the power may be of God and not of us" (2 Cor. 4:6–7 NKJV).

Ideas for Reflection & Application

Something to Try On

- Look for a small stone that you can carry in your pocket. Carry it for one week or more. Now memorize Revelation 2:17: "To him who overcomes I will give some of the hidden manna to eat. And I will give him a white stone, and on the stone a new name written which no one knows except him who receives it" (NKJV). Every time your hand touches the stone remember God's promise to transform the ones who believe in him and love him. Let this promise, by the reminder of the stone, encourage you to endure in faith.

- "Having work done" is a popular phrase that means you're getting a face-lift or liposuction or a hair transplant. Everyone can see the results, because you can look twenty years younger. How about getting some "spiritual work" done? Start a new plan for sacred reading and prayer. If you stick to the plan, those practices will renew you and make your spirit beautiful, so that everyone can see.

- For a whole day, go without looking in a mirror. Brush your teeth without looking up, dress and comb your hair by feel, not sight (you'll probably save this exercise for a day off), and ignore or cover all the mirrors in the house. At the end of the day, still not looking in a mirror, write in your journal at least two sentences about how you feel.

2
You in the
Salon

Calling Up Beauty

I think miracles exist in part as gifts and in part as clues
that there is something beyond the flat world we see.

Peggy Noonan

Pretty Is as Pretty Does

Linda: Of all the topics Christian women talk about, appearance is the thorniest. We can't decide when looking clean and healthy turns into vanity. Here we are at God's spa, and yet I'm not sure how much attention to pay to my appearance.

Kris: We go over and over this, year after year, but we don't come to a universal conclusion. I guess every woman has to make her own decision about beauty and glamour and appearance.

Linda: You're right, but every woman also must strike a balance between looking good and taking care of her spiritual beauty.

Kris: How does a woman do that? What's the balance point?

Linda: You stop when beauty or plastic surgery or tooth veneers become addiction.

Kris: I saw a woman on *Oprah* who had endured twenty-six plastic surgeries and still wanted some more. She talked about the times she went through her house, finding things to sell so she could have more surgery. She had a beautiful young daughter who apparently got attention only from her father, because her mom was so preoccupied with her face and body.

Linda: That is addiction. I wish I could tell her that God loves her.

Kris: You don't think she knows that?

37

Linda: I'm assuming her insatiable quest to improve her appearance is a spiritual problem. If she could understand how much God loves her, maybe she could be more satisfied with her face and body.

Kris: I'm still not certain where you stop or start. Most Christian women think it's okay to wear makeup and stylish hair, but they would probably stop at having breast implants. I dunno, Linda. What we're saying is that if you seek the kingdom first, you'll be beautiful in God's eyes. Is that enough for you?

Linda: Well, pretty is as pretty does. Right?

In the Salon

Linda Clare

Does God Host
Extreme Makeover?

Beauty of style and harmony and grace and good rhythm depend on simplicity.

Plato

Watch any of the popular television "makeover" shows—from *Trading Spaces* to *Oprah*—and when the new look is revealed, the reaction you'll often hear is, "Oh, my God!" Are many of the participants really thinking about God? Probably not. It's a shame that people use God's name so casually, but if God did host *Extreme Makeover*, I wonder what it would be like.

The Bible says, "So do not worry, saying, 'What shall we eat?' or . . . 'What shall we wear?'" (Matt. 6:31 NIV) and "Your adornment must not be merely external—braiding the hair, and wearing gold jewelry, or putting on dresses" (1 Pet. 3:3 NASB). Does God ask us to give up fashionable clothing and stop wearing makeup? Does God want us completely plain?

Some think so. That's their right. Yet most of us land someplace between Tammy Faye Bakker's opulence and Amish simplicity. God created beauty along with everything else, and many women believe God wants us to be the best we can be.

There's no denying that the modern Christian woman is involved in a cultural tug-of-war: she can either distance herself from any form of outer adornment, separating herself from worldly pursuits of beauty and fashion, or she can bow to the pressure exerted by media and strive to look slim, chic, and in step with the latest trends.

Both beauty experts and the Bible often give conflicting advice. On one hand, psychologists sometimes chide women for putting too much stock in appearances, reminding us it's what's inside that counts. Scripture says that God looks at the heart.

But just as you and I start to gain comfort in our plain selves, the women God created, we hear the other side of the argument. We've been told to look as attractive as possible in order to emulate Proverbs 31, or at least keep ourselves fit and trim. By the time we reach adulthood, and sometimes long before, most of us know beauty is much more than a simple matter. It's the gray area of how we look and what we aspire to possess that is much more complex. And it is the complexity of appearance that keeps some of us in a spiritual quandary as we navigate our way through Western life.

In the fitness movement of the 1970s, women began to challenge the notion that when they reached a "certain age" they could abandon their bodies to the aging process. Jane Fonda gave women a perhaps unrealistic view of how they should look, even if they had celebrated one too many birthdays. Today, in the twenty-first century, those early changes have been taken to their extremes.

No longer are women content to be physically fit. I heard somewhere that the average American woman is five feet, four inches tall and a size twelve, yet magazines typically feature models who are five-foot-ten and wear sizes four to six. Young girls are tempted to alter their bodies permanently through plastic surgery or destructive eating and exercise regimes, while fast-food eating habits hurtle them toward obesity. Women of any age must come to terms with a culture that stresses fatty foods and at the same time exhorts them to remain waiflike.

Even in churches across the country, Sunday services become fashion shows. Sometimes the idea of "Sunday best" becomes a competition for the most stylish clothes or the most expensive car in the parking lot. Sermons may be punctuated with golfing anecdotes, as America's middle class becomes more class-conscious.

Some would say that women should stick to no makeup and plain clothing as a way to eliminate these problems. Certain sects of Christianity, such as the Amish and Mennonites, have dealt with the question of beauty in this way for centuries. Yet for many women, their denomination and values don't call for such strict measures. Women who desire to climb higher spiritually often ask the same question: *Where do I draw the fashion and beauty line?*

The real question becomes not what rules God demands you and I uphold—whether to wear makeup or jewelry, color our hair or get liposuction—but instead, how does the attention we pay to our bodies influence our relationship with others and with God?

Vanity and self-absorption are usually only desperate attempts at overcoming inadequacy or feelings of inferiority. We all need and want to be loved, and we have no doubt that God created beauty to help us enjoy and appreciate life. It's the niggling details that can trip us up: Is it okay to straighten our teeth but not our noses? How can a woman justify a breast reduction or implants? How much is too much?

Transformation requires radical questions. It forces you to dare to think of God in bigger ways than you've ever been able to do.

"I am convinced that the calling to spiritual transformation is a call to freedom," Ruth Haley Barton says in *The Truths That Free Us*—"the freedom to be completely given over to God and to others in love in any given moment. It is the freedom to live from an inner security that leads us beyond self-interest, self-consciousness, and self-protection. It is the freedom to live beyond the expectations and limitations placed on us by others."[1]

You owe it yourself to see what kind of freedom you can grow into, a freedom balanced by biblical principles and common sense.

Here I am with you, volunteering for an extreme makeover. We've arrived at the place where God invites women to be transformed. This first stop is the Salon, where we may change our appearances as well as our attitudes. Here you'll hear honest conversations about those issues.

The Salon is all about trying to find balance. We don't pretend to know all the answers about beauty. We don't want to become self-centered and vain, but we don't want to cringe when we see our reflections either. If you struggle with the boundaries and barriers of our physical world and sincerely want to strike a balance that pleases God, you've come to the right place.

In the physical aspects of your Christian life, it's okay to start wherever you are. Just don't worry too much about it. The grass of the field is alive today and tomorrow is cast into the furnace, Jesus said, so we ought to have faith that God will take care of us. Besides, God probably never will host *Extreme Makeover*. He's more interested in makeovers of the heart.

Reflection

People are like stained glass windows: the true beauty can be seen only when there is light from within. The darker the night, the brighter the windows.

Elisabeth Kübler-Ross

The Bride's Story

A Reflection on Esther

The king said to her, "What is it, Queen Esther? What is
your request? It shall be given to you, even to the half of
my kingdom."

Esther 5:3

She had to be so beautiful, intelligent, and agreeable that even a
king could not resist her, because God intended her to be the queen
of Persia.

Xerxes, ruler of all Persia, needed a wife. His previous wife, Vashti,
refused to come into his important banquet unveiled, to display her
beautiful face and the crown jewels; and he was a suggestible man
who constantly sought the advice of his courtiers. But after his anger
cooled and he had exiled Vashti, he realized he missed having a wife,
so he followed a courtier's suggestion to "appoint commissioners in all
the provinces of his kingdom to gather all the beautiful young virgins
to the harem in the citadel of Susa" (Esther 2:3). The decree further
stated that the young woman who most pleased the king would be
the new queen.

This was the world's first beauty contest. And one of the contes-
tants was the cousin or niece of a Jew who held high clerical office in
the court. His name was Mordecai; the girl, known in Jewish circles
as *Hadassah*, which means "myrtle tree," was called Esther, after the
evening star (to which the myrtle tree was sacred).

The beauty trap has always snared people and did so even four
hundred years before Christ. The palace appointed yearlong beauty
treatments for the queen-hopefuls: six months with oil of myrrh, and

42

six months with perfumes and cosmetics. Persians didn't have breast implants or Botox treatments, and they didn't worry too much about lipstick that could last all day, but they used every possible emollient and mineral coloring. They rimmed their eyes with *kohl* and antimony, rubbed their cheeks with red-iron oxide, and ground the precious stone *lapis lazuli* in a pestle to make blue eye shadow.

When Esther finally went to the king, the Bible says, the girl pleased him and won his favor, and he put the crown on her head. She was then officially the most beautiful woman on earth. Esther's hopes for the future lay not in her character or morality or faith; she had to lean on her beauty as the center of her life and vocation. And she had to be aware that someday, when her beautiful face aged and wrinkled, she would live alone in the harem.

Living life around her looks wasn't peculiar to Esther, or to women of the fifth century BC. Recently, Oprah Winfrey devoted a program to women whose entire lives were consumed by looking good. They could not leave their houses without makeup or without wearing attractive—sometimes almost coquettish—clothes and attitudes. A forty-year-old woman, who couldn't bear to say her age aloud, dressed in the same clothes as her thirteen-year-old daughter. She spent two hours every day on her hair and makeup, then had to primp in the car for fifteen minutes before she went into a store. She believed her duty was to be attractive or even seductive.

Life was much the same twenty-five hundred years ago. Esther had a *responsibility* to be beautiful and sexy. Though Pericles, ruler of Greece at near the same time, fell in love with and married Aspasia, his intellectual and politically clever *hetaira* (concubine), kings of Persia in those days weren't known for their interest in a woman's mind. So what made Xerxes choose Esther as queen had to be the will of God. God knew what evil was about to befall the chosen people; Esther was God's vessel in the palace, whether she knew it or not.

Haman, the courtier, then convinced Xerxes to commit genocide on the Jews. Esther's maids and her eunuchs brought her a message from her cousin Mordecai, saying that she must go to the king and plead for her people.

Poor Esther! The king hadn't sent for her for a month. Maybe this was just after his defeat by the Greeks at Salamis, where he'd sat on a throne on the cliffs and watched a woman, Artemisia, queen of Halicarnassus, ram and sink his greatest ship. Or maybe Esther and Xerxes were madly in love and fought often, as lovers will. She sent a message to that she was afraid to go.

Mordecai's reply read, "Do not think, Esther, that you will escape because you're in the king's palace. You're just another Jew, now. And if you don't speak up to the king, God will somehow save the rest of us but you and your father's house will perish. Maybe you became queen for just such a time as this."

Esther put aside her cosmetics and perfumes. She defiled her body with ashes, put on rags, and lay on the floor, fasting, crying, and praying. On the third day she bathed and perfumed herself, put on her finest clothes, and slipped into the throne room. She wore her beauty again, this time in the service of God.

As soon as the king saw her, he held out the golden scepter, saying, "What is it, Queen Esther? What is your request? It shall be given you, even to the half of my kingdom" (5:3).

This time Esther used wisdom as well as her beauty, so instead of asking for half his kingdom, or begging on the spot for him to lift his edict against Jews, she invited him and his wicked courtier, Haman, to a little feast in her palace apartment. They arrived, dressed for a banquet and in a celebration mood, and Esther served delicious food and plenty of wine. Finally, the king said, "All right, Esther. I know there's something. What is it?"

"If you're pleased with me, please come back tomorrow night for another banquet, and then I'll tell you," she said. We don't know her reasons for delaying, but God had a good deal of work to do between the two feasts.

Haman left the palace in especially good spirits, but his joy was tainted by passing Mordecai at the gate. Everybody bowed down to him except Mordecai, who bowed to nobody except God. Like Henry II of England, who incited his barons to murder when he told them he would have no peace until Thomas Beckett was dead, Haman told his family, "But none of these good things will give me any happiness until I no longer see Mordecai at the gate."

His wife said, "Then build a gallows so high you can see it from the palace, and ask the king to hang Mordecai. Then you can go to the banquet and be happy." So Haman ordered carpenters out in the middle of the night to build a seventy-five-foot gallows.

Meanwhile, the king, perhaps suffering from indigestion after the banquet, couldn't sleep. Just before dawn, he asked a servant to read the annals, the record of his kingship. When the droning voice came to the heroism of Mordecai in uncovering conspiracy against the king, the ruler jolted upright. "How did I reward Mordecai for this deed?" he asked. The servant searched the page, then said, "Nothing has been done for him" (6:3).

About that time, Haman made an early morning visit to the palace, hoping to suggest the hanging of Mordecai. Xerxes, troubled that he had let Mordecai go unrewarded, cast about and said, "Who's here in the court?" Haman had come into the chamber, so the king asked him how to reward a man the king wished to honor. Haman thought, *The king wants to honor me!* So he described a group of appropriate ceremonies, puffed out his chest, and waited for Xerxes to clap him on the shoulder and call someone to bring his prizes.

Instead, the king said, "Good. Go do all those things for Mordecai, who has served me well and who is sitting out at the palace gate." Haman had to take a royal robe the king had worn, to vest his nemesis; he had to seat Mordecai on Xerxes' own horse, which wore a crown; and he had to lead the Jew through the city, shouting, "Thus shall it be done for the man whom the king wishes to honor" (6:11). Haman had to venerate the man he'd hoped to hang that morning, and he must have glanced over his shoulder more than once at the gallows he had erected.

At the end of the day, he rushed home with his head covered, threw himself down in humiliation and grief, and blurted out the whole story to his wife and his advisors. They said, "A Jew? The man you hate is a *Jew?* Then you have no chance. He will win."

Before Haman had time to digest that bit of bad news, servants from the palace fetched him to the banquet, where he arrived just in time to hear Xerxes say to Esther, "What is it you want, my queen? Anything! I'll give you half my kingdom."

According to the Bible, Esther answered, "If I have found favor with you, O king, and if it pleases your majesty, grant me my life—this is my petition."

"Your life?" The king's brows were knit in puzzlement.

She added, "And spare my people. This is my request. For a man in this court has sold me and my people for destruction and slaughter and annihilation. If we had just been sold as slaves, I wouldn't have troubled you, but we are to be slaughtered."

Xerxes rose, his face ashen. "Who—who has dared to order such a vile deed?" And Esther pointed at Haman.

Like all the stories God writes, this one has a just ending: the Jews are saved from annihilation, Haman gets the punishment planned for Mordecai (who becomes the king's head counsel), and Xerxes and Esther apparently live happily ever after.

The story of Esther, who saved her people through the king's love for her, is also the story of the church, past, present, and future. God fell in love with Israel long ago, perhaps smitten by the beauty he alone had created in her. Over and over, Israel did what was wrong in the sight of God, and over and over, God reprimanded, then restored her. Finally, the King himself came to earth and offered her, now called *the church*, a course of beauty treatments. First, a time with oil of myrrh, the spice most often used to anoint the dead, and thus a sign of Christ's own crucifixion for our self-centered sinfulness. And then, cosmetics and perfumes.

In Scripture, "perfume" and "incense" usually stand for prayer or an act pleasing to God; "cosmetics" *enhance* beauty, they don't create it, so the church's cosmetic treatment has to be whatever glorifies God's beauty within us: love, piety, compassion, and purity.

Your outer beauty may draw people to you, but your inner beauty is what may change your world.

Breck Girl

> Your hair is like a flock of goats that have descended from Gilead.
>
> Song of Solomon 6:5 NASB

When I was in high school, I thought I was going to be a famous actress or a supermodel. Either way, I was going to stun the world with my beautiful, long, brunette tresses, rivaled only by Liz Taylor and my best friend, Carolla, who thought her hair was prettier than mine. I imagined myself winning pageants and screen-testing with famous Hollywood directors, tossing back my locks coquettishly. Believe it or not, I really did have nice hair.

And hair is a very important part of being an American woman. We spend thousands of dollars to cut, lengthen, curl, straighten, tint, or strip color from our locks. We sit for hours with aluminum foil or plastic bags wrapped around our heads and hope aliens or the Prize Patrol doesn't show up while we're beautifying our crowns of glory. And if you've ever gone through cancer treatment or known someone who has, you know that hair loss can be devastating.

Beautiful hair, no matter who tries to tell you otherwise, is an attribute we all want. I know from experience that hair can be a saving grace when it comes to overall beauty.

The first time Grandma brought up her great idea, I was fifteen, reading a *McCall's*, one of the top women's magazines of the sixties. "Linda," my grandmother said, looking up from the hem she was sewing on a dress for me, "you could be a Breck Girl."

For younger readers, a Breck Girl was an ad campaign for Breck Shampoo. Magazine ads featured cameo portraits of young women with flowing, healthy hair. My grandmother, bless her soul, said I would make the perfect Breck Girl.

I was flattered for a moment or two—didn't I wash my hair in beer, rinse with vinegar, condition in mayonnaise? *The painstaking attention I lavish on my head three times a week must show,* I thought. I tossed my hair, ran my fingers through the silky strands in typical teen fashion.

Something cut away inside me, though. At first I didn't know what. Samson's beautiful hair had gotten him into big trouble. Maybe I was being conceited. Although I spent my share of time primping at my reflection in store windows, vanity didn't seem to be the reason. Perhaps it was my style—I wore my hair straight instead of rolling it on orange juice cans or bristly curlers. No, everyone said my coarse, thick mop was suited to a straight look. There was only one reason left: the pictures showed the models only from the neck up. I thought my grandmother was being kind in not pointing out the obvious, that even if I had been as gorgeous as I fancied myself, I was far from picture-perfect. I was a polio survivor.

I got sick at age nine months, just a year or so before the vaccine. After Sister Kenny treatments and lots of rehabilitation, I had residual paralysis in my left arm. It hasn't prevented me from doing almost everything I've wanted, if you don't count playing the violin.

But with a less-than-perfect arm, how could I become a model or a movie star? This was the burning question for me at age fifteen, when looks really, *really* mattered. My grandmother must have remembered that adolescence was a tough time for any girl, all about breasts or the lack of them, moodiness and menstrual mishaps. Nobody ever mentioned my disability to me, maybe because I was supposed to try hard to be normal. Only on the inside, I knew it wasn't true.

In my life I've told myself a lot of things that weren't accurate. I've stood before the mirror and pronounced my image "disgusting." I've berated myself for not being able to shed those extra pounds, whiten my dingy smile, or get a wardrobe that puts me in the *chic* category. I've scolded myself to stand up straighter and cruelly pinched my own thighs to shame them into melting the cellulite. Above all, I've lied to myself about what I think others must see: a crippled person, with way too many flaws to be liked. All the beautiful hair on earth wouldn't have helped me see the truth.

My tresses *were* lovely. People stopped me on the street to admire my "flower-child hair," as my dad liked to call it. Yet I was stunned by the suggestion to model my hair for one reason: I had to face the fact that not only was my body flawed, but also that my family realized those flaws would keep me out of any beauty contest.

I had never considered that reality. Everyone made such a big deal of telling me I could do anything that I must have started to believe it. Years later, Marlee Matlin, the deaf girl in *Children of a Lesser God*, showed the world you could be disabled and still become famous. Yet I hadn't heard of many roles calling for a one-armed actress. I began to think about a career in art instead of acting.

As a teenager, I couldn't accept my flawed self, so I imagined all sorts of wacky fantasies about stardom. Grams did her best to bolster my crippled self-esteem, but I was suspicious—maybe she felt sorry for me, she tried so hard to help. I needed to find my own way out, and for me this included a great performance in looking normal.

And though Mom and Dad and Grams swore I was as normal as anyone, the Breck Girl incident proved the opposite to me. There were barriers, ones I wouldn't be able to cross. I'd accepted that I couldn't play the violin but not that I might be excluded from a beauty contest. Under the weight of physical limitations, I realized that my self-image would crumble altogether if I didn't find a way to look past the surface of everyone I met—including my own reflection.

Luckily I found a place where inner beauty is what it's all about. Some people in the church still put the emphasis on outward appearances, sure, but I have never felt more normal than I do when I'm singing God's praises along with the rest of the congregation. The love and acceptance I've experienced as a Christian have helped heal the hurts of self-inflicted lies and half-truths. Drawing near to God instantly refocuses the light from me and my problems—lame arm, poor posture, cellulite—onto the Son of Man and of Woman. When I am frustrated by my nonworking arm or lamenting the effects of gravity on everything else that is me, I sit at God's feet and hear the truth that you and I are unique and God loves us, with no conditions, no exceptions. I read how Jesus cares about our physical bodies—he healed people everywhere he went—but he also made it clear that our outer flaws pale in comparison with the flaws within. Most women don't go around with paralyzed arms, but every woman must face her own imperfections, real or perceived.

I want to confess that some days I feel more okay with my body than other days. Most of us don't get zapped with any self-acceptance miracle. I still bristle when I can't do something because of my disability, and I pray for healing. But most of the time I'm at peace. I accept me, because I am the only me there is. If I'm learning anything, it's that my body, soul, and spirit all matter to God, that my bad arm is just as important to God as my bad attitude.

Every day you and I must decide how we will deal with our short-comings. Will we tell ourselves another pack of lies? Or will we allow Jesus, who is the truth flowing in and through each cell of our bodies, to transform us anew every morning?

I don't know if I would have made it as a Breck Girl. I guess I'll never know if I would have felt more like a true beauty from the neck up. But Jesus is standing next to me as I brush out my now-graying hair.

Reflection

The eye by which I see God is the eye with which God sees me.
Meister Eckhart

What God Says about Beauty

A Reflection on Psalm 50

Out of Zion, the perfection of beauty, God shines forth.

Psalm 50:2

Oscar Wilde, in his novel *The Picture of Dorian Gray*, wrote about a corrupt, perverse but beautiful young man whose face never changed or grew older; instead, a portrait, painted by his friend Basil, bore the burden of his evil. While Gray continued to be handsome and charming, the portrait showed his true depravity and the results of his murdering wickedness. The portrait became a horror, diseased and degenerate, until one night he stabbed it; the constable found a splendid portrait of the young Dorian, and lying on the floor below it, a hideous, deformed old man. Only his rings revealed that he was Dorian Gray.

But God's portrait of *you* is just the opposite. Your face may show lines and the rewards of stress; your body may be scarred or your spine scoliosed; you may, like Linda, think you're deformed even though nobody ever notices your handicap. (She's so self-sufficient that I'd known her three years before I realized her left arm didn't work.) But while you're scowling at your image in the mirror, God is gazing at a woman whose beauty surpasses any known on earth. As you struggle through life and grow in your faith, God's picture of you grows more lovely, because he suffuses it with light: God is not only love, but the light of the universe. Even though you can't see the light of God, you are surrounded by it, engulfed, swimming, baptized in it.

When you pray, when you shoot God a quick "Thank you!" for the sight of fir trees with snow or a sand dollar or a windswept wheat field, you're in the center of God's own beauty and light. Despite theologians' efforts over the years to create either an enraged God who wears black with a high, white collar and hates almost everyone, or an unrecognizable mass of benevolent energy that cannot or will not *be*, in the way humans think of being, God was, and is, and will be. In the beginning, there was that surge of light, an explosion of love, and God created a universe of ineffable splendor.

Philosophers and spiritual writers and poets always hook beauty to goodness and truth and an abandonment of the physical. "Beauty is truth, truth beauty, that is all / Ye know on earth, and all ye need to know," says the poem "Ode on a Grecian Urn" by John Keats, written in May 1819. Plato says in *The Republic* that the body "distracts the soul from beauty, justice, and goodness." The Greek idea was that humans are imprisoned in bodies that are needy and demanding and bestial. Not only Greeks perpetuated that fraud: even Saint Francis of Assisi called his body "Brother Ass."

But I think the clue to what is really beautiful isn't just about truth or goodness; it's that beauty has innocence. Babies are beautiful not only because they've sweet lips and tiny fingers, but also because they've not yet eaten from the tree of knowledge and don't contemplate any evil. Brides are beautiful because in their white gowns and veils, they at least symbolize virginity and innocence. The Hubbel photographs yank the tears out of us by their beauty because for us they are the face of God.

"Well, then," says a woman treading the waters of separation and, with her children, clinging to the last splintered plank of her faith, "I can't go back and be a baby, nor reclaim my virginity, and I certainly don't know how to be God. Do you mean I can hope for beauty again? Are you saying that if I suppress some badness in myself and speak only truth, that I will be lovely and acceptable, not only in God's sight but in the world's?"

No! One of the reasons women get restless and unhappy in their Christian lives is because they don't want to recognize the devils that try to set up housekeeping inside them. Suppressing evil within oneself is the best way on earth to make shallowness burst forth, pretending to be beauty.

Jesus said to agree with your adversary quickly, before you get to court; so, when the adversary stands before the throne of God and accuses you of selfishness or lust or dishonesty or harshness with your children, say—as fast as you can—"Yes, yes, I did those things." And your beauty treatment will have started, because when you confess your inner or outer sin, someone stands nearby and whispers that you are made whole, and therefore lovely. And when you own up to the fact that yes, you could perhaps commit a murder of passion or make war on an enemy or break up all the furniture in your house (or at church), the better you become, and the more spiritually beautiful.

And then you can let God shed his light on you again. Ralph Waldo Emerson said in his book *Nature* that nothing on earth is so repulsive that it won't become beautiful under intense light, which means that to God, in whom there is no darkness at all, ugliness doesn't exist. God is love and also light, the kind of light that creates beauty wherever it shines. He shines on anything—or anyone.

Did God make you or not? And with the capacity for imperfection? The devil certainly didn't make you; he has no creativity and couldn't make a woman if God handed him a rib. If you're less than perfect, that will make you long for God, yearn to be one with God. When you confess that you're bad, you become good, and full of laughter. God may have laughed the universe into being, may have made everything out of his burgeoning joy. So a laughing, sin-forgiven woman is godly, and therefore breathtaking. Everyone will see it.

Lonnie Hull DuPont

I Need a Pentecostal Woman to Braid My Hair

She'll wear a full cotton skirt and a clean face,
her own rope of braid never touched
by a blade. I need this holy ghost woman
to lift a blanket of hair off my hot neck
and baptize it in a cool river,
to sing about Jesus and miracles
brought about by raised arms,
to weave wet tangled strands
into something strong enough.

Reflection

*Lonnie's powerful poem isn't just about her hair but has several
layers of meaning. It's about the need for women to minister to
and strengthen one another and, at the deepest level, about the
longing for the Holy Spirit in everyday life.*

Ideas for Reflection & Application

Something to Try On

- Maybe you can't change history with your beautiful face. But in
  your journal, write down the way your inner or outer beauty has
  changed for the better something in your household or workplace.

Don't be afraid that you're bragging on yourself, because you'll follow that journal entry by writing about gratitude to God for giving you the experience.

- Linda believes she's deformed, even though nobody notices that her left arm doesn't work. Do you have some small defect that you try to hide? If it isn't physical, maybe it's an emotional imperfection, like crying too easily or talking too much. Maybe you feel a spiritual deficit, not knowing how to pray or read the whole Bible on your own. Whatever it is, memorize this verse that God has sent you: "You are altogether beautiful, my love; there is no flaw in you" (Song of Songs 4:7). Every day for the next week, recite those words to yourself, realizing that God sees only your beauty, because he sees Jesus in your place.

- Do you harbor a secret sin? Are you afraid to say it? Kneel down by a chair or your bed and confess that to God and ask him to forgive you and send his beautifying light down on you.

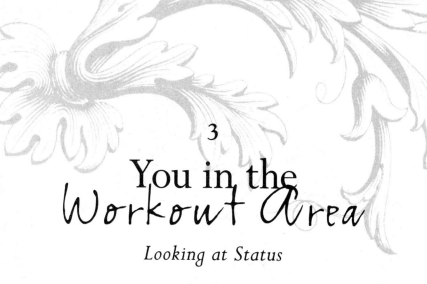

3

You in the Workout Area

Looking at Status

Fame is a pearl many dive for and only a few bring up. Even when they do, it is not perfect, and they sigh for more, and lose better things in struggling for them.

Louisa May Alcott

Satisfaction and Status

Kris: Status is a sticky business. To be honest, sometimes I'm not satisfied with being a princess in God's world. Sometimes I'd rather be a rich, best-selling author.

Linda: I won't lie: I struggle with the same thing. Although I know that nothing on earth will last, I have a drive to succeed, to meet goals, to achieve. I want to be the best writer I can be, not just for God—for recognition and money. Not necessarily in that order.

Kris: Money can give you status in this society. How did we get this way? If we were made for God's pleasure, why do we have these yearnings for status and importance?

Linda: For me, it has to do with competition. We can't all be leaders and chiefs, but we all want to be, so we compete. And I want to be God's favorite too, just like several of Jesus's disciples wanted to be his favorite.

Kris: Yeah, James and John even got their mother to put in a good word for them, which did no good at all. Status in God's world is conferred; in this one, it's earned or bought or even grabbed. But I want to know how I began wanting to be important—and rich. Don't leave out rich.

Linda: Our society has put the emphasis on appearance and performance. "Good, better, best, never let it rest," as my mother used to say.

Kris: What we all have to learn is relinquishment. I say to God, "Take me and make me over," but God expects more on my part. I have to consciously live a life of relinquishment, abandoning status or riches.

Linda: Sounds as if relinquishment might take some practice. In my mind, I want to be fit for God's kingdom, but my actions are directed toward earthly status.

Kris: We've still got a way to go.

In the Workout Area

Linda Clare

The Christian Ladder of Success

Everyone wants to be somebody. You have a need for acceptance, love, and admiration. You have a need for status. God has never been impressed by the kind of chariots, oxcarts, or autos people drive, whether you sniff out day-old bread or have a live-in chef, which exclusive order or country club you join. Class-consciousness didn't cross Jesus's radar screen. He treated tax collectors, prostitutes, and lepers with respect usually reserved for "somebodies," although the royal Somebodies and other high-ranking folks weren't happy about it. The Bible says "God is no respecter of persons" (Acts 10:34 KJV).

Still . . . you want others to respect you.

In twenty-first-century America, the status trap is set and ready to snare the unwitting. From designer clothing to luxury cars, Americans are targets of advertising. The pressure comes from all angles.

You're bombarded every day with the prospect of raising your social position with a better job, a bigger home, a newer boat. The girls at your workplace all join a spa or club. Your kids ask for the same toys all the other kids want. It's an endless circle of trying to buy one's way into being somebody.

Like children in a playground sandbox, we know whether or not we fit in. And many of us secretly feel as if we're spiritually defective.

While everyone who's Somebody tools along in life driving a better car than you do, here you are, stuck in a dented-up Yugo, spinning your wheels in a miserable rut that's going nowhere. Not only that, but somewhere on the road your love, joy, peace, and other fruits have gone bad and need to be thrown out.

You convince yourself that if you only had that special something, you'd be okay. You'd be Somebody then, all right. So you fall for a kind of performance-based Christianity to secure your place in the group. You keep up with the Joneses, even if Jones herself is the "top" missionary or tither or prayer-chain warrior. In your American zeal for excellence, you must be upwardly mobile, even in your Christian walk.

But do you? In high-school gym class, when you chanted, "We must, we must, we must" while toning up your chest muscles, you were already a prisoner of status, sure about your own ranking in the group. Pecking orders, while often cruel and unfair, are thought to be natural, as are friendly competition and the desire for self-improvement. Most of us want to rise to the top whether we admit it or not.

But there's Jesus, holding out his hand. He knows that status seeking only slows you down. He's ready to accept you right this second, no entrance requirements other than your acceptance of him. With Jesus your status is that of beloved daughter.

If you strive for higher status, you might be tempted to tell God to wait while you improve yourself a little more, put God on hold while you work on finding your place. If you look only at another person's social position, you could end up being insincere, or worse, a snob. Status consciousness may tempt you to preach grace without practicing it.

That's what this workout area is all about: getting down on the mat to wrestle with your own attitudes about status. Just as starting a new fitness regimen requires you to get real about the shape you're in, rethinking your ideas about status may leave you breathless at first. So while you're working new muscles, you lean on the inspirations in this Workout section. They're from women who learned their hardest status lessons from a brush with racism, a snooty church member, or the type of car they drove.

Maybe you always head to the back row in aerobics class because you're sure you don't belong up front. If you long to escape the status trap, here are stories from women who've learned that to break free from status isn't always easy or quick, but they've discovered someone who makes them feel like Somebody. It's as simple as reaching up for Jesus when he extends his hand.

Kristen Johnson Ingram

Desperate for Success

A Reflection on Jezebel in 1–2 Kings

Her eyes are wide and knowing, her hair is in the Egyptian style, and a gold hair circlet indicates her royalty. She leans forward through the triple frame of the window, staring with intense dark eyes, a Mona Lisa smile on her lips. She is an ivory artifact, a furniture decoration found at Nimrud but made by Phoenician-Canaanite artists. Some scholars think the artist modeled her after Jezebel, queen of Israel, who painted her eyes and adorned her head, then looked out the window before her death, and who was part of one of the Bible's most bloodthirsty stories.

Although she is always associated with wickedness, Jezebel was probably twelve or thirteen when she married Ahab, and possibly as young as eleven; most girls were married off before their second menstrual period. It's hard to imagine a girl that age having enough capacity for evil, or enough power, to wreck a kingdom.

Jezebel's reputed beauty was enhanced by her status as the daughter of a king; when she married Ahab, she was part of a truce and trade agreement between the northern kingdom of Israel and Sidon, the coastal city-state. Ahab, the king of Israel, was, according to the Bible, already the worst leader who ever rose in that country. And the marriage completed Ahab's moral failures. First Kings tells us, "And as though it were not enough to live like Jeroboam, he married Jezebel, the daughter of King Ethbaal of the Sidonians, and he began to worship Baal" (1 Kings 16:31 NLT). Ahab's allegiance to Baal was probably part of the marriage contract, but he was no doubt only too glad to oblige. Dabbling in the dark arts of the Canaanite gods and goddesses must have been much more satisfying than sacrificing to Yahweh, who was invisible and unpredictable.

Jezebel began a campaign to kill the prophets of Israel, perhaps to flout the authority of the one God, or because Ahab manipulated her. He apparently knew how to make her do nearly anything; he bears responsibility for Jezebel's cruelest act, the murder of Naboth. The Bible says that Ahab went home sullen because when he tried to buy Naboth's vineyard for a vegetable garden, the Jezreelite answered, "I will not give you my ancestral inheritance." So Ahab plodded home and flung himself on his bed; Scripture says he "turned away his face, and would not eat" (1 Kings 21:4).

That was a grown man who just wanted someone's garden! As Ahab knew she would, Jezebel asked, "Why are you so depressed that you will not eat?" Ahab whined, "Because I spoke to Naboth the Jezreelite and said to him, 'Give me your vineyard for money; or else, if you prefer, I will give you another vineyard for it'; but he answered, 'I will not give you my vineyard." *What can you do for me, Jezebel? You know I have to have my own way.* Jezebel said, "Do you now govern Israel?" *Are you king or what, husband?* You can almost hear her sigh as she says, "Get up, eat some food, and be cheerful; I will give you the vineyard" (1 Kings 21:5–7).

Jezebel wrote messages, signed them with her husband's name, and stamped them with his seal. She ordered officials to set up a kangaroo court, to accuse and convict Naboth of blasphemy, and to stone him to death. As soon as he was dead, Jezebel told Ahab to take possession of the vineyard.

Did all this happen because she was evil? Probably. But the implication that she led Ahab astray when she was thirteen and he about forty has a suspicious sound. Ahab was a manipulator who repented only when it was to his advantage and imprisoned the only prophet who told him the truth. He died in battle because of that disbelief, certainly not because of his wife.

What is the key to Jezebel? Maybe she loved Ahab.

First Kings 21:25 says, "Indeed, there was no one like Ahab, who sold himself to do what was evil in the sight of the LORD, urged on by his wife Jezebel." A woman usually urges the man she cares about. She killed Naboth for Ahab's sake and apparently took on the prophets of Yahweh because they had condemned her husband. In fact, she did what we often tell Christian wives to do: support your man, affirm his ideas, be a "helpmeet" for him, assist him to achieve his aims. You can think of her as evil, because her deeds were wicked beyond measure; but add into that her love for Ahab and the effect of his inherited evil, the Phoenician lifestyle in which she grew up, and you have a young girl who was set up to be bad.

Jezebel was an example of a greedy woman, but what she wanted wasn't just money or things. She wanted to remind the whole world that her husband was king over Israel; in fact, she even had to remind him of it. She didn't want the vineyard for herself, but for Ahab. When she greeted Jehu, at the time of her death, she called him "murderer of your master" (2 Kings 9:31). In all likelihood Jezebel killed the prophets not because she hated them but because their honesty threatened the king. And what she *did* want for herself was him, and her position as queen.

The end is sorrowful. Jehu had conquered Israel and the king of Judah when he rode into Jezreel. The Bible says "Jezebel heard of it; she painted her eyes, and adorned her head, and looked out of the window." She was a widow now, she knew she was doomed, and she wanted to die with dignity in her regal clothing. Like that famous Phoenician carving, she leaned through the window and as Jehu entered the gate, she said, "Is it peace?" (2 Kings 9:30–31).

Jehu glanced up to the window and said, "Who is on my side?" (v. 32).

Two or three eunuchs looked down at him from behind the queen. Jehu yelled, "Throw her down," and they didn't hesitate. They threw her out the window over the wall. The bloody description of her death can be found in the Bible, but Jehu went in, had supper, and said, "See to that cursed woman and bury her; for she is a king's daughter" (vv. 33–34). He didn't say because she was queen, because she was the king's wife, or because Ahab had loved her. But because she started life as the daughter of a king, she had to be buried; and if for no other reason than to keep peace with Sidon.

In one of its most horrendous passages, the Bible says the dogs had been at her and when they went to bury her, they found only her skull and feet and the palms of her hands. That strange array of remains is a perfect symbol of how Jezebel used wickedness: with her brain for evil thoughts, her feet, or *going*, and her hands, or *doing*.

Perhaps Jezebel loved her husband, but she loved her status more. And her horror story reminds us that evil rises out of ordinary longings.

All God's Cadillacs

But now faith, hope, love, abide these three; but the greatest of these is love.

1 Corinthians 13:13 NASB

I wonder if God teaches us all about status through the cars we drive.
I didn't think so until 1983, when my husband had lost his job and
we had two young boys to feed.

A local church advertised supplemental food boxes, free to anyone who
needed one. I was eager to stretch my meager pay from a job at a Christian
bookstore, and the bare cupboards at home attested to our need. There
was one hitch: this was a drive-through giveaway. You stayed in the car
while a church volunteer handed a box to you through your window.

I queued up in our silver Pontiac Trans Am, the only vestige of our
former abundant life. The Trans Am rumbled as we inched forward
in the line of battered station wagons and junk heaps. I felt all eyes
on me. After an eternity, I lowered the power window, took my food
box, and got out of that parking lot as fast as I could.

I wanted to explain to all the other poor folks that I only looked
well off—that that car was more a burden than a blessing, that it was
all we had left. Appearances, I would have screamed, are deceiving.

Other cars I've owned were just as embarrassing. My first set of
wheels was a Chevy Malibu. My grandmother donated it to me when
I was a poor college student. It had cloth seats and air conditioning. If
my high school sweetheart hadn't totaled it, I'd still be getting around
in that gem of a car.

But my high school sweetheart did wreck the Chevy, so Grams
helped me get another ride. In no time I found myself driving the
ugliest but most reliable Plymouth Valiant on earth.

I hated that car—a dark blue shoe box on wheels. The Valiant thought it was a patrol car, but it wouldn't go over fifty. I was late everywhere I went, and my friends refused to get in. They worried someone would see them riding in a little-old-lady car.

But it never broke down, and if my husband hadn't wrecked it (don't ask), I would probably be driving it into my grave. The Valiant gave way to a miserable parade of awful transportation—from VW buses that caught fire to a rusted-out Oldsmobile we called Betsy.

Of course, during the food-box fiasco I didn't have a chance to detail our circumstances. I'm sure some thought I had taken advantage. I had to admit that the Trans Am made me appear to be wealthier than I really was. The next time, I vowed, I'd go through the food box line on a bicycle so people wouldn't get the wrong idea.

That incident made me wonder: in God's eyes, am I a Cadillac or a Chevrolet? America, the Land of Opportunity, still promises everyone can make good if he or she works hard. But in at least one area of the American Dream, status is easy to recognize. Every day, whether we're aware of it or not, we size each other up. I might be highbrow or lowbrow, or somewhere in between. It all depends on the car I drive.

According to one psychology professor at Trinity College,

> Beyond its utilitarian functions, the automobile has come to carry considerable symbolic significance for its owner and/or operator, as is the case of many social roles. As O. B. Hardison noted, cars "are status symbols, coming-of-age symbols, symbols of virility, symbols of independence" (1989). Consider the similarities between your aging mother and your sixteen-year-old son in terms of the meaningfulness of having access to an automobile. For both, the auto symbolizes mobility, independence, and an adult status. The elite may choose to transport themselves in cars costing more than the homes of Mr. and Ms. Average American, while those at the bottom of the social order travel in older, often less reliable vehicles.[1]

If I pull up for valet parking in a luxury car, chances are that the valet will treat me differently from the way he treats the woman in the beat-up junk heap. I might get the red-carpet treatment, while the other patron gets a terse "Pull around to the back."

Americans judge each other by their transportation. I'm a Christian, but I struggle with car consciousness too.

Ask five Christians what kind of social position God wants us to have, and you'll get five different answers. Some say we all should shun technology and ride a horse or walk. This attitude, while extreme, makes more sense as global warming and traffic congestion take their toll on the environment. But for most, automobiles are a necessary fact of life. So if I must drive a car, what kind of vehicle fits best with the Christian ideal?

Many Scriptures—in both the Old and New Testaments—describe how riches trip up people. Jesus instructed a rich man to sell everything and follow him. We are told to be good stewards of our money, to refrain from boastfulness, and to lay up our treasure in heaven.

Other Scriptures tell of God's generosity: Ask and you'll receive. The Father knows what you need. It is God's pleasure to give you the kingdom. Those who hold a more prosperous view of earthly riches don't think God wants to be stingy. They say God has unlimited wealth and can spare a shiny new Mercedes as easily as a Pinto with a faulty muffler. Why not ask for something nice?

The answer may not become clear until we meet God face-to-face. But one thing is for sure: here on earth, people do judge each other by their cars.

If I'm really doomed to own one beater after another, I suppose I'll always need to worry about breakdowns and snickers from passing drivers, not to mention smiles from other little old ladies. Unless God drops a car out of the sky, I'll be driving a hunk of junk that gets eight miles to the gallon and might be rejected by Rent-a-Wreck.

Meanwhile, I tell my friends I plan to live vicariously through my daughter. Last week she purchased her first car. It's a shiny red Honda and she bought and is paying for it herself. She endured the shame of being one of the only kids at her high school to be wheel-less, but now she's on her way to college with a decent car. Her status was definitely lower when she had to be seen in public driving the family wagon, lovingly called the Boat.

In much the same way, my status on the road of American society has followed whatever models I've had the privilege to own. The Trans Am was undoubtedly the most prestigious car, but it didn't reflect my true economic status. I felt embarrassed to drive through a church charity line when the car itself seemed to contradict our need.

But at least I could have left the Trans Am home. Skin color or ethnicity isn't as easy to hide. I doubt that my small chagrin in the church parking lot is anything like being stared down or refused service for being a different race or ethnic group. Those kinds of status indicators are much harder to disguise—you can't exactly leave your heritage parked in the garage.

Maybe it's only human to elevate each other based on our automobiles. In some ways they are, as Freud maintained, extensions of our egos. But surely God knows that things are not always as they seem.

That got me wondering: if there are freeways in heaven, will we still rank each other by our vehicles? If I drove a model called Faith, what qualities would pass God's inspection?

First, I'd want something reliable. That's what Grams always said—while I drooled over the cute little foreign jobs, she steered me toward the sensible Valiant. Likewise, faith ought to be able to withstand all sorts of adversity. Grams reminded me that I didn't want to break down on a lonely highway, unsure of where to get help. No, she said, I wanted something that would keep going when the going got tough. Faith that's the evidence of things not seen, faith that can go the distance and doesn't overheat.

Next, I'd want my heavenly car to make the top-ten list for hope. Maybe a car with a high-miles-per-scary-life-challenge rating, so when I'm running on fumes I can still limp home. If my Bible were a car manual it might say that hope gives faith a good cleansing, one that scrubs out doubt and makes sure all the cylinders are firing properly. Hope costs a little more but cuts down on faith maintenance in the long run.

Last, I'd want Faith wheels that hold resale value—and the only thing that would fetch high blue book is love. Not just any love. This love would need to come from God, and it would have to be renewed each day before I went tooling off into the traffic of life. Without love, my spiritual chassis might rust and the engine would gum up. Pretty soon, a loveless ride would be worthless, to me and everyone else.

Okay, so maybe God doesn't have freeways of gold in heaven and maybe there are no spiritual cars. On earth you don't always get to choose what kind of car you drive either—you go with what you've got, whether it's a sporty Trans Am or an ugly Valiant.

In that line to get a food box, I believed that right or wrong, people were going to make judgments based on what they saw me drive. I no longer pigeonhole others according to the make and model of their automobiles—for all I know a fancy car might be the last thing that person owns, just as a millionaire might be crazy about his Pacer. I've found that status of one's heart with God is sometimes easier to control than the social status of our cars.

Yet I can decide to cultivate the qualities mentioned in 1 Corinthians every day. I can keep my faith in good working order, praying and seeking God with each new day. I should check my hope as often as I check the oil; maybe by deciding to treat others with kindness, I can transfer my hope to them. And waxed and buffed with the greatest of these, love, even my most scratched and dented places can be forgiven, as I forgive those who've bumped into me.

I tend to think God sees all of us as Cadillacs, complete with all the extras necessary for a purposeful Christian life. While that first Chevy was a peach of a car, I'd venture to say I'm much richer spiritually now. With the Holy Spirit as my chauffeur, my Christian life can be chock-full with all the options available through the sacrifice of Jesus, God's only Son. So whether I end up as a Rolls Royce or a Pinto, a Cadillac or a Chevy, I will always be looking for a model loaded with faith, hope, and love.

Reflection

Life asks that women be free to define themselves—instead of having their identity defined for them, time and again, by their culture and their men.

Susan Faludi

Love and War

War was a card game—I learned
in second grade and the loser had to give up
all his marbles: even clearies.
We all knew where Japan was—
where tiny tea sets and those barrels you
opened and another was inside, (forever)
came from.
I didn't give a hoot for rice,
but did like this boy who walked me home
(he gave me all his good marbles for no reason)
and showed me sticks to eat with
if you're Asian.
He asked me if I thought
he was a dirty Jap. I said
I thought his name was Richard.

Reflection

Linda reminds us love and friendship can transcend status.

What God Says about Status

A Reflection on Psalm 75:4–7

I say to the boastful, "Do not boast,"
    and to the wicked, "Do not lift up your horn;
do not lift up your horn on high,
    or speak with insolent neck."
For not from the east or from the west
    and not from the wilderness comes lifting up;
but it is God who executes judgment,
    putting down one and lifting up another.

Psalm 75:4–7

When I was a little girl in an Arizona mining town, four people lived in our house: my mother, my father, Julia, and me. Julia and I had our own rooms, and we usually ate breakfast and lunch together. My mother bought clothes and bedding and treats for both of us, and Julia and I walked to school together. My parents were polite to both of us and gave us both plenty of time to do whatever we wanted.

But Julia wouldn't have dared to stamp her foot at my father or sit in my mother's lap. She didn't join us at the dinner table, and after she walked me to school, Julia (whose name was pronounced *Hool-ya*) returned home to start her day's work. Because in that house, I was the daughter and Julia was our housekeeper.

Julia, who wore a light brown uniform, cleaned and did laundry and ironed. She helped in the kitchen and served our dinners, and she was the one who brought me through a hundred childhood asthma attacks. Those were hard times for young Mexican women in Superior, Arizona, and she probably worked for four or five dollars a week plus her room and board. The limits of her status were defined, whereas mine were not. I was the only child in that household, and I *could* stamp my foot at my father; I might get in trouble, but he wouldn't fire me as he would have Julia for the same thing. In fact, he probably would have laughed.

My story matters only because faithful Christian women sometimes replicate my situation, but in reverse. They expect God to load them with burdens and pray to be faithful servants. But if we are daughters of God, why are we trying to be the housekeepers? "I will welcome you, and I will be your father, and you shall be my sons and daughters, says the Lord Almighty" (2 Cor. 6:17–18). And how about this? "For you did not receive a spirit of slavery to fall back into fear, but you have received a spirit of adoption. When we cry, 'Abba! Father!' it is that very Spirit bearing witness with our spirit that we are children of God, and if children, then heirs, heirs of God and joint heirs with Christ" (Rom. 8:15–17).

We are God's daughters. God has the angels to be servants, and God's powers are unlimited, so we don't need to take on a spirit of slavery. Your status is as a princess in the court of the King of Kings. The prophet Joel said, and Peter repeated, "Your sons and your daughters will prophesy" (Joel 2:28; Acts 2:17).

Virginia Ramey Mollencott, well-known writer and speaker on women's spirituality, says, "First of all, then, who are these daughters whom the prophet Joel and the Apostle Peter proclaimed as prophets on an equal basis with God's sons? Judging from the Pentecostal context in which Peter quoted Joel, the daughters and sons are everybody upon whom the Holy Spirit descends. And eventually that would include literally everybody, for God says 'I will pour out my Spirit upon all flesh.'"[2]

Mollencott reminds us of the flashes of love and promises of salvation in Scripture and adds, "This is one of them. 'In the last days it will be, God declares, that I will pour out my Spirit upon all flesh,' flesh without regard for gender or age or class or any other barrier." And she adds,

> The Bible says everyone who calls on the name of the Lord will be saved . . . So the daughters who prophesy are ordinary women

just like us, rendered extraordinary only by the fact that the Spirit of God is poured out upon all of us. And such in-spirited or inspired women have always prophesied.

Biblically speaking, to prophesy does not necessarily mean to foretell the future; it means to respond to God's call and to speak the Word of God, calling for justice and for action in the face of injustice, challenging the way things are, and bringing hope that a way can be found where there is no way. The Bible is full of such daughters.[3]

Not housekeepers or handmaids, not servants or sewing experts, not the busy Proverbs 31 woman or Ruth, who gleaned so humbly after Boaz. We are daughters, princesses, heirs of Christ's kingdom.

Someone said once that if you put two seven-year-old boys in a room, they'll wrestle, but two girls that age will start a secret club. The female of our species naturally gravitates toward equality, bonding with other women to shut out the pain of the world, while the males struggle for one-upsmanship. Men, even Christian men, compete and struggle for earthly status, but the Christian woman who knows she's God's daughter doesn't have to. She and her sisters and mother and daughters can join that secret club, the one in which worldly status is worthless and where her position as Princess of Heaven is so assured that she's looking around for new members. Because the kingdom is big enough for *all* God's daughters, including Julia, who is, by now, in her Father's house, her work finished at last.

Something to Try On

- Do you really believe that you are a royal princess, daughter of the high King? Dress up in your very best clothes and visit a Starbucks or other coffeehouse for an Italian soda or latte. Or if you can't leave your home or workplace, sit down for a cup of tea. Finally, ask a favor from God, the King and your Father. You can write it on a little scroll, or chink it into a rock wall, or burn it along with a stick of incense.

- At the next church event, volunteer to do a menial task: washing the dishes, mopping the restroom floor, or straightening up all the music in the choir room. Even if you're a liberated lady and president of your circle, humble yourself to a lower status, remembering that Jesus, though he was God's Son, took the role of humility on earth.

- Wash and wax your car. Not only will you get some exercise, you also can thank God for the car you drive, even if it's not a Cadillac.

4

You in the
Wind-Chime
Atrium

All You Need

Happiness is not in the mere possession of money; it lies in
the joy of achievement, in the thrill of creative effort.

Franklin D. Roosevelt

Treasure Hunt

Linda: People often look back on their "poor years" as the best times in their lives, but when they're going through those times, they feel awful.

Kris: Uh-huh. I remember when my husband and I were both finishing college, and we had three small children. He worked nights at an aircraft plant and I taught piano. Sometimes I cried at night because the kids didn't have the toys they wanted, and I bought my clothes at a thrift shop. Now that time is perfumed by sweet nostalgia.

Linda: What I don't get is why God lets us struggle and suffer to make ends meet, and yet Jesus apparently wants us all to give everything to the poor and follow him.

Kris: I think the struggle is what brings you to God. To your knees. You don't understand, so you pray. And when you pray, you realize someone is making a demand on your attention.

Linda: The Rolling Stones sing that you get what you need.

Kris: I think I often *choose* what I need, without knowing it. I think God guides you to what will round out your life and personality—not necessarily money.

Linda: Shh! I think I hear God whispering right now.

Avoiding the Treasure Trap

For where your treasure is, there your heart will be also.

Matthew 6:21

Stuff. You have lots of it. From the absolutely vital to the embarrassingly absurd, you and I and everyone we know have more things than we know what to do with. If you are alive and watch TV commercials, you understand that American culture is all about life, liberty, and a good shopping experience.

We've put material goods and the consumer atop a pedestal so tall it's hard to see the top. While most Christian women spend wisely and give generously, some of us love our things more than we'd like to admit. Truth be told, it's almost too easy to land in the Treasure Trap. Whatever we do, we shouldn't look back, as Lot's wife did, and end up as a pillar of salt.

"Well," you say, "we have to live. Even the most dedicated or ascetic Christians have to have a few things." True. But marriages, families, even entire churches have split over the issue of possessions. When it comes to our treasures and their pursuit, it's hard to decide exactly what God has in mind for us. Especially us women.

Women, the adage goes, love to "shop until they drop." The stereotype says we brake for garage sales, mob bargain bins, and can never own enough pairs of shoes. Like Lucille Ball in the old sitcom *I Love Lucy*, we buy things behind our husbands' backs and can't resist a good deal. We know these financial foibles are not limited to women, but the image of a crazy-eyed lady in a shopping frenzy persists. Yet as Ruth Haley Barton writes, "We also need to realize that remaining unaware of the undercurrent of materialism can be dangerous."[1]

Even if too much consumerism isn't your problem, you may wonder at times how to balance Yankee capitalism with what God says about possessions. You try to figure out how you can be charitable if you don't inch up the ladder of success to earn money to give away. Doesn't God want us to be happy?

Debates have raged for centuries, and so far no one has come up with precisely what things are all right to own and what things are not. The Bible does, however, provide a blueprint. God tells us that the love of money, not money itself, is the root of all evil. Over and over, Jesus commands us to love one another, care for one another, and give to the poor. In Genesis God declares that humans are to cultivate earthly resources in order to prosper. And speaking of prosperity, the Bible also mentions that God wants people to do just that. Yet the question remains: how much treasure is too much?

Whenever earthly things drown out God's voice, the advice is always to "be still, and know that I am God" (Ps. 46:10). Here in the Wind-Chime Atrium, God invites you to slow down and enjoy the soft sounds of the bells as they sway in the breeze. As you quiet your soul, the clamoring ads fade and God's still, small voice emerges out of silence. Then you can explore the inspirations written by women like you, who've wrestled with their attitudes about material goods.

These inspirations are honest accounts of their attempts to align the American quest for things with the desire for obedience to God. For some, unburying themselves has been very difficult. But no matter how entrenched in this wily trap, these women, like you, sincerely seek God more than any treasure. Stroll through the Wind-Chime Atrium and let God speak to you.

Choosing Fool's Gold

A Reflection on Sapphira in Acts 5

> But a man named Ananias, with the consent of his wife
> Sapphira, sold a piece of property; with his wife's knowl-
> edge, he kept back some of the proceeds, and brought only
> a part and laid it at the apostles' feet.
>
> Acts 5:1–2

Her name means "beautiful one," and maybe she was. We have no
personal information about Sapphira except that she was a member
of the early church in Jerusalem and she tried to lie to God; and we
find her story in Acts 4:32–5:11.

Most people don't like this story, not only because it doesn't reflect the mercy of Jesus Christ on a pair of ordinary sinners, but also
because it sounds more like magic than God in action. Maybe you
could imagine *one* of these two people getting so scared that he or
she had a heart attack and dropped dead. But both? Well, the nar-
rative made it into the canon of the New Testament, which means
you have to take a long look at Sapphira and her spouse and decide
what the lesson is.

When the couple joined the Jerusalem community, they understood
that living was communal and all money went into one pot. People
with nothing got the same benefits as the most generous benefactor;
the early church had no needy members because everyone got the
same. People sold their homes and fields and handed the money over
to Peter and the apostles.

Joseph, a Cypriot Levite, sold a farm and turned the money over to
Peter; perhaps the new couple wanted to look as good as Joseph did. All

we know is what the Bible tells us: Ananias sold a field *with his wife's consent*, which probably means, in the language of the time, she was the actual legal owner of the field. Then, "with his wife's knowledge," he banked some of his profits and took only the remainder to the apostles. You know the rest: first Ananias and then Sapphira lied to Peter, and they fell dead and were buried.

Sapphira would fit into twenty-first-century society just fine. She and her husband engaged in accounting practices that whisper the names of Enron and Worldcom and a few other big corporations. Today, showing a loss while reserving bonuses for CEOs is a common practice. Greed has been around a long time, and it isn't the invention of modern-day cheaters. But somehow we expect members of the early church, only a few years after Jesus died and was resurrected, to be above all that.

Nowadays, few Christians are asked to throw everything they own into the offering plate, whether it be a widow's penny or the profit from selling a field. In fact, most of us even fall short of the traditional 10 percent. There have been exceptions. The late R. G. LeTourneau, who invented and manufactured earth-moving machinery, made more money than he thought he needed, so he tithed 90 percent, saying if 10 percent was enough for God, it was good enough for him. And C. S. Lewis gave away at least 75 percent of his income. But they were anomalies, and 10 percent of LeTourneau's income wasn't hay. Most evangelical Christians tithe up to 10 percent and subscribe to the principles of capitalism, which considers saving and dispersing money wisely to be as important as tithing, including saving so that family or the government won't have to take care of them when they're sick or old.

We don't know Sapphira's motives, but hers was a treasure problem. Instead of laying up riches in heaven, she and her spouse put aside an earthly buffer, maybe against future hard times. They didn't trust God to take care of them. What killed Sapphira wasn't just going along with the program. Not only was she a partner in the scheme to defraud the church, but she lied with her own mouth when Peter asked if they had "sold the land for such and such a price" and she said, "Yes, that was the price" (v. 8).

83

O Sapphira. O Beautiful One. O lady whose name is applied to gems of the deepest blue, lady who could have been remembered for honesty and generosity, why did you lie?

We might like to assert that Sapphira and her husband were counterfeit Christians who wormed their way into the church for the wrong reasons, that they were nonbelievers who planned to mulct the other members. But that's too pat. And if we say that, then we've got to chalk off millions of Christians, especially American Christians, who live in nice houses and have more than two garments and invest in stocks, market accounts, and savings, and who don't give *all* they have to the church.

Maybe Sapphira was afraid. Christianity was new, and though believers *said* they trusted God to meet their needs, that must have been scary. Maybe Sapphira was destitute as a child, born to poor parents during some kind of depression, raised in wartime, and frightened of the future. Of course, she didn't know at the time of her lying that her husband had already died; maybe she was trying to keep him out of trouble.

Whatever her reason, she lied, and when she was confronted, her heart or brain or circulatory system couldn't take it in, and she fell down dead, just as her husband had done. We don't know how old the Beautiful One and her husband were at the time of the transaction. Was Sapphira an eighty-year-old who went into shock and had a stroke? Did God snuff out her life? Probably only indirectly. We're usually punished *by* our sins more than for them. At the moment she beheld her own life, when truth rose up in protest against what came out of her mouth, she could no longer abide her own life.

We now live in a lying society. Not only did we have a president who waggled his finger at the press and said, "I did not have sex with that woman," we have tobacco processors who look the Senate straight in the eye and swear they had no idea nicotine was habit-forming. We had another president who proclaimed, "I'm not a crook!" and we have company officers who mourn the loss of their companies' assets, chuckling all the way to the bank. Truth is not the ethos of our society; our cultural norms pay more homage to success, no matter how you get there.

Sapphira and Ananias were like Cain of the Old Testament. They brought an inferior sacrifice to God and then lied about it; but this time, they weren't allowed to kill the one whose offering was worthy but instead died themselves. And their greatest sin wasn't the holding back, wasn't the lie they told. The sin that killed them was their belief that they could fool God, could lie to the Holy Spirit and get away with it.

Greed, falsehood, and folly: they are what killed the Beautiful One, deprived her of life, maybe of children, maybe even of an eternal crown for her virtue. The choice is always there.

Wind-Chime Inspiration
Linda Clare

Frugal to a Fault

If our hearts are where our treasures lie, then pardon me while I fish mine from the recycling bin. I am a compulsive saver of orphaned socks, things-that-will-be-urgently-needed-the-moment-you-toss-them, and other valuables. I'm doing it for the environment and because it's godly to be frugal. Isn't it?

"Waste not, want not," Grandma used to say. So I wash out smelly cat-food tins and carefully bundle newspapers for our weekly pickup. I keep black, overripe bananas in the freezer for banana bread. I tear the fabric softener sheets in half. I even retrieve cardboard wrappers from the trash when my husband forgets to recycle. While I may not be as thrifty as Amy Dacyczyn, the Frugal Zealot, who wrote *The Complete Tightwad Gazette*,[2] I may be a close second.

Like Dacyczyn, I wanted to stay home with my kids. All four of them. So I focused on saving money instead of earning it. I recycled, bought in bulk, and gave home haircuts until the children grew up. Lots of moms are thrifty, but my kids call me McMom, after Scrooge McDuck, the cartoon miser. They think a mother who darns their socks and washes out plastic sandwich bags is positively Scrooge-like.

But when I came home from a garage sale with a shirt that I'd once purchased new for one of my boys, he said I'd gone too far. Called me "cheap." "Not true," I said. "I'm simply frugal." Maybe frugal to a fault, but Grandma is partly to blame.

Thriftiness didn't find me until I was around ten years old. Grandma would say if cleanliness was next to godliness, then penny-pinching should be pretty high on the list too. No matter that the cleanliness adage wasn't really in the Bible—God and Grandma had plenty to say about money and how I managed it. I was told to "be on . . . guard against every form of greed" (Luke 12:15 NASB) and that I couldn't serve both God and money (Matt. 6:24). In Luke I read about a faithful and sensible steward who was in charge of his master's possessions (12:42). I decided right then that it was important to wisely use the resources God provided.

In biblical terms this is known as *stewardship*. When I was younger I thought it was Steward's Ship. I wondered about that ship—I thought maybe it was the same one for which my grandma was always waiting. She was pretty old, and so far nothing had come in for her. But she could teach me. Grandma taught me that stewardship means not spending your allowance on poorly made toys that break or those wax lips that taste great for only three seconds. How simple.

But stewardship was much more complicated than I thought it would be. Grandma showed me how to break my savings up into fractions: one-tenth for the Sunday school offering, another tenth for higher education, some for a rainy day, and some more for that shiny pair of roller skates on which I had my eye. After Grandma was finished, I knew that stewardship meant you learn to get along with what you have, and never mind the wax lips. I became the youngest tightwad in the family.

In my teens, the famous Rolling Stones hit "Satisfaction" reinforced my stewardship ideals. Hadn't Grandma always told me to ask myself, *Do I need this, or do I just want it?* The Stones were right—I did usually get what I needed, although Grandma wasn't thrilled to be paraphrased by Mick Jagger. I arrived at adulthood armed with a hundred ways to reuse gift wrap, tin foil, and tuna casserole.

My skills did not go unused. After college I taught elementary school art, and I collected empty margarine tubs and cardboard toilet paper tubes until I had nightmares about junk taking over the world. The students made bats, turkeys, and Christmas trees out of the tubs and tubes, as well as Valentine holders and Mother's Day flower vases. A third-grade boy named Derek constructed a toilet paper tube hamster run, but his pet gnawed through the maze and got loose. The principal wasn't happy, and Derek accused me of hamstercide. I cleaned out my collection of junk art and moved to California, where people are tuned in and understand important things like recycling.

Then I got married, and frugality landed me in all sorts of trouble. My new husband loathed tuna casserole almost as much as he hated turkey burgers. He thought I was silly for taking an hour to unwrap a gift to keep from tearing the paper. He definitely didn't understand recycling, especially if he'd already pitched the empty milk carton in the garbage with the remains of last night's spaghetti. I tried to overlook his environmental irresponsibility as I plucked items from our trash can. Carefully, with gloved hands, I separated the plastics from the glass, then white paper from the colored. I stomped the cans flat, put our bin at the curb. Then I watched in horror as the garbage man dumped everything together in the black hole of the truck's receptacle.

Even at church my efforts weren't appreciated. I thought it would save our congregation money if we washed the plastic communion cups instead of polluting the landfill with them. The health department informed me that sanitation was more important than saving a dollar and a half every month. And the pastor wasn't interested in exchanging the Mogan David grape juice for purple Kool-Aid, although it had stretched my home food budget on many occasions. The pastor said it was enough to be substituting juice for wine, and also would I please stop emptying the paper vacuum bags—the church could afford a new bag now and then.

So I turned instead to educating my children in stewardship the same way Grandma had me. As a stay-at-home mom with lots of time but no money, I earned my McMom nickname through diligence and hard work. I forced the kids to pick up empty soda cans on our walks to the park. We never used Styrofoam products. I taught them to bundle up to save on the winter heating bill, and they dutifully turned off the water while they brushed their teeth. We parsed their allowances to the nearest decimal, and I helped them tithe to the church and save for rainy days.

I was relentless in my crusade. The kids got toys from thrift stores and ate day-old bread. They learned not to beg for things they saw other kids receive. My children knew the difference between needing something and mere want. My kids were frugal.

I wouldn't even allow them to waste time. We were one of the last families on earth, my son tells me, to own a video game system. No cable TV, just three local stations and rabbit ears. The kids learned to appreciate reading. Grandma would have been proud.

But one day in the store my daughter saw a candy necklace she *had* to have. I reminded her of how fleeting a reward candy can be, but I was willing to indulge her sweet tooth. Suddenly she was quiet. Instead of the excitement kids show when they're about to get something good, Alyssa seemed anxious. "What's the matter, honey?" I asked. "Don't you want the necklace anymore?"

Alyssa pursed her lips and looked very serious. "I want a candy necklace," she said, "but I wonder if I really need it. Maybe I'm not supposed to have this much fun."

I felt an immediate zing inside, the kind only God can bring. We bought the candy, but I didn't feel much like teaching the kids to be frugal anymore. I wasn't having much fun either. For the first time I saw my thriftiness for what it had become: a treasure. I was frugal to the point where I sucked the joy out of living.

This was no laughing matter. I wasn't a compulsive shopper. I had little interest in fancy clothes. Expensive cars and homes? Not necessary. Even romantic island vacations didn't appeal to me, except in those awful last days of summer when moms can't wait for school to start. How did I go wrong?

For starters, I should have looked beyond the biblical warnings about riches and remembered the most important thing: Jesus asks us not to worry or fret or get too involved with things, lest we obsess about getting and forget about the Giver.

If I'm such a frugal zealot that my family is miserable, then I've missed the point entirely. Jesus came to bring us life, an abundant life. A book from the 1970s called *The Richest Lady in Town* illustrated beautifully the real wealth we ought to pursue: the fruits of the Spirit.[3] Love, joy, peace, patience, kindness, goodness, faithfulness, gentleness, self-control are the qualities that transform us on the inside. No mention of frugality. I began to see that it's hard to feel rich if you are constantly counting the number of paper towels your kids use in an afternoon.

In my determination to be a good steward, I missed the lesson Grandma wanted me to grasp. Concentrate on dividing your allowance to the nearest decimal and it's no wonder you don't feel content. Refuse to part with your savings for any reason and it may always seem like a rainy day. Dive into enough old spaghetti to retrieve a milk carton and you'll feel slimy, with or without rubber gloves.

Like many people, I let a good idea grow out of control. I listened to the biblical warnings against riches so often that I forgot that God wants us to enjoy life as well. If my focus is on money instead of God, like Scrooge McDuck I'll find it easy to get engulfed. I never intended to pass along stinginess to my children, and I don't want them to live unable to enjoy God's generosity.

I want them to follow the advice that Charles Swindoll gives in his book, *Strengthening Your Grip*. Swindoll writes that with money there are three principles: First, don't be conceited; second, don't trust your wealth for security; and finally, become a generous person.[4] At the root of all of these is the idea that giving is the true basis for Christian stewardship. While we are not to waste resources, hoarding what we have prevents us from enjoying life and replaces God as the center of our activities. Giving allows joy to rise up from the dumpster of obsession with treasure—treasure that Proverbs 23:4–5 warns can sprout wings and fly away.

My husband is finally getting the hang of recycling—last night he rinsed a milk jug and set it in the bin. The kids are more relaxed because

I'm working on my compulsion to recycle everything I own. And I tossed a couple of freezer bananas that were too far gone for bread.

If Grandma were alive I think she'd be proud that I'm still frugal. But I'm learning that God's supply of everything is unlimited, that hoarding and saving forever can take the fun out of life. I think I'll go buy some wax lips and get my three seconds of flavor before Steward's Ship comes in.

Reflection

Never work just for money or for power. They won't save your soul or help you sleep at night

Marian Wright Edelman

Wind-Chime Poem

Luci Shaw

Confession

for Susan Bergman

In your presence, at no great urging from you,
I hold my purse bottom-up over a cascade
of scraps, myself turning inside out
as though my need, too, were bottomless. A tissue
floats to the table. A shopping list and an old
Safeway receipt (food already eaten). A wallet
full of worn green, outgrown photos of my children,
the California driver's license that seems

to confirm my West Coast existence. Tarnished coins
varnished by a thousand palms. Tablets to ease heart
burn. A scarlet comb tangled with a disconnection of hairs.
The keys to house, car, and all the locked doors
in my life. A datebook that foretells the multiple
expectations of the future.
Inside-out, and the leather interior
is naked, visible as skin, seams as ragged as my
laugh lines, the emptiness behind the glossy calfskin
and the gold-tone metal: I will discard. I will purge.
I will erase, scour, reverse a reamed-out
waiting heart. See, at last, I am hollow for you. See
how I need to be filled.

Reflection

*Noted poet Luci Shaw discards every earthly treasure in order to
be filled with God's Spirit. And she waits for God to answer.*

Wind-Chime Inspiration

Marlee LeDai

Courage Is God's Currency

My climb, a rage against pain, is one of those insane things you do in
utter disconsolation. The nine-thousand-foot volcanic crater is covered with snow and ice. Leaning in to the heart of the earth, I feel it
pounding. Pines tower against a hoary sky. Frozen wind sears my cheeks.
At the lowest place in my life, I've decided to climb a mountain. Not

just any mountain, certainly not a metaphorical mountain. My climb is both a dare to God—and a scream.

Somewhere along the way, I realize that what people call a "mountain-top experience" is dead wrong. The mountain top is not blissful. The mountain terrorizes me. The mountain pushes me back and down. I fake resolution, exhaustion tangled with grim hope. The two wrestle all the way until, in the wrestling, they weave a kind of three-strand cord. It is composed of fear, passion, and grim desire. The cord gives me leverage to climb.

To make a climb is to throw down a challenge to everyday life. It is to understand that what matters is to grow and change in order to help to heal the world as well as yourself. To climb is to make a pilgrimage, and "pilgrimage is always an inward journey," writes world religion expert, Huston Smith. "The art is to learn to master today's unavoidable situation with as much equanimity as we can muster," he says, "in preparation for facing its sequel tomorrow."

Yes, I say. And I think of Joshua.

Joshua was on his way over Jordan when the Lord promised that every step to fall under the soles of his feet—through fortified hill country—was a gift.

A gift?

In the same breath came the declaration that the pilgrims would be required to fight for every square foot of land they wanted. Hardly a gift! Yet, the Hebrews were to learn that in the divine economy, the struggle *is* the gift. How far would they go? How high would they climb? Reaching for new heights was limited by nothing except their faith. Faith is walking to the edge of everything known and taking one step more. That one step often brings struggle.

I have found that struggle is the process God uses to prepare my way into new territory, within as well as without. Long before Messiah Jesus articulated the words, it was implied for the chosen people: the kingdom of God is within you. The kingdom of God is apprehended by faith, passion, and often as not, grim desire. *Do you want it or not?* God asks me so often. *Oh? Okay, maybe not this time, then,* he says when I balk, feigning lack of resources. *Be strong and of good courage,* he says. Is it a reprimand or an encouragement? Either way, his words imply that when I climb, these qualities are already there, waiting to be appropriated.

Atop the mountain at last, I sit on an icy slope and slip first one strap, then the other into its buckle. I ratchet my feet, one in front of the other, tightly onto a long board. Lifting my body precariously over it, the board slips away. Gravity has its way with me. There is nothing to do but surrender to its authority. Careening down the mountainside, I fall against it again and again, thundering through snow. I stand again and fall again because, unable to keep my balance upright, it is the only way down. My body endures a variety of odd twists and turns. Eventually, I learn to use the jolt of the fall itself to propel me up and off again. I glide. I fall. I get up. I fall again—until falling itself becomes the process. And then things change for the better.

I learned to snowboard at age fifty-one, with my primary goal on that mountain merely to survive. My secondary goal was to turn life itself on edge. This is the legacy of thriving in high places.

Since I learned to snowboard, people often give me credit for being one of two things: either courageous or crazy. *Imagine*, they must be thinking, *a menopausal woman whizzing down a mountain in her baggy pants and spiked fleece hat.* Maybe I am crazed, but it is intentional. Maybe I am courageous, but if so, I do not know it at the time. Neither climbing, nor boarding down, is at all about the kind of bravado associated with daring-do. "Courage doesn't always roar," writes Mary Ann Hershey. "Sometimes," she says, "courage is nothing more than saying, 'I will try again tomorrow.'"

Hours of focus, faith, and falls on the mountain—all of it a struggle—brought a gift to me as it did to Joshua when the walls of Jericho finally fell. It brought the understanding that life itself is meant to be lived on the edge. In high places, the challenge of transitions are what make it difficult, and what make it possible.

Courage is the currency of God's kingdom. Your climb will grow daunting or more awesome according to your courage. I doubt you'll recognize courage if you go looking for it ahead of time. Are you trying to decide whether you have courage or not to make your dreams come true? To accomplish what you set out to do? To apprehend the will of God for your life? To climb a mountain? Of course you do.

I'll tell you how to know it's there. Look your dream straight in the eye. Do you feel fear? That's what courage feels like. Do you foresee negative consequences if you fail? Courage looks like the possibility of defeat. Is there pain in your life you are trying to overcome first? Pain forces courage to take a stand. When the pain of staying where you are is greater than the pain of taking a risk, it will force you into new territory. Are fear, anxiety, or pain present in your life? Yes? Okay then, there's the evidence; you have all the courage you need. It is already within you, as is the kingdom of God.

It's high time to step out and dare to be remarkable. Take that first step into the Red Sea. Hang the scarlet cord from your window on the wall of the city. Stay tight in your ruby slippers. Careen down a mountain, crimson blood rushing through your veins. Live the delicious raspberry-truffle life that is manifest only when you willingly, or unwillingly, take a risk. Take the risk of the next step. Then take the next. Never give up.

I've been back to the mountain of my fear many a time, paying the required price: a fight against the anxiety that pulls me back and down like gravity. But each time, I understand better the illusion of power that fear wields. Each time, I climb higher. No longer will I be stuck in low places, wistful for a better view. Unthreatened by the potentiality of worst-case scenario, the beautiful mountain surrenders itself as a sensual experience beneath the soles of my feet. The physical high places—and the climb to reach them—have taught me to reclaim my own poise, and in that, my own power. I am mastering the art of confronting the unavoidable situation and facing its sequel again and again. As I do so, the dynamics of height are turned on their head.

The cord that I used to climb the mountain the first time, fashioned of fear, passion, and grim desire, has become a rope, tough and strong. I tell myself, *I can use this for something.* And I do. I use it to climb other, higher mountains. I use it to survey new horizons. I use it to help lift others who, climbing behind me, are quaking like an Aspen leaf in the wind. Living in the heights is not a once-and-for-all achievement, however. It is about making the climb over and over again, learning to take the edge more gracefully each time. It is about mastering difficult transitions—in spite of terror and failing strength.

Courage becomes "good" courage, the kind God admonished us to have, when we move forward and engage ourselves in the climb. To be "of" good courage means that you go despite dire consequences. Despite other people making fun of your dream. Despite voices in your mind whispering you'll be a loser if you try. Live the be-afraid-but-do-it-anyway consequences of womanhood and pilgrimage from a higher level of calling. Live them from who you know yourself to be in God. Live them because it is the right thing to do. Live them because Jesus challenged you to explore the boundaries of the kingdom.

I want to see the kingdom of God come to earth. I want to glimpse the sunrise of his purpose for me in all its passionate splendor. I want to feel the heart of God pounding against my own. He invites me to pilgrimage. He invites me make a climb. It's my gift. It's my life. I want to view it from a higher place.

Reflection

Living is a form of not being sure, not knowing what next or how. The moment you know how, you begin to die a little. The artist never entirely knows. We guess. We may be wrong, but we take leap after leap in the dark.

Agnes de Mille

What God Says about Treasure

A Reflection on Luke 12:15

And he said to them, "Take care! Be on your guard against all kinds of greed; for one's life does not consist in the abundance of possessions."

Luke 12:15

Freedom from want . . . means economic understandings which will secure to every nation a healthy peacetime life for its inhabitants, everywhere in the world.

Franklin D. Roosevelt, "Four Freedoms" speech,
January 6, 1941

When President Roosevelt made his State of the Union address in 1941, he named four freedoms he wanted to see all over the world: freedom of speech, freedom of religion, freedom from want, and freedom from fear. All wonderful dreams for the world. But I need freedom from a new kind of want. The kind that says "I want, I want, I want." And it's connected to the freedom that Franklin Roosevelt proclaimed, because when I want, someone somewhere may have to go without.

I used to take my pleasure in small things. A fresh cup of tea in my grandmother's china cup, a walk in the snowy woods to look for spring's first violets, rereading a favorite book, identifying birds, visiting with a friend—all these were where I found my joy. But somewhere, I jumped on the world's bandwagon and began *wanting*. A bigger house, a newer car, a cell phone, a quieter printer, more expensive clothes. Faster computers with unbelievable memory systems. I want, I want,

I want. Somehow, living in this society, I learned greed. And greed, avarice, is a sin.

Not everyone is at the top of the cupidity scale, but they may not admit that *wanting* can be a source of sin in their lives. Some women are keepers: women who have two or three closets in the house full of clothes they can't wear because the styles have changed or because they've gained weight; they tell themselves they'll get back into them someday or the style will return.

They keep their clothes for several reasons. I know a woman in her fifties who still has her high-school prom dress, the suit she was married in twenty-five years ago, and little velvet shell hats from the early sixties. She is reluctant to let go of her youth and its trappings; every time she opens a closet, the perfumes and textures of her girlhood surround and embrace her. She is, in her mind, the icon of a certain time and space that she can occupy at the same time as this one. Her Christian life is also overlaid with her youth: she speaks in an electric, urgent voice about the day she went forward in church, the day she was baptized, and the wonderful young people's group she attended. Now she goes to church on Sundays but the rest of the time she cooks and crochets and smokes, not noticing that her two teenage daughters have the same romantic stars in their eyes that she had when she wore the pale blue chiffon dress to the prom.

Other women, who know deep down they'll *never* be thin enough to wear their size-eight dresses again, believe that so long as the tiny clothes hang at the back of the guest-room closet, they can pretend that they *are* losing weight—they've just hit a little plateau right now—and one of these days they'll wear the beautiful garments again. Those women aren't just greedy with clothes; they also have an abnormal relationship with food, and ultimately their own bodies. They need to eat less and move more, but keeping those clothes helps them hide the truth from themselves.

Of course, wanting isn't just keeping old clothes. It's shopping and shopping and shopping, it's bargain hunting or cruising Saks, it may even be theft, shoplifting. Women spend millions, probably billions, every year on cosmetics, clothes, and "notions," to use the word from another time that describes the stuff we buy. A woman who would never steal, never even take paper clips from her office, a woman who wouldn't wear a bracelet to an opening and then return it to the store—that woman probably wouldn't think it's a sin to buy so much and have so much.

A professional woman who behaves normally most of the time has her cupboards so crammed full of food she can't find the can of string beans she's looking for, because twelve cans of beets are on top of it. She goes to warehouse discount stores and buys cases and flats and mammoth jugs of everything, but because she works long hours and comes home exhausted, she never gets anything organized. Her cupboards are an experiment in madness: you have to move a gallon jar of dried cranberries to look for the flour, and she has so many kinds of olive oil you could use one daily for a week without repetition.

Others have to have a new dress or blouse or scarf for every occasion; if they're poor, they shop at thrift shops, but by heaven, they shop. Literary types often have a guilty stack of brand-new books they haven't read, and the beauty-conscious woman has drawers full of makeup: eye shadows and lip liners and lengthening mascaras, some still in their shrink-wrap. They and the book buyers and thrift-store shoppers buy to feel better, to forget their real lives, to punish their husbands. Some people hide things from their spouses and partners for a while, which reveals a lot about the sin of greed, compounded by the sin of lying, at least by omission.

You can take ownership to extremes. I know a woman who can't get rid of anything because she might use it. She washes and saves her used-up moisturizer jars and spray bottles. She has a stack of about a hundred plastic lids, one of which she might need someday. Every room in her home is filled with boxes of unopened Avon products that someday might be collectors' items, oil filters that she found on sale, and hundreds of magazines from which she plans to cut recipes. Bedrooms and even the bathroom are lined with brown cardboard cartons and big plastic bags of clothes or towels or fabric, and she won't let anyone even look under her beds.

Across town, another woman wants the cupboards bare, the windows uncurtained, and the tables unornamented. She regularly goes through her husband's closet to pitch out clothing, invades the kids' toy boxes and dressers on a search-and-discard mission, and shops for every day's groceries on her way home from work, because there's no food in the house.

Both women are object-centered, both participating in a pathological relationship to objects and ownership. The first woman has closeted herself and her family with belongings; she is passive-aggressive, forgetting or putting off the big throwing-away she says she plans. The other is more openly controlling: she wants to own and manage all the space in her home, irrespective of her husband's and children's wishes, wants to be the one to fill it with her ego. Just as overeating and anorexia are the two ends of gluttony, or a sinful relationship with food, the two women in this story both dwell in greed, the sinful relationship with things. And their husbands often enable the practice of greed by surrendering to it.

How did America get so greedy and controlling? We eat too much. I heard someone say the other day that more than half of all Americans, including very young children, are considered obese by doctors. We buy too much: bankruptcies are rampant, and many Americans owe thousands in credit-card debt. We own too much, both in size and amounts. You can find whole subdivisions of huge houses that look like medieval castles and sell for upward of a million dollars. We use too much: we're exhausting the earth's finite amount of oil, old-growth forests are disappearing off the planet, and we'll soon run out of air to breathe.

Because of human irresponsibility, we are faced with the earth's demise: every day, at least ten species of animals or plants or insects disappear forever, largely because of human occupation. Every few weeks, a wildlife officer has to shoot a cougar or a bear that appeared in its own territory, but into which humans have built new housing developments. Every day, about 1 percent of the tropical rainforest is slashed and burned so people can mine gold or grow quick crops. "I want, I want, I want" has turned into "We take, we take, we take." And I think we'll have to answer for our destruction of God's own creation. When God gave human beings dominion over the earth, he made us caretakers, not destroyers. I think God said to Adam, "The buck stops with you."

Forget the psychological part of greed or enabling. It doesn't matter in this moment why you shop or acquire or keep or use. The *spiritual* effect of greed can turn us all into devils if we don't stop. So what's the cure? Love.

If I give away my worldly goods, if I sell my house to relieve suffering in African countries, will I be healed of wanting? If, as Saint Paul says, I bestow all my goods to feed the poor, and give my body to be burned, what will happen to my greed? According to Paul, nothing—unless I have love. Love is the transformative element, the wedge that can split my soul and remove my urge to own the earth. God's kind of love, that is, God's kind of total beneficence and care. Love preceded by a conscious act of relinquishment, a surrender to what I know is right.

If I love the earth, I can't pollute it or use up all its resources. If I love my neighbor as myself, I have to make sure my neighbor has as much to eat and drink and wear and dwell in as I do. If I love God, I'll spend more time in prayer and *mitzvah*, acts of goodness and kindness, than I do in shopping or eating or using. That's it.

But of course, that's not it. Getting from here to there isn't just a leap: It's a flight over the widest, most yawning chasm in all the geography of the soul. Only an informed heart can turn love into action, so I'll have to start investigating the living conditions of my neighbors worldwide, next door or in Rwanda or Estonia. I can no longer turn on my electric range without finding out how that electricity is produced. And most of all, I can no longer buy or use or honor anything that deprives natural resources or a single hungry soul.

So here is my prayer.

Invade me, God. Convert my greed into wanting to help, turn my owning into giving, my arrogance to concern. When I am tempted to buy or own something that would ultimately cost the earth or even one of its people, warn me. Teach me to quit stuffing my body with too much or frivolous food. When I think about replacing something that still works, like a car or a computer, explode in my head and remind me. Siphon off my belief that I have any rights here, and help me to understand that I live by your pleasure, not mine. Help me to make "freedom from want" a worldwide reality. And keep me saying "Amen" to this prayer as long as I do live.

Ideas for Reflection & Application

Something to Try On

- Think about the part treasure plays in your spiritual life. Do you have a tithe or pledge to your church? Do you donate money or other goods to the poor? How do you think God wants you to offer him more of your time, talent, and treasure? Light a candle, and then write down two or three ways in which you want to be more generous to God and God's people.

- Have a garbage bag or other large container ready as you clean out your closet. Toss in anything you haven't worn for a year, including shoes or hats or coats. Dip into your dresser drawers and discard the frilly camisole you've kept for three years. Don't spare purses or belts either. Keep your wedding gown if you like, but send all those too-small, too-large, out-of-style garments to charity. If you can get the contents of your closet down to half, or at least two-thirds, of its former size, give yourself a reward: rent a DVD you've wanted to see, or give yourself a manicure.

- Pray Mary Gordon's "Prayer for the Wasteful":

   O God, in your benevolence look with kindness upon those who travel first class in high season, on those who spend whole afternoons in cafes, those who replay songs on juke-boxes, who engage in trivial conversations, who memorize jokes and card tricks, those who tear open their gifts and will not save the wrapping, who hate leftovers and love room service, who do not wait for sales. For . . . collectors of snowman paperweights, memorial cups, and souvenir pens. For those who take the long way home.

We pray to You, whose love is prodigal, who multiplied the loaves and fishes so that there were baskets upon baskets left, who turned plain water into wine of a quality no one required, who gave Your life when You need only have lifted a finger, protect these, Your servants, from afflictions of the hand, cover their foolish bets and greet them with that mercy whose greatness is unearnable by calculation or by thrift.

from *God Is Love: Essays from Portland Magazine*,
edited by Brian Doyle

5

You in the Aromatherapy Alcove

De-Stressing Your Life

A woman under stress is not immediately concerned with finding solutions to her problems but rather seeks relief by expressing herself and from being understood.

John Gray, author of *Men Are from Mars, Women Are from Venus*

What Wrecks Your Calm

Kris: When I was younger, we didn't have stress. We had bad cases of *nerves*. Later on, we got *tension*. *Stress* appeared in the country around 1980, I think.

Linda: I recently read about a study that said broken hearts, usually from the loss of a spouse, can kill people. People have heart attacks even though they have no chronic heart disease. Even if the name *stress* is a recent invention, it reaches into every corner of our lives. And the busier I get, the higher my stress level becomes.

Kris: You mean like writing this book? Is that wrecking your calm?

Linda: I guess I have to say yes, even though I'm enjoying the work. In all those stress tests, points are added for positives such as Christmas or getting married, as well as for negative stress such as death or loss.

Kris: I almost never feel stressed. Even when I'm in the middle of terrible problems, I don't have much conscious reaction. I feel perfectly fine, but I just calmly drive into a tree. This is almost like having that dangerous disease that makes a person immune to pain. I need some better detection mechanism or something.

Linda: Something like God?

Kris: You mean God should say, "Kris, you're stressed. Go lie down"?

Linda: (sharply) Well, maybe. But how about casting all your cares upon him?

Kris: No problem. He can have them, and some more stuff I'll dig up.

Linda: Stop it! You're stressing me out!

Taking Time to Listen

> Everybody today seems to be in such a terrible rush; anxious for greater developments and greater wishes and so on; so that children have very little time for their parents; parents have very little time for each other; and the home begins the disruption of the peace of the world.
>
> Mother Teresa

Hectic, overcommitted, frenzied, harried—could these words describe your life? In addition to retaining child-rearing duties, cooking, cleaning, and chauffeuring, many of you hold full-time jobs. You volunteer and make time for church work too. You've been urged to do more and more, until *busy* doesn't begin to describe your pace.

Welcome to the Aromatherapy Alcove, where you can put your feet up and breathe in calming scents to de-stress your busy life. This is the place to release tension and reevaluate priorities, to slow down and literally smell the roses.

So far, it's been all you can do to keep up. No time to say hello-good-bye, as the White Rabbit said in Lewis Carroll's *Alice in Wonderland*.

Unrealistic expectations for women, both in society and in the church, persuade us that we can "do it all." You suspect the world is spinning faster than it once did, but you have no idea how to slow life down.

Our lives do seem more frantic. Cell phones, instant messaging, and email make us available 24/7. Today's cutting-edge technology is tomorrow's dinosaur. We don't send our children out to play—we must schedule their lives too. But are today's women actually busier than those of centuries ago?

Thousands of years ago, our ancestors needed built-in protection against predators, the elements, and natural disasters such as floods, volcanic eruptions, and earthquakes. Today, we no longer need to flee from wild animals, but we still react to situations by producing substances that speed up the body's reaction time. We may be trying only to escape rush-hour traffic or a cranky boss, but our bodies still react to modern life as if we were running for our lives. We call it stress, and too much of it can make us sick.

In pre–Industrial Revolution times, a woman was expected to take care of the cooking, cleaning, and child rearing. In addition she kept the home fires burning, made soap, candles, and other household products, and tended the garden. She might sew the family's clothes and keep them mended and darned to extend their wear. She taught the children to read and was in charge of their spiritual upbringing as well. The only time this woman had to herself was perhaps a few minutes in prayer. She rarely lived past sixty.

You say you're glad you didn't live then? Well, today's women have only traded a full day of backbreaking housework for a full day of brainbreaking deadlines, traffic jams, and day-care woes. It's enough to make you sick.

Intent on buzzing around like busy bees, we often neglect our physical and emotional health. The Proverbs 31 woman dangles in front of us like a carrot, luring us to try harder. Squeeze in another assignment, take on one more project, until one day we simply can't do anymore. We're physically sick or at best overwhelmed. Busyness has claimed another victim.

Stress has been shown over and over to influence our mental and physical health. Dr. Steven L. Burns of UCLA says, "To your body, stress is synonymous with change."[1] He claims that any life change, whether good or bad, taxes your body. Even imagined change, or worry, causes stress.

If you feel harried, hectic, frenzied, or frantic in your daily life, your body may be giving you a warning: slow down. Stopping to smell the roses isn't just good advice, it may be crucial to your well-being. Nobody can really do it all—but even at church we keep trying.

Can we become too busy if we're serving God? There are so many hurting people, so many worthy and wonderful projects. We may say to ourselves, "If Mother Teresa can do it, why can't I?"

The answer to that question comes in two parts: priorities and callings. First, there's a high probability that Mother Teresa had her priorities straight—she sat at God's feet before she did anything else. And while many admire her accomplishments, she always claimed God was responsible. "Before you speak," she said, "it is necessary for you to listen, for God speaks in the silence of the heart."[2]

Mother Teresa may have been busy, but she had God's help.

Getting help with our busy lives may be the key to transforming stressed-out women who stagger from one task to the next into real women who know their limitations and are willing to listen to God. Relax here in the Aromatherapy Alcove, with a soothing bouquet of lavender. Ponder the inspirations of women who know how easy it is to be too busy at work, at play, and at church. While you're there, let God's sweet aroma enfold you with peace.

A Bee's Life

A Reflection on Proverbs 31

Her lamp does not go out at night.

Proverbs 31:18

It is not enough to be busy . . . The question is: What are we busy about?

Henry David Thoreau

You've probably had the Proverbs 31 woman held up as an icon, an example for you to emulate. She labors from before dawn to late at night, feeding, weaving, selling, buying. She makes her well-dressed, well-fed husband proud among other men. She runs a home and a business that make him rich. And she balances her time without any effort or complaint of fatigue. But does she live in the average Christian home? Or anywhere else?

Probably not, but that doesn't mean women don't struggle to attain that kind of perfection, and they may feel miserable because they're failing. I discovered that chapter of the Bible all by myself, when I was a young girl, and I began trying to copy the woman's personality and lifestyle. The era I grew up in, even secular society, pointed at the virtuous woman as an ideal: Jacqueline Kennedy. Madame Curie. Eleanor Roosevelt. So I can't blame a church, a Sunday school teacher, or my mother when I say that every time I reread the passages about the perfect wife, I vowed to try harder. And of course I failed and felt guilty. Until I finally saw the truth that transformed me: the paradigm for womanhood shouldn't come from the author of Proverbs, but from the Gospels.

The way Jesus treated women was new and still is. He preaches to us, teaches us, eats supper with us, and begs us to sit down and visit instead of scurrying around with housework. The famous Proverbs woman is not present in the Good News of Jesus Christ. The women he loved sometimes had bad reputations or disliked housework. He had a whole covey of women with him who, instead of investing their money and giving their husbands or brothers the proceeds, supported the Messiah in his travels; Matthew tells us they stood at the foot of the cross, even after the disciples had run away: "Many women were also there, looking on from a distance; they had followed Jesus from Galilee and had provided for him" (27:55).

If you've been trying to become the Proverbs lady, stop it. Yes, stop it. Turn your eyes toward Jesus Christ. Can we really believe God gave men the new covenant but left women in the old one? Look at the differences between that woman and the message of the Gospels.

Proverbs says, "She is far more precious than jewels . . . She seeks wool and flax, and works with willing hands. She is like the ships of the merchant, she brings her food from far away . . . She considers a field and buys it; with the fruit of her hands she plants a vineyard . . . She perceives that her merchandise is profitable" (vv. 10, 13–14, 16, 18).

Hoo, boy. Her immense value was in her performance and products. Besides weaving and embroidering and cooking, she made a profit in real estate and wine making, and she dolled up in purple every day. She looked good, and she worked and worked and worked.

But remember, that woman had slaves and lived in a slow agricultural society. If she rose while it was still night and provided "food for her household and tasks for her servant-girls" (v. 15), that meant a slave probably cooked breakfast for the field hands and housemaids, and then the wife handed out a list of the day's duties. How could a modern woman, maybe with a family and a job, keep up with her schedule?

Jesus wasn't too impressed by wealth and profit. He said that where your treasure is, there your heart will be also, so women should quit being overachievers and get real.

While Proverbs insists, "She looks well to the ways of her household, and does not eat the bread of idleness" (v. 27), Jesus is critical of such concerns when he says, "Consider the lilies of the field, how they grow; they neither toil nor spin, yet I tell you, even Solomon in all his glory was not clothed like one of these" (Matt. 6:28–29).

We could go on and on, comparing every phrase of the Proverbs 31 woman with the words of Jesus, but it's already clear that God is more interested in what you *are* than in what you *do*. And not only in the Gospels: the "Be still" psalms say, "Be still before the **Lord**, and wait patiently for him; do not fret over those who prosper in their way" (37:7) and "Be still, and know that I am God!" (46:10). And that "be" is, in Hebrew, similar to "stand still." Quit doing and start being. Wait patiently in the presence of God. "Sit down and visit with me," says Jesus. "Ponder these things in your heart."

But after years of striving and doing and producing, can you switch from the definition in Proverbs to that in the Gospels? Can you abandon one way of life for another without having mental or emotional consequences? You may have trouble breaking your habit of always doing, giving, and planning. Sitting at the feet of Jesus, perhaps deep in meditation, or savoring the Bible a slow verse at a time, or just sitting on a rock, staring at the sunset over the ocean, may feel artificial or even forced. But think back to the day you decided to become the Proverbs woman: that was even more artificial. Science says it takes three weeks to form a new habit, so start today. Honor Jesus by making tea in your best china, then meditating on his name.

How about the people around you, who may be used to your busy-bee, cheerful, do-it demeanor? What will happen when your co-workers, husband, children, parents, and siblings see you transformed from Proverbs Woman to Gospel Woman?

First of all, Christ goes before you. When any woman becomes intimately involved with him, he fights the battle, even with those who try to drag you back to your old life. Maybe your family will wonder or even get mad. On the other hand, they might enjoy the fact that you have more time to love them. They might like your drinking an after-dinner cup of coffee with them instead of leaping up to clean the kitchen. If you have a husband, he will value your attention and easy affection more than your being a woman who salutes him and marches to the kitchen or the loom or the bedchamber.

A man wrote her description, yet women have taken on his burden without whimpering. So read the first words of that Old Testament passage: "A wife of noble character who can find?" (NIV). Even the writer of Proverbs knew she was just an idea. She didn't exist.

Aromatherapy Inspiration

Linda Clare

Sitting Down for a Silent Movie

My husband claims that in more than twenty-five years of marriage, I have never seen the beginning or the ending of any movie we've ever watched at home. According to him, I always find some excuse to miss either the all-important opening scene or the film's climax. It confounds my movie-loving spouse when, just as the bad guys get caught or the good guys save the day, I jump up from the sofa and yell, "I'm busy!"

He's exaggerating, of course. I admit that I can't sit still for two hours (or longer if he rents one of those five-hour sagas), but I don't leave the room to irritate him on purpose. Most of the time my sudden departures have had more to do with getting the last load out of the dryer before the clothes wrinkle or checking on the kids because they're too quiet. Recently I noticed my husband's disappointment—after I popped in and out while the DVD played on—and realized I'd fallen into the Busy Trap.

I didn't mean to become overextended. Every opportunity—to be the best wife, mother, or servant of God—felt doable when I agreed to take it on. And prayer and meditation don't come easily for me. The moment I close my eyes, a thousand thoughts clamor

112

for attention. In no time, I can think of something that must be done right away.

My neighbor can't understand why being quiet and still is so hard for me. I said I'm a Type A personality, but she didn't give up. She once handed me a calming meditation cassette so I could learn to relax, and I promised I'd try it. Needless to say, I returned the tape unused because I couldn't find time to listen to it.

In my zest to be everything to everybody, I somehow lost sight of God's idea of balance. When it comes to juggling work, chores, kids, and church service, I'm no different from a lot of women.

We all live hectic lives. More women work in addition to keeping a home than in any time in history. Wives and mothers feel the pressure to do it all. And Christian women gladly dedicate themselves to church ministry, mission work, choirs, or Sunday school. We've all known a Superwoman or two, and many of us have lived like one at one time or another. She's the one who always seems to be flying low, the one with never-ending energy and time for "one more thing." *Superwoman* might even describe your own role in your harried life. But I'd bet my bag of popcorn that most of these wonders long for the chance to at least catch their breath.

When does Christian service become busy-ness? How many of us wish we could slow down and watch the dust bunnies (or a movie) once in a while? I asked myself these questions and soon found that as long as I kept up my frenetic pace, I couldn't hear the answers. Then came my first self-revelation: I am not Mother Teresa.

While this might not be news to most people, I was shocked. How could I not be able and willing to take half the world (and an assortment of stray animals) under my wing? Why was I bone-tired after working my day job, cooking, cleaning, helping with homework, sticking in a late load of laundry, and getting lunches ready for the next day, when I'd do it all over again? Why was I surprised if I dozed off in the dentist's waiting room or in church?

Of course, there are times in our lives when busy comes with the territory. New mothers, those caring for elderly parents or a seriously ill family member, or those who still think they can have it all must keep schedules that would exhaust any sane person. When I remember those late nights from my kids' infancies, I shudder and wonder how on earth I lived to tell about it. During those ultrabusy eras in life, you cling to the adage "This too will pass."

Then it really does pass, and suddenly you're alone again. The kids grow up, parents pass away, a divorce happens. For years you've poured your energies into your family's needs, and now you're not needed much at all.

Anne Morrow Lindbergh, in her memoir, *Gift from the Sea,* says we must face our God and ourselves with no one else beside us. "Woman must come of age by herself," Lindbergh writes, "she must find her true center alone."[3] Women cannot expect their relationships to be a substitute for a relationship with God. A woman who sacrifices herself in order to care for her loved ones will, at some point, be abandoned.

And what if you're the one who needs care? If you are a woman with a debilitating disease or if you're disabled, getting your basic needs met can be hectic. If you must depend upon someone else to help you make your wheelchair transfer or get you to the bathroom, you're familiar with the cliché "Hurry up and wait." If you struggle with depression, you may feel embarrassed to ask for help, so life may seem out of control because you're too ill to take care of your affairs. You may even feel like a malingerer because you're not doing your share in life.

I know what I'm talking about. For more than ten years I've struggled with a fatigue-inducing, pain-filled syndrome as a result of the polio I had as a child. I'm not supposed to overdo it, and when I do, everyone suffers. I get so cranky when the syndrome flares up that I can't stop feeling guilty about resting. Even from my bed I think I should be up mopping the floor or some other idiotic chore.

One dear friend says I am a Puritan at heart. She chides me all the time because I make others' problems my own. I've adopted homeless teenagers, only to wonder why I can't keep milk in the fridge for more than ten minutes. I take in kitties that appear at my doorstep. I feel compelled to donate my time to things my four young-adult children should do for themselves.

Okay, she's got me. My friend is right. But I don't want to be an idle time-waster. "Busy hands ward off worry," my grandmother used to say. Grandma, however, never taught me how to balance busy-ness with common sense. And I have never figured out how to be Mary instead of Martha.

Everyone knows the story. Martha supposedly scurried around, getting a meal ready, while Mary sat at Jesus's feet. The way I learned it in Sunday school, Jesus told Martha to seek the spiritual before she focused on the details of life. Get with God before you worry about the small stuff. Makes a lot of sense—self-revelation number two.

When I realized this one day, I sat down on the sofa, stunned by the simplicity. All I'd have to do was park my bottom in front of God's throne and pray for direction. Add one more thing to my overflowing, messy life, Lord? I could practically see God's head shaking no. Get rid of some things that aren't really my problem, such as wayward kids and cats? Common sense. Listen to God's suggestions about when to ignore the housework and enjoy time with my husband? A no-brainer.

I closed my eyes to pay closer attention to what God was saying. I tried hard not to nod off. Then I felt a tug at my sleeve. My daughter said, "Mom, I'm late." I'd promised to give her a ride to work. Maybe spending time with God would be harder than I thought.

Self-revelation number three: balancing busy-ness is easy to say, much harder to do. I sighed, whispered to God that I'd be right back, and grabbed the car keys. When I returned, I thought, *So much for neat and tidy formulas.* I returned to the couch and pondered. Jesus must have realized Martha's dilemma, and I don't think he was saying she ought to let the place turn into a pigsty while she joined Mary at his feet. Yet I wonder if the Lord, in his admonition to Martha, was hinting that life is more than an orderly set of how-tos. We can toss out the unnecessary, but other unnecessary things will rush in to fill up our days. I know I'll never crack the code of a perfect life during my brief time on earth.

If I ever believe I've got everything in order, that I've achieved a pristine balance between busy-ness and simple being, for me that won't be real living. Yes, I can and should simplify my life—especially when it comes to collecting—and I'm working on it. Why, just last week I closed my eyes and held myself back from sweeping the kitchen floor, even though a muddy-pawed cat had just left a trail on the linoleum. For me, life demands that I make mistakes, occasionally overextend my capabilities, and ultimately face my own selfishness. Learning to walk the balance beam of activity without falling into chaos or a nervous breakdown is, for me, all part of the process.

I looked up and realized I'd been sitting there for nearly an hour. It felt so good to hang with God and with God's help decide how much I should be doing, for others and myself. I didn't have to beat myself up, because getting the right level of busy takes practice. Some seasons of life would be busier than others. And what a relief to find out that God didn't mind if I wasn't a saint!

But that day I decided I wouldn't give up on prayer and meditation either. My neighbor would be overjoyed. When God said, "Be still and know that I am God," I felt an awesome tug of love, pulling me to stick around a little longer. Even if all I do is watch the funny shapes on the inside of my eyelids, I'm determined to be silent and still for at least ten minutes a day. You have to start someplace.

My husband walked in and saw me, still camped out on the couch. His mouth fell open when I said, "Honey, let's watch a movie." I smiled, knowing God was nodding yes as we dimmed the lights.

Reflection

Any concern too small to be turned into a prayer is too small to be made into a burden.

Corrie ten Boom

Finding Time for God

I don't think I ever worried about *becoming* real as much as I wondered where and when I would find time to be real. I was looking for a space apart from my daily life, or a time when there wouldn't be so many demands. Because demands on my time come from roles that have rules. Wife, mother, keeper of the home, editor. How can you be real at work if you can't have a temper tantrum? The real me loves to sit and be still, read and think. But at home lunches must be made, laundry must be done. Do those chores, and that time, take away from who I really am? I have always known there is more to me. But I did get desperate about the fact that no one, not even God, might be able to tell.

Within the space of two years I went from young married woman to mother of three—having twins makes that happen fast. The thing I resented most was that my quiet time was now not quiet, and it wasn't mine. There literally didn't seem to be time to sit, let alone sit, read, pray, think. I tried getting up earlier, staying up later, but that mostly led to guilt. I couldn't do it and be awake at work.

And then came a day I think God was waiting for. I sat in the grocery store parking lot, and just cried. *I just can't do it, God. There is too much to do and too little of me. I can't do it, so you have to*, I said like a stubborn child.

And he did. Of course he did, but you wouldn't have guessed it from my reluctance to let go. God swept in with a blanket of peace. Nothing really changed in my daily life. My children still needed their mother. Work was still demanding. But in the midst of all that dailyness, I began to find suggestions and invitations to make daily life a prayer.

At work, Robert Benson's *Venite* came across my desk. One chapter was a lyrical description of his year. The people, places, and rhythms

117

that read together became an act of worship. So I set out to write my own "perfect year."

What would I put?

In March we fly kites in the hills behind our house.

In July we stay up late to hunt fireflies, and crisscross the country to visit our family, making a great strong web of people that take time to be together, to touch each other.

In September we steal a few more summer moments, collecting shells at the beach with the warm sunset on our faces.

You know what I found out when I wrote about my year? I found it full of concrete things. Actual places and events and actions that glorify God. I never once wrote about "squeezing in" quiet time with God. He was all over that year, in every idea.

At church, I stopped trying to be a different part of the body than I was. The church is a body, but I believe most of its parts tend to think if there were more parts like them, it would function better. Sunday schools always want more teachers. Choirs always want more members. Coffee hour hosts want more volunteers. They are organized. They have charts, and lists, and it is usually easier to just join in and say yes than listen to what God might really have in mind.

I began to recognize myself a lot easier when I learned to be honest about my role. I believed in prayer, and really wanted to be a part of a concentrated time of prayer for our congregation. It turned out I had to be the first pray-er to get it going! I believe God will not brook any argument when we meet him face to face and explain we were too busy to look after orphans and widows, even though we kept him very busy looking after us. We didn't really have a way to move funds and volunteers to the people who needed them most, and that's what I wanted to make happen within our local body.

Mainly though, I learned to embrace my time with my family. I have been learning, these years as our children grow, to stop struggling against the demands on my time and energy. When I stopped trying to get "done" whatever it was they asked, I could finally see the gifts that they were all along. Okay, it doesn't always feel like it. But I have seen now enough times that performing a service for them, or my husband, can be an act of worship. Making lunches turned out to be a great time to pray for my children's days. Ironing my husband's shirts is a very physical way to talk to God about him. That heavy iron presses down, and my concerns for him go with it. Then like magic the wrinkles are gone, taking my cares and worries with them. And my need for time with the Father has been answered in a hundred disparate minutes, rather than a set block of time each day.

Finding time for God, as Brother Lawrence taught us centuries ago, is not about doing more with less. And it's also not about doing less. It's about living life knowing God is present. He's not waiting for you at one time of the day. He's up and out and on the move, his schedule in hand, leading you on.

Scripture Salon

Kristen Johnson Ingram

What God Says about Being Busy

A Reflection on James 1:11

In the midst of a busy life, they will wither away.

James 1:11

In 1721, a book of proverbs appeared in Boston, and one of its adages proclaimed that "the devil finds work for idle hands." (I've also heard versions that say "Idle hands are the devil's workshop," or "Idle hands do the devil's work.") Since the Boston reading audience was made up of Puritans and a few other strict Protestants who were already oriented toward a strict work ethic, and who were certain that a wrathful God would throw them into hell at the slightest provocation, the maxim became the eleventh commandment. Especially for women.

And that tacked-on commandment still rules the lives of too many women. I went to a pre-Christmas party at the home of Connie and John, a churchgoing couple who have four children; energetic Connie also works part-time at a brokerage. Their home was like a gift-shop display. Two Christmas trees graced opposite ends of the big family room, one pink with silver ornaments, the other silver with pink. The buffet table looked like something from *Better Homes and Gardens*, with food and decorations that should have required the services of two chefs and an interior designer, but all were the handiwork of my friend, whom we call Martha Stewart Jr.

The guests took home pink-and-silver-wrapped gifts, which turned out to be satin tree ornaments Connie had made from real eggshells, open on one side and crusted with "jewels" and glitter. Inside were tiny embroidered ribbon roses and teeny white-wax candles. Each one of those ornaments must have represented at least three or four hours' intensive industry. They were exquisite. Works of art. With forty guests, that must have meant more than a hundred hours' work for just the gifts; and none of the food was catered. When I remember that party, I have to lie down, just thinking about the amount of labor.

A few days after the party, I was doing last-minute shopping and ran into Connie's eighteen-year-old daughter. I invited her to the hot-chocolate bar. We sipped our cocoa, and I remarked what a perfect party her mother had given. "You're lucky to have such a great mom," I said, and the girl sighed.

"Yeah, if all you want out of life are beautiful clothes and party favors," she said. "Mom makes all my clothes, and she's a wonderful cook, but *she's* never around to have a cup of cocoa with me, like you are."

Being too busy does more than make kids like Connie's daughter or friends or spouse feel left out. Too much busyness can do spiritual damage to a woman because it keeps her out of the stillness and silence where God wants to meet her.

Since many Christian women place more value on virtue than they do on holiness, they depend on their good works and their dutiful daily prayer list to be offerings to God. Which they are, of course: God accepts anything you want to offer. But are those things alone sufficient for those women? Because if you quiz the busiest Christian woman you know about her deeper spiritual life or her intimacy with God, she may answer that she finds God in Scripture (which she doesn't have a lot of time to read), that her spiritual life is lived around obedience, and that worship means the music part of the Sunday service.

God wants more. God didn't create the dishes in the sink or the long list of parents to call about the school Harvest Fair so women wouldn't do "the devil's work." And nowhere in the Bible do you find that a woman has to clean her oven once a week, enroll all four of her kids in soccer at different schools, and volunteer in the Women's Hospital Auxiliary gift shop to be worthy of the kingdom

The unhappy writer of Ecclesiastes blamed God for the problem, saying, "It is an unhappy business that God has given to human beings to be busy with" (1:13). Well, he was a bored king who had compromised God's commandments with his foreign wives and his bower to the goddess; no wonder he saw the business God gave him as a burden. But Jesus's resurrection proved that God doesn't send an unhappy anything, and "Thy will be done" is really a request for peace, justice, and love between people.

"Keep busy" and "The devil finds work for idle hands" aren't in God's call to be still and know his gracious presence. The devil can't find *any* work for idle hands that are folded in prayer, by a woman who is willing to let God draw her into holy silence. And *busywork* is an insult both to God and to the woman who engages in it.

I've searched the Scriptures for the Puritan work ethic and find only a few verses in Proverbs—said to be written by that same bored, sinful king—that qualify. On the other hand, Deuteronomy commands, "Keep silence and hear, O Israel! This very day you have become the people of the LORD your God" (27:9). Elijah had to quit working, quit running, stand in silence on the mountain in order to hear God's whisper. In the Psalms we read, "For God alone my soul waits in silence; from him comes my salvation" (62:1). Scores of verses in the Bible call us to a holy kind of idleness, to emptying oneself in order to be filled with God. Nobody can hurry that event. And several Scriptures mention being patient instead of trying to fill every minute and improve each shining hour.

We are not made to be frantic, scurrying ants or goal-driven worker bees. God didn't create us to labor day and night; the creation of the Sabbath, which requires complete rest, was a glimpse of what perfection is like. Not only did people have to observe the day of rest and joy, but slaves and servants and animals had to refrain from work. And in Hebrews God calls "his rest" the life beyond this one. God's rest, God's peace, God's ineffable joy: none are gained by being busy but can happen only as a result of being still and knowing God.

Did Jesus want us to be busy all the time? Here are his words: "Come to me, all you that are weary and are carrying heavy burdens, and I will give you rest" (Matt. 11:28).

Something to Try On

- Think about the stress in your own life. Is it caused by people or circumstance? Sick kids, lack of money, or physical limitations? Cast all your anxiety upon Christ, says 1 Peter 5, because he cares about you. What happens to you matters to God; he may be unable, by the restrictions of divinity, to change your circumstances, but he will take your anxiety and hang it on the cross like a crown of thorns. Take some time today to tell God how you feel and ask God for relief. Strength. A breath of fresh air.

- Do you hoard your anxiety or fears until they turn into anger and make you explode? Maybe it's time to sit down with your significant others and tell them the truth about what you're worried about, and apologize for your short-tempered outbursts. Make a covenant to tell the truth before it boils over.
- Do some exercise every day. Whether you join a gym or start by lifting two cans of tomato soup, let the magic of exercise help you dump your tied-in-knots stress. While you're lifting or swimming or dancing, sing a hymn or praise chorus.

6

You in the Mud-Bath Room

Cleansing

Purge me with hyssop and I shall be clean;
wash me, and I shall be whiter than snow.

Psalm 51:7

Reaching Outward for God

Kris: Linda, sometimes you sound as if God has you on a hit list. I wonder if you're the only one on the roster of the unloved, or if you think you're in a great company of people who didn't make the grade in God's eyes.

Linda: Leave me alone and don't ever mention God again! Seriously, it's a good question that will no doubt reduce me to looking like an idiot. I don't think I'm alone in my feelings of unworthiness—as if God thought I was so awful that God had to stop and think up a punishment exclusively for me. How pathetic, right? Many people believe, way down deep, just that. How I got to this dumb and illogical conclusion is a mystery to me. My biggest mistake is I keep trying to argue my way out of this false assumption, as if logic and information will cure a broken heart.

Kris: Wait a second. Are you equating your feeling of worthlessness with the conviction that God can't or won't love you? Of course you feel worthless. You *are* worthless. *We all are.* Unless you have a tame God in a petting zoo, you're wise to feel a little scared in the presence of his immense mystery. There's no little wizard behind the curtain manipulating the sounds and colors of God. And we're worthless to God as far as God's needing us is concerned. Maybe the trick is getting empty enough of judgment on ourselves to allow God to fill every wrinkle in the shabby bags of our souls. And maybe

127

you have to turn off the tapes playing in your head so you can hear Jesus saying, "You are precious in my sight."

Linda: I was praying and praying and praying yesterday—so worried about my son—and I heard myself talking to God in "Christianese," worrying about whether I remembered to say "Thank you," "Praise God," confess my sins—to make sure my prayers didn't bounce off the ceiling. I thought, *If I claim to know God, why shouldn't I speak to God as if God is a treasured friend or my most beloved confidante?* It was so silly, I laughed at myself. Why do I sometimes think I must use special words or abuse the word "just" when I talk to God?

Kris: We all grew up under the impression that we have to talk to God differently than we do to anyone else. Actually, we should talk to God differently, but in more intimate, loving language.

Once I got past "Now I lay me" and "God bless Mama and Daddy," I thought I had to address God in formal, King James, Book of Common Prayer words: "Almighty God, I beseech Thee to succor me." I didn't learn "Christianese" and I never put "just" in a prayer, but I still kept God at arm's length with my words. The author of the fourteenth-century classic *The Cloud of Unknowing* says we should call on the name of God for help in the same voice and tone in which we'd cry "Help!" or "Fire!"

Linda: Grandmother Gypsy used to tell a story on my daddy: she said when he was little, he got stubborn if told to do something. He crossed his arms and scowled, saying, "Hum, me do it." I think I'm like that with God—who keeps trying to tell me Christ tore up the hit list—and still I get so stubborn. "Hum, me do it," I growl. So much scar tissue has grown that no wonder I can't open the door, even a crack. My prayer? "Help me, Jesus."

Kris: Ah, but could God hate anything he has made?

Linda: The longer I live, the more I see the arbitrariness of human rules. We race around here on earth, passing laws upon laws that mean well but are never 100 percent enforceable. We postulate political and social opinions that are right while those opposed to our views must be wrong. Christians try to use the Bible to navigate life, but, in the process, we mistakenly assign some arbitrary or cultural laws to what God absolutely wants or demands of us. We get tangled up with the details and miss out on the love God waits to shower upon his children.

The process of writing this book has helped me open my mind and heart to the God I seek so desperately. The old forest-for-the-trees adage applies to me. All the while I see God peeling away layers of rules and regulations I cling to, gently assuring me that God's love and acceptance transcend human constructs.

If I choose to remain uptight about the way I look, how I perform, how I compare to others, well, then, that's the sum of my spirituality. And if I'm so careful to judge everything by my human standards—even if they are biblically inspired—then that's all I get, as far as my Christianity goes. God seems to be telling me that if I focus solely on whether or not I am doing it right—and so many times I'm not—I might miss my God experience altogether. I don't want that to happen, so I'm willing to search the sky above God's head to see as big a picture as I can.

Kris: Good answer, good answer! Not too long ago I reread *Sinners in the Hands of an Angry God* by Jonathan Edwards. I wanted to rename it *Sinners in the Hands of an Angry Edwards*. Am I deluding myself, refusing to see God's dark, angry side, or is that god a human construct?

I wonder how many of our readers believe that when they get to heaven's gate, God might buck, snort, and send them to hell? But can a Christian go to hell? Sometimes I can almost see the logic in purgatory. That's also a human invention, maybe because nobody really feels clean and good enough to go before the throne without washing up. I take that back: I know one woman who said she now was able to lead a sinless life. Since her children were terrified of her sharp tongue, and her husband positively hagridden, I suspect she meant she didn't break any commandments about sex, alcohol, or theft, but couldn't see the serious sins of her mouth.

Linda: I'm sure my mouth sins often; I don't think anyone dares believe she doesn't flub up with the words she utters. And yet since this is so common—we don't all drink or smoke or steal, but most of us talk—there must be a way God looks at the sins of the mouth and forgives us much. Otherwise I doubt any person would make it to paradise.

Kris: In childhood, one of my best-loved responsive readings from the Psalms started with "O Lord, open thou my lips," and we answered, "And my mouth shall show forth thy praise." If I waited for God alone to open my lips, would I ever speak again?

Linda: This really gets to the core of my relationship with God. If I try to speak only in Scripturisms or "Christianese," I'll be a phony. I don't think this is what God meant about guarding our lips. By being more and more aware of God in my life each moment, I may bring my tongue into line. The Hippocratic oath should apply to what we say in most cases: first, do no harm. The truth may hurt, but it doesn't destroy what is good—yet the truth can be wielded too harshly. Refuse to respond to those around you in terms of what's "nice," and you may wound others without meaning to. I think the psalm you mentioned is advising us to be careful with the sword of truth, lest we be too zealous and critically injure others and ourselves.

Kris: Okay, okay. I'll be careful. But I don't think being ultrasweet or surly are the only two choices either.

In the Mud Bath

Linda Clare

Detox Me, God

Christian women want God and their moms to love them, which is a good thing. Yet many of us don't stop there. We aren't happy unless everybody on earth thinks we're swell. We must be kind to everyone. We want others to like us, because we think being a Christian is about being nice, not real.

You pull into the open parking spot without realizing someone else had been waiting for it too. When the other driver honks or swears, you apologize. You might even let the impatient fellow have the spot, though you have to park in Outer Mongolia. You don't want anyone to be offended.

You and the other members of the church decide to conduct the service a certain way lest You-Know-Who get her knickers in a knot. You-Know-Who wields a lot of power because she's confident no one will want to make a scene. You've gone along with her absurd wishes for years.

Or maybe you dress or act a certain way at church so you'll present a "nice" image. You wear dressy clothes—not too racy or casual—and your shoes have a heel that's just so. You smile a lot, because the Bible says we are to be cheerful. You may agree to do things you hate or take on a burden that isn't yours, all in the name of being a nice Christian woman. The secret is, you know you're not being real, but your strong desire and training to be accepted prevent you from considering a change.

Here in the Mud-Bath Room, we're all about washing away what clogs our pores or keeps us from having that healthy glow. When we're wrapped in seaweed or a blend of dolomite and fine corundum, those nagging impurities rise to the surface. Under a masque of avocado or mud, we can soften, purify, and polish our bodies and our souls.

Most of us who are slaves to "nice" already know our aims are unreasonable and not healthy. Some of our friends might use words such as *codependency* or *people pleaser* to describe our condition. But even Jesus had lots of enemies—folks who were out to get him in the worst possible way. Perhaps all this is really a supersized version of the wish most of us harbor, secretly or not: to make nice, no matter what. Even with people who are impossible.

If you're a nicemaker, you know you spend lots of energy trying to preserve and nurture others, maybe at your own expense. You keep your true thoughts a secret lest someone think you're not a nice Christian.

But God wants something more, and down deep, you know this. Allowing God to exfoliate the faux nice side of you is risky and might feel as pleasant as microdermabrasion or an acid bath. After all, many of us have a hard time grasping the idea that God did not put us on earth to be loved or even liked by every single person. Yet something inside us longs to be real.

If you're willing to go for the mud pack, the exfoliating scrub, or the seaweed wrap, you know you'll come out a different person. Change sometimes rubs people the wrong way and might take some getting used to. But keep in mind that in the spiritual spa, God will always wrap you in his love. In the end you'll look polished and glowing—and real.

Kristen Johnson Ingram

Peace at Any Price

*A Reflection on Euodia and Syntyche
in Philippians 4:2–3*

I urge Euodia and I urge Syntyche to be of the same mind in the Lord. Yes, and I ask you also, my loyal companion, help these women, for they have struggled beside me in the work of the gospel, together with Clement and the rest of my co-workers, whose names are in the book of life.

Philippians 4:2–3

Separate yourself from all twoness. Be one on one, one with one, one from one.

Meister Eckhart

Nobody ever said what the quarrel was about. Maybe the problem began with one of the women making a personal remark about the other. Maybe they struggled over beliefs about angels or miracles in their early church. Euodia could have thought Syntyche was too friendly to strangers, or perhaps Syntyche told someone that Euodia was overbearing. Two godly women who had served the church at Philippi, spreading the gospel and whose work Paul considered to be apostolic, had fallen into a dispute. And their quarrel was beginning to affect even the thriving church at Philippi, of whom Paul had said earlier, "I thank my God every time I remember you" (1:3).

Pastors sometimes think they should ignore problems between a couple of women, but Paul knew better. He was on first-name basis with both these women, who were spiritually mature, hard workers, and valuable to the spread of the faith. He includes their names along with that of Clement, who was an important figure in the early church, so both of them were godly. Tradition says Euodia was the older, but we have no proof, nor any word from God about their ages. Maybe they were sisters, which might explain a lot if they got into a power struggle.

Church schisms occur more often because of personal strife than they do over theology or Bible interpretation or pastoral failure. Many a church has split after two people had a fight and the congregation fell into two camps. And the fight usually starts inside the inner circle, in those close to the leadership, people whose spiritual lives are more mature. Oftentimes it involves the pastor's wife or women who teach or minister. And frequently they are people jockeying for position or feeling slighted by the board or the clergy.

Syntyche's name means "fortunate" and "affable," while Euodia's meaning is "perfumed" or "of good odor" (a common phrase during Roman times, indicating the political or social position of an individual). Now just how did an affable woman, and one whose personal and social perfume was so good, get into a state where they were not of "one mind in the Lord"? And why did the church report the problem to Paul instead of settling it themselves?

Several years ago a church in Oregon was ready to splinter apart over what started with a quarrel between two women. One of them was the pastor's wife, Amy, and the other was Ellie the organist. Ellie believed that Amy had snubbed her, and Amy said Ellie was hypersensitive and imagining things. Ellie told her friends that Amy implied that she was mentally ill, and one smite led to another. These two educated women, both devout Christians, turned into a pair of wildcats, spitting and snarling.

The congregation chose up sides; one or two families left to go to another church, but the rest hurled themselves into the standoff. By the time the church had called in a Christian arbitrator, the parish was in disarray.

The mediator didn't even try to retrace the steps that had led to the disorder. He called an all-church meeting and said that if the problem was tearing the congregation apart, it was destroying the body of Christ. He asked everyone present to kneel and confess his or her participation in the schism, even if that participation was unspoken thought or opinion. And then they sat in silence and waited for the Holy Spirit to do his work.

Finally Amy began to cry. "I never meant to hurt you, Ellie," she sobbed, and within an hour the church was a church again. Or was it? This kind of dissension leaves scars that may never look like new skin. Sure enough, within the next year, several families transferred out, and Ellie's husband never went back to his job as treasurer.

Since such scars are real, the best medicine for schism is prevention. Counselors and pastors should make sure their congregations know they can call on them to arbitrate, or at least listen to grievances, and if that doesn't work, they should appeal to someone outside the church to assist.

And that's why the Philippians reported their problem to Paul. He had been with the flock and knew Euodia and Syntyche, but he was also an authority whose word they considered inspired by God. We might suspect just his words, "I urge Euodia and I urge Syntyche to be of the same mind in the Lord," were enough to solve the problem. Imagine the women's consternation: Paul himself, writing from Rome, with greetings from the emperor's household, the great Paul whose mission had empowered church after church, had named them in his concerns. And had asked the others to help them avoid choosing up sides.

Peace at any price is not peace; it's shutting someone up. Winning and losing are human inventions that leave at least one person feeling like a victim. Sister Mary Bennet, a Benedictine nun who travels the country helping school boards and church leaders solve the issues that have them at each other's throats, says that every person should be heard, and feel as if he or she has been heard; and she advises never to solve a split by anything but consensus. Quakers have a rule that if the board or group cannot agree on an action, they will take no action.

Problems don't work out, people work them out, and talking is the best way to let God's will reveal Godself. People need to talk when they're happy with things and talk to the pastor about the sermon they didn't like, instead of telling everyone else. Christians should talk to the lady who runs the kitchen about her being so bossy; and if talking to that person doesn't work, get a reliable third party to help uproot the problem. Remember what Archbishop Desmond Tutu said to those who were seeking reconciliation between angry Zulus and their former white torturers: "Anger and jealousy and revenge are particularly corrosive, so you try . . . to enhance the humanity of the other, because in that process, you enhance your own."[1] And ultimately, you enhance the church.

Apparently the women in the church at Philippi solved their problem, because Polycarp, who was an associate of Clement and Paul, wrote to the Philippians: "I have greatly rejoiced with you in our Lord Jesus Christ, because ye have followed the example of true love [as displayed by God], and have accompanied, as became you, those who were bound in chains, the fitting ornaments of saints, and which are indeed the diadems of the true elect of God and our Lord."[2]

Not bad for a church that two women had threatened to split.

Cleansing Inspiration
Kristen Johnson Ingram

Handle with Kid Gloves

So then the Lord Jesus, after he had spoken to them, was taken up into heaven and sat down at the right hand of God.

Mark 16:19

When I was four years old, I ran away to Sunday school.

We woke late that morning, and since my mother was the church organist, a lot of rushing around ensued. Mama said she'd get me ready soon, but that I wouldn't be going to Sunday school that day. I put on the previous day's clothes and went outside to my sand pile near the kitchen door.

But, as I sat there pouring sand into a sieve, I listened to the sounds of water splashing and coffee percolating indoors, and I thought about Mrs. Duncan. She was the pastor's mother, a white-haired lady who taught our preschool class, and she wore kid gloves. The touch of her hand in one of those smooth gloves was like a caress from an angel. Suddenly I wanted to be in my class circle, listening to Mrs. Duncan's easy voice as she showed us pictures of Jesus and the other Bible people, of the beautiful tabernacle, and of donkeys and doves.

The church was only about a block away, so I went. In a soiled sunsuit and with bare feet, I ran down the sidewalk to the little white church, stepped through the back door, and slipped into my classroom. Mrs. Duncan looked up and, after a moment, smiled.

"Here's a chair right here by me," she said and held out her hand. She said nothing about my clothes or dirty face and sandy feet. She just welcomed me, and as I climbed onto the dark green folding chair beside her, she took my hand and held it.

I don't know if the other kids noticed my appearance. I don't even remember what the lesson was about. I only remember Mrs. Duncan's smooth, kid-gloved hand making me welcome until my father showed up, grinning, and took me home. I had been at the right hand of power that day. Not only did Mrs. Duncan take my hand, she never let go until I left.

I grew into your basic church kid, appearing at every choir rehearsal and potluck and youth activity. I was baptized and confirmed. I prayed for God to make me his own, to make me feel something I thought I should feel. Yet, in truth, I never listened to the lessons or sermons carefully; I went to church more to be with my friends and to sing than for any other reason.

Then, when I was fourteen, I heard a sermon that took me right back to Mrs. Duncan and the old Sunday school room with its brown beaverboard walls. I don't remember most of the words, just the pastor's saying at the end of each example he gave, "But Jesus is whispering, 'No condemnation.'"

And God touched me with smooth, gentle hands, drew me into the throne room, and reminded me that I was welcome—no, more than *welcome*—I was *honored* by that angelic company.

I wish I could say that from that day forward, I was perfect, that all my choices were godly and wise, that I grew to be a lovely Christian lady without incident. But that's not what happened. Of course. "Without incident" isn't a true story for any man or woman. I grew up in jerks and sputters, making progress and sliding back. I finished school, married unhappily, and bore three children who got the brunt of it. I wanted desperately to be like the stylish, pretty women I saw at church or on Christian magazine covers, women who knew what they were supposed to be, women whose lives were peaceful and perfect. They didn't have a lot of depth, but they sure had a handle on looking and being beautiful.

During those stormy years, though, I still hung out at church a lot, read my Bible, and prayed and listened, listened hard for the voice that whispered "No condemnation."

After many years, one Sunday morning I knelt in church with my own children, singing the communion hymn. I watched one kid crawling under the pews and listened to the birthday pennies rolling down the aisles, and the kids whispering and the badly played organ blaring behind the choir that stumbled through the notes. And as I knelt, something happened. A candle flickered. Or a sunbeam broke through the clerestory windows. Or maybe the organ suddenly expressed a note of exquisite sweetness. I don't know—but I felt the touch of Mrs. Duncan's kid gloves, heard the pastor's sermon, and remembered once and for all that not only was the Jesus story true, but I was written into the story. I was welcome here, this mysterious, beautiful place, full of squirming kids and off-key singing voices . . . donkeys and doves . . . the presence of God.

What happened that day in church was a mystery, just as God is also the mystery I dare to engage.

Reflection

Our natural will is to have God, and the good will of God is to have us, and we may never cease willing or longing for God until we have him in the fullness of joy. Christ will never have his full bliss in us until we have our full bliss in him.

Dame Julian of Norwich

Cleansing Inspiration

Linda Clare

The Paper Dolls of Niceville

When I was a little girl, I played with paper dolls. My younger sister Leslie and I spent hours carefully cutting out the wardrobe of the Lennon Sisters and Pollyanna. I scolded Leslie if she accidentally snipped off a tab or the hem of the doll's dress. Then Mom hollered from the kitchen, "You girls play nice."

At school, things weren't much different. By fourth grade I knew what nice girls didn't do, such as talk out of turn or take cuts in the jump-rope line. Nice meant you waited to be called upon to speak, and you kept your knees together when you sat down. We were expected to be nice and follow the Golden Rule.

Now, in the twenty-first century, has anything changed? Is it possible to be too nice? Can we strike a balance between taking care of ourselves and taking care of others? I think so. Like many women, I've fallen into the Nice trap, where nurture becomes torture and selflessness is riddled with resentment. But when I decided to plan my escape from my hypocritical life of Nice, I didn't know it would be so hard. Or so worth it.

Elizabeth Hilts, author and editor, says there is something called "toxic niceness." What starts as good manners or compassion grows beyond social decorum, creating a fear of being what you really are. You bite your tongue instead of saying what's on your mind. You're quick to smooth over any unpleasant event, often at your own expense. You go so far out of your way to help others that your own needs are neglected. Toxic niceness can render you flat as my sister's paper dolls.[3] Yet many women have learned these behaviors from an early age. Mine started with that pesky Golden Rule.

The Golden Rule was God's idea, so how could I go wrong? The familiar "Do unto others" Scripture was emblazoned across my memory, eager to assist me in any relationship decision. Before acting, my sister and I were taught to think about how we'd feel if that action were turned upon ourselves. I got plenty of practice.

For instance, if I did something mean to my unwitting little sister—say I hid her favorite Janet Lennon paper doll and told Leslie that Mom had vacuumed it up—I heard a booming voice in my head quoting that verse. I knew what I was doing was wrong, but I had so much fun that it was almost worth it. Until I had to copy that verse one hundred times as punishment.

My grandma spouted adages such as "You catch more flies with honey than vinegar" and the dreaded "If you can't say something nice, don't say anything at all." With those rules it made sense for us to be nice—even when it wasn't in our best interests. So I grew up to be a nice, people-pleasing woman who hates confrontation and has a terrible time speaking her mind.

But is that so bad? In this era of rude and aggressive behavior, it's hard to fault anyone for showing kindness and civility. Road rage is a real threat to ordinary drivers. People shout and make crude gestures for minor infractions; we race to beat each other into parking spots. And everyone sighs if you let someone get ahead of you in the supermarket checkout line. Everywhere we go, it's unusual to observe the most basic of social graces. So how can anybody be too nice?

Toxic niceness is really about being less than honest, and it takes many forms. Some women think they must be completely selfless, doing for others while completely ignoring their own needs. They run ragged doing good deeds—even when they're too tired, sick, or inconvenienced themselves. Others believe they must be a combination of Superwoman and Proverbs 31 in order to be pleasing to God. Caring and selfless giving are wonderful qualities, but when self-neglect rises to the breaking point, niceness can develop into unhealthy habits.

One way to tell if your nice has turned to Nice is to think of the oxygen masks that pop down in front of you if an airplane is in trouble. Airline personnel always instruct passengers to put their own masks on before trying to help anyone else. If you can't breathe, how can you help others?

The same holds true for our relationships. If we give so much that we feel resentful, hypocritical, or far from God, we may have forgotten to take care of ourselves. We must put on our own oxygen masks before we can afford to help others.

Sounds easy enough, but I'll admit that my own mask often gets lost or misplaced. I struggle with toxic niceness even when I try to stop. Nice is so ingrained in me that I feel awful twinges of guilt if I so much as disagree with someone. I'm so attuned to the "as you would have them do unto you" part that I can't stop trying to assist people. But when I look around, I notice that I'm doing all the giving.

I also notice that I'm miserable. Like many women, I end up kicking myself for being such a pushover. Time after time, I avoid conflict until I fear my own emotions. The Golden Rule imprisons us if we ignore the opportunity for transformation. There is a way out, as God calls us to live a fuller, more authentic Christian life.

When I discovered that I was caught in the Nice trap, I couldn't see any escape. If I became assertive, would I be accused of feminism or worse? If I took care of myself, physically and emotionally, would I fall prey to a "me first" mentality? And if I drew boundaries for myself, would people whisper "selfish" behind my back?

Then I looked at my problem in a different way. If all my relationships are based on master-servant models, I have no choice in anything.

It doesn't do much good to disagree if I have no part in the decision. If, however, I decide what I do or don't do, I must set my own limits.

This does not amount to selfishness. It's about boundaries. There's only so much of you and me to go around. If we are constantly doing for others while neglecting ourselves (or our spouses or our God), we may find we have little energy left at the end of the day. Keeping our niceness in check involves drawing an imaginary line around the things we think God wants us to do and not stepping over the line.

Drs. Henry Cloud and John Townsend have written a series of books about boundaries, maintaining that "boundaries are a 'litmus test' for the quality of our relationships."[4]

Setting boundaries does not mean being aggressive. Aggression takes many forms—yelling, belittling, stonewalling, even violence—but assertion requires a calm demeanor. Pent-up anger and resentment sabotage many attempts at assertiveness. That's been my problem too—I act Nice (even when I'd rather not) until I explode. Like the man in the classic movie *Network*, I'm mad and I'm not going to take it anymore. No in-between. I'm working on saying what I think without resorting to a volcanic eruption.

Being assertive means you are calm and you state your answer to a request in simple, nonemotional terms. The phrase "I don't think so" is nonjudgmental and doesn't give an excuse. No lengthy explanation and no "I'm sorry." That's right. I have to remove "I'm sorry" from my vocabulary if I wish to get beyond the Nice trap. But even this was too difficult for a nice person like me.

I simply couldn't do it on my own. I had to admit I couldn't change. I had to get prostrate and tearful and tell God I wanted a deeper, more authentic life, and I needed a lot of help to do it. Like a person in a 12-step program, I had to "let go and let God."

Knowing I wasn't in it alone gave me confidence. God and I would lick the stupid Nice problem. "I don't think so" was firm but gentle. How could anyone argue with it? Then one of my children tested me.

My teenage son was speechless when I said it, after he'd asked for a ride somewhere just minutes into my nap. I was groggy, but somehow I managed "I don't think so." When he began to argue, the trap was sprung.

"Mom," he said, "why not?"

I launched into a bunch of reasons and even apologized for resting. Before it was over I was pulling on my shoes and grabbing the car keys. I blew it and was resentful with my son in the car. As I said, de-Nicing takes practice. Next time, I'll keep repeating "I don't think so" until it sinks in. Assertiveness isn't easy, and I have a ways to go until I succeed.

Confusing assertiveness with aggressiveness is a common reaction for those of us who've stuffed our true feelings for a long time. We've smiled through clenched teeth when asked to squeeze in another meeting or bake another batch of cookies. We don't want to do it, but we say yes because that's the Christian way. Or is it?

The Bible describes the power of the tongue to hurt or heal in James 3:8–10. We set the tone for how nice we can be. Yet according to author and psychologist H. Norman Wright, we often poison and wound each other with the words we use.[5] That's when our desire to "play nice" gets contaminated with toxic weapons.

But Jesus wants us to be nice, doesn't he? In addition to the Golden Rule, Jesus spoke about loving one another, bearing one another's burdens, turning the other cheek. Can we be good Christian women if we aren't nice all the time?

Absolutely. Jesus *is* love and he loves us—the Bible tells us so. He was sinless and helped thousands of people in biblical times. But was he always nice? And did he say yes to everyone? Now and then there were times when Jesus showed emotion to get his point across, as when he tossed money changers out of the temple.

Even though Jesus was God incarnate, there were, no doubt, those who didn't receive what they wanted from him—rather like the bank teller who closes her window when you finally get to the head of the line. Jesus as a man had to draw his own boundaries, and he was assertive (not aggressive) to the very end. When we limit the extent of our niceness, we are only acknowledging our humanity, just as our Lord did during his time on earth.

By now you may be asking, as I did, "Can I be nice without being toxic?" Yes. Jesus doesn't want us to be mean. He wants us to be firm. He wants us to be reasonable. And most of all, he wants us to be honest and sincerely nice, not Nice. There is a huge difference between being nice and being Nice. Jesus doesn't want us to be phonies. As the *Boundaries* books explain, it's all about when to say yes and when to say no. Sounds simple, but once identified, the toxic brand of Nice takes practice to eliminate. Try saying "I don't think so" next time you're tempted to say yes when you'd rather say no.

The journey out of toxic niceness is scary because it requires us to change. If I set boundaries, I risk losing the love and acceptance I enjoy as the nice lady who will "do anything for anyone." My family may not understand if I am honest and say, "I don't think so." Yet I am convinced that God wants vibrant people who joyfully extend grace to others, not tired and resentful followers who feel put upon.

I've outgrown paper dolls—although I still follow the Golden Rule. I'm reaching for a more genuine brand of nice instead of the toxic, phony kind. Escaping the Nice trap won't be instantaneous. It will be hard and I may stumble, but I'm not giving up. For any woman who desires a closer connection with people and with God, it's a worthwhile journey.

Scripture Salon

Kristen Johnson Ingram

What God Says about "Nice"

A Reflection on Ephesians 4:15–16

> But speaking the truth in love, we must grow up in every
> way into him who is the head, into Christ, from whom the
> whole body, joined and knit together by every ligament
> with which it is equipped, as each part is working properly,
> promotes the body's growth in building itself up in love.
>
> Ephesians 4:15–16

I was wandering around the World Wide Web looking for information
for an article I was writing about new techniques in healing fractures.
I ran across a French site and tried to translate what was there. My
French had deteriorated from lack of use and I didn't know some of the
words, but at last I saw a tiny British flag in one corner and clicked.
Voilà! I could read the following words in English:

> About five percent of fractures do not heal or heal badly. In
> these cases the shock wave therapy could be helpful. With an
> electric device applying a voltage up to 28,000 V an underwater
> explosion is evoked. The resulting high-energy waves can be
> focused and guided exactly to the points of fracture. The enor-
> mous forces destroy the shell of the bone endings. Microscopic
> tears and bleeding occur. These injuries stimulate the tissue to
> growth and to close the gap between the bones. The therapy
> continues 20 to 90 minutes and is quite painful. Therefore it is
> applied under an anesthetic. Further, patient and physician have
> to wear protectors for the ears because of the explosions.

Yeah, I thought. *Fracture.* The church, the body of Christ, is fractured and not healing all that well. Will God send us some kind of shock wave? Will it be painful? And will it work?

I wondered about this treatment and finally had a physics discussion with my husband. I was reluctant, not because he won't answer questions, but because he tells me a great deal more than I want to know and continues talking, making pencil sketches, comparing my question to unrelated things without noticing that my eyes have glazed over ("A minuscule shock wave is actually what makes your printer jet ink," he said triumphantly). I did finally comprehend that the voltage, which is considerable, doesn't enter the person's body but only creates the water wave that bangs against the joint or fracture, tearing it up so it can begin to heal, the way you might hammer the ends of a twig so it will root.

Shock wave therapy is "quite painful," the medical paragraph says, and requires an anesthetic. And therein lies the flaw: I think one of the problems with healing the church is that we're gulping the anesthetic but dodging the shock, in the same way that some people are hooked on ether or nitrous oxide ("laughing gas") or midazolam and don't have a dental or medical procedure that requires it. The church, which needs its fractures healed, is snorting the anesthetic called Nice but not letting God slam it with the wave. We want the sweetness without the pain.

Throughout the church, the most anesthetized group are the young girls and women. Nice, one of the first attributes most little girls learn, smothers the intellect, dulls the pain of relationships, and covers anger or frustration. Nice substitutes sentiment for love, cuteness for beauty, shallowness for honesty, and charm for truth. Nice is more destructive to real Christian behavior than a thousand sins, because Nice is, even in people who believe in it, a falsehood. A Nice Christian woman who has never spoken her deepest feelings is living a lie that can become a pain-killing, brain-numbing habit that's as bad as sniffing nitrous oxide or shooting up morphine.

I'm not sure which is the prevalent fear that sends us looking for the anesthetic: are we most afraid of hurting someone, or of being hurt? Or do those two opposites feed on each other to produce a sweet-tempered woman who keeps her intellect in check, her temper filed away, her appearance perfect—and who believes that she's living a life of biblical proportion? What she is really doing is stifling the magnificent spirit with which God endowed her. And she is helping to fracture the church because she's not living an authentic Christian life.

When the shock comes, I hope we recognize it as a gift from God to heal the fracture of Christ's body. I'm not talking eschatology: God won't rapture up a church with as many splinters and fissures and breaking joints as ours. I'm talking about God's correction, which we need desperately. And though Christ's shock-wave ministry to the church may be abrasive or even painful, and though the explosions might hurt our ears, we have to welcome them.

We have to give up Nice and become women who speak the truth in love and are willing to become Christian grown-ups. Now let's get those joints and ligaments knitting. Let's forget being nicey-nice while we struggle with dispensationalism or baptism or predestination. God would much rather see us talk to one another until we really resolve our differences, or at least come to open terms with them, than see us snorting Niceness and drifting into apathy.

Ideas for Reflection & Application

Something to Try On

- Pray today for peace on earth, peace not as the world gives, nor peace to keep things nice; instead ask for God's peace to fall on nations and cities and houses, including yours.

- If you're in an abusive marriage or other relationship, quit being nice and leave. Do not live in a home where anyone hits you or abuses you verbally. Yes, you made marriage vows, but you didn't promise to be the object of brutality, physical or verbal. If that's going on, you don't *have* a marriage. Leave. Take your kids, go to a women's shelter, and listen to what they have to say about self-destructive niceness.

- Civility rises out of the need for people to be together amicably. "Niceness," on the other hand, is someone's desperate need to please others. When you are polite and kind, why are you doing it? Fold a piece of paper in half, then write the things you do to appease everyone and the things you do because you love doing them.

7
You at the
Massage Table
Community

There can be no vulnerability without risk; there can be no
community without vulnerability; there can be no peace,
and ultimately no life, without community.

M. Scott Peck

Is Community Necessary?

Linda: Getting along with people in church is the hardest part of being a Christian. No matter what church you attend, it seems as though there's always somebody you can't stand. You don't want their cars bombed or anything, but if they don't show up one Sunday, you're kind of glad.

Kris: I'm glad you don't want their cars bombed. I rarely see someone whom I dislike that much. I can think of one woman who's a church menace, because she wants to control anything she works on. She dang near drove our Habitat for Humanity house out of business. But since it says in Hebrew not to neglect our community, we have to find a way to make her an important part of our assembly.

Linda: It's hard to remember that someone you dislike is someone God loves. And God wants me to love as God does, even if people are controlling or gossips or even liars. Or people in the church who try to sell you home-care products or some other pyramid scheme.

Kris: How come you're so harsh in your opinions? And how do you get past that when you're trying to be part of a faith community? Do they have to change, or do you?

Linda: Obviously, *I* have to change. For me, change can happen only when I try to see God in every face I look at. No matter what opinion I've formed of that person, I don't want a barrier between God and me.

Kris: How about someone who has hurt you terribly? I've encountered a few of those. In fact, I've had more hurt and betrayal from Christians than from anyone in the secular world. You and I have to try to get God between us and the people who hurt us, because they may need God's love worse than we do. And they turn up everywhere we go.

Linda: Maybe it's like a deep tissue massage that's going to hurt before it feels better. Forgiveness and love are hard, painful, but once I've forgiven, I feel so much better. I *want* to love everyone, and I'm trying.

At the Massage Table

Linda Clare

Getting Along with God— and Everyone Else

You've made it this far in God's spiritual spa. Now you arrive at the Massage Table, after purifying yourself in the Mud Bath. You lie face-down on the bench, not sure you're up for another challenge. What area of your life is God going to fiddle with this time?

Well, if you had any doubt about laying aside false niceness back at the Mud Bath, you'll be glad for this station. God wants to help you massage away the sore spots as you deal with the relationships in your life—your community. God knows that getting along with others is one of the knottiest problems in our lives.

You're an ordinary Christian woman, struggling with your relationships. You truly desire to live as Jesus wants you to live, and yet at times this seems impossible. At every turn you meet people who have their own ideas about life. When their agendas collide with yours, sparks fly and you may forget the Golden Rule. You feel awful and you vow to change, but then it happens again. Is there an answer?

In Psalm 91:2, David says God is "my refuge and my fortress; my God, in whom I trust." Throughout the Psalms, David thanks God, rejoices in God, and loves God. Even when David himself makes mistakes, he readily admits them to God. But when David speaks of other people, things get complicated.

Relationships will do that. Some have said that being a Christian would be far easier if it weren't for the people. For it's in our dealings with others—spouses, children, church members, or that third cousin twice removed—where life can be the most challenging.

King David had trouble with relationships, so we know that problems in getting along with each other have been around for a long time. Across history the church has divided and divided again because people couldn't agree. And here we are in the new millennium, still trying to negotiate our relationships without destroying them.

On Sundays, when the pastor asks you to turn and greet your neighbor, do you inwardly groan? Do you make nice even when you'd rather tell off someone who has hurt or angered you? Is there someone in your social circle who gets your goat no matter how hard and often you pray that you'll suddenly like her? Or do you deal with relationship hassles by staying so busy you don't have time to think about them?

Hard questions, to be sure. You know the right answers: Treat others as you would be treated. Turn the other cheek. Don't let the sun go down on your anger. Love your neighbor as yourself.

Tall order. Jesus surely must have known how difficult it can be to practice his precepts. He must have watched as his own disciples argued about everything from the best fishing spots to how to distribute their resources. Since they were human, they must have murmured about each other too. Maybe someone didn't pull his weight or took more than his share at the dinner table. If they were married, maybe they occasionally fought with their wives or got busy and forgot an important anniversary. We can only imagine their conflicts, but we must allow for them because they were all ordinary men, called to an extraordinary purpose. Jesus asked them to open their arms and minds to the possibilities of spreading the Good News, in spite of their shortcomings.

Look to Jesus for the answer to relationship woes, and you may be surprised. While we often think Christ was always gentle and nice, the Bible tells a different story. He never stopped loving, but he was often firm; a few times he even became angry. As God's Son, Jesus's reach was unquestionably wider than any human's, yet he was also an ordinary guy. He saw the pain of love when it becomes all-consuming, the guilt of covering true feelings with a niceness mask, the numbness of substituting activity for relationship. No matter the situation, we know for sure that Jesus understands.

When you lie on the Massage Table, God and you can explore common pitfalls in your community, because connecting with others is the first step in loving your neighbor as yourself. You may be tempted to flinch, but remember that God isn't interested in causing you more pain. Instead, God's touch is more likely to gently melt away hurt or bitterness and help you begin to reconnect with the people in your world.

Reflection

I had not loved enough. I'd been busy, busy, so busy, preparing for life, while life floated by me, quiet and swift as a regatta.

Lorene Cary

Kristen Johnson Ingram

The Community of Christ's Body

A Reflection on Hebrews 10:24–25

> And let us consider how to provoke one another to love
> and good deeds, not neglecting to meet together, as is the
> habit of some, but encouraging one another.
>
> Hebrews 10:24–25

Waves crashed and then receded, their last ripples swirling foam on the sand and my bare toes. I had walked several miles, and it was time to turn back. The last smidges of sunlight danced on the water, and as darkness began to creep in from the east, I watched the stars and planets appear, dressed in light. There was no moon that night, so the spangle of the heavens was breathtaking. I opened the gate to our beach house and sat on the front step, adoring the one who made the ocean, the stars, and the lacy phosphorus that now decorated the dark ocean waves. The night was full of God, and for a long time, I worshiped just by sitting on that step while creation revealed itself. An experience I will never forget.

Are occasions like that enough? Moses went up to Mount Sinai alone, and Jesus went off by himself to pray. So can I be a church here, all alone, reading the Bible, singing hymns and sitting in awe of what God has created?

Unless I live in a forestry lookout station in the Yukon or am so disabled that I can't move out of my bed or chair, no. I'm supposed to mingle with my sisters and brothers in the faith. The Bible tells me so, tells me that community and assembly and meeting are articles of

155

my belief. We don't just encounter one another in church and Sunday school; we meet Christ there too, in the faces and the words of those men and women.

Think of the holiest person you've heard about in modern times. Maybe it was Mother Teresa or Billy Graham or even Mahatma Gandhi. Whomever you choose, imagine that the person was going to sit with you in church, at your table at potlucks, and in your study groups, where he or she would pay special attention to you. If you were certain Billy Graham was going to be your study partner, or that Mother Teresa was going to pray with you, would you be more or less likely to go to church? I feel certain you're saying "More often," because you want to encounter Christ in those persons. You long for holiness, or you'd be reading something else. Maybe the company of someone who has given his or her entire life to God would satisfy some of your longing.

Well, guess what? Your faith community contains unsung heroes, people who have indeed sacrificed their lives for the sake of the Savior. Maybe that mousy little widow who always sits in the third row of pews gives more than half her income away. Perhaps the old guy with a face like a Shar-pei can read the Old Testament in Hebrew. Holy people are everywhere! As the children's hymn says, "The world is bright with the joyous saints who love to do Jesus' will."[1]

Then what is my purpose, what is your job in the church? It's to be there. To be a holy person who can satisfy someone else's longing. Because the kids' hymn ends with "For the saints of God are just folk like me, and I mean to be one too."[2]

Yes. You and I. We're God's saints, and we've got to contribute our sainthood to the faith community, to keep the body of Christ alive and in communion with its members.

Linda Clare

A New Look

We need others physically, emotionally, intellectually; we
need them if we are to know anything, even ourselves.

C. S. Lewis

Love is blind, they say. And knows not how to fill an empty toilet-
paper spindle. Whether you're talking about your spouse, child, parent,
a friend, or an enemy, the relationships that make up your world are
probably precious as well as problematic. You can't live without others,
but living with them is sometimes a huge pain in the neck.

Women have always tended to look for ways to compromise, to
maintain peace, to work things out. Yet in the quest for smoothing
things over, we have also trapped ourselves in a cycle of making nice.
We have tolerated unhealthy unions for the sake of the children. We've
given until it not only hurts, it's life-threatening. And we've done it
all for the sake of relationships.

A wife said ruefully of her failed marriage, "When I look at my
wedding dress it hurts that all that care is taken to preserve a dress
when so little care was taken to preserve a family, but I guess it's easier
to store a dress than to make a marriage work."[3]

Marriages and other relationships do take work—lots of it. This is
the area of life where we hope for the most happiness, where we never
anticipate failure. Every person we know—from mother to daughter
to friend—makes up a complex web that can be the source of joy, but
just as often it creates friction. Then we seek out counselors, write to
advice columnists, and pray, hoping for improvement.

We all need love in our lives, and when things go wrong we look
to God for answers. One of the most important ways God shows love
for us is through our relationships. Life without them would be lonely

indeed. But conflict is common, and some people go through life with emotional machetes, hacking their way through their relationships. These are the crisis junkies, who don't feel alive unless something is wrong.

Sometimes a relationship simply can't be saved. The church has become more realistic about spousal abuse and no longer forces women to suffer in the face of physical or mental mistreatment. Those are the times when we may step back and see whether love has played its part.

Loving others as Jesus loved is a monumental task for even the most well-intentioned Christian woman. We don't expect each other to turn water into wine or to walk on water, but we often assume we should be able to maintain a perfect love—even if the person in question has wronged us in a most grievous way. While godly love is a worthy goal, it may be a little like catching butterflies without a net.

So you're human. That's step one of any relationship improvement program. The sooner you admit that you and everyone else you know are bound to make mistakes, the easier it will be. You sometimes say things you wish you hadn't said, or you act mean without really thinking. Relationships run best on large doses of honesty, and the first place to get real is with you.

While you're at it, you might decide that God's love has no use for phony niceness, the sort that politicians use when they're stumping for votes. If you don't think it's lying when you say your friend's awful new hairdo looks terrific, think again. The mask you wear while trying to like and be liked by everyone will one day wear you down. Public displays of piety to groom a friendship will backfire. Being nice to your husband while you secretly fume at him for forgetting an important occasion only fortifies resentment. Paul says if I speak with the tongues of men and of angels but I lack love, then I am "a noisy gong" (1 Cor. 13:1). Leave out love and eventually relationships collapse.

While many marriages and friendships fizzle for lack of love, some get smothered by unhealthy clinging and dependency. Even in the face of physical or emotional abuse, some women can't or won't leave their spouses. Addictive relationships can be just as harmful as lifeless marriages for the same reason: real love is absent. In addictive love, an idolatry of sorts takes place, and one or both partners gets caught in a cycle of abuse and neglect.

And what about your enemies? It's hard enough to get along with your friends and family. How about those in your life who are constant thorns in your side? Barbara Johnson suggests that we can give ourselves love homework, ask God to help us love someone we don't like. We don't have to make that person our new best friend, but we can decide to stop disliking. Johnson says God will bless us for our obedience and replace animosity and hostility with patience and forgiveness.[4]

Loving our enemies sounds very difficult, and maybe it's something with which only God can assist us. While thorny people will always invade our lives at times, it's our attitude that counts. God uses available people—those whose minds and hearts are open to change. Difficult relationships may always be difficult, but in trying to see them as God does, we shed attitudes that hold us back.

You may recognize yourself here and truly want to have honest, more meaningful relationships. You aren't afraid to look at your own attitudes to be sure they're healthy and productive. You seek God for the answers. Like you, I want to learn more about God's love, a love that isn't blind and keeps the tissue roll full.

Massage Inspiration
Jo M'Gonigle

In the Garden

Pastor Bill expressed disappointment about previous years' low attendance at our Ascension Thursday service, and at the same time some parishioners had been looking for a reason to have a service in their garden setting. This seemed like an Amen kind of combination, so the worship committee planned it as such for that feast day.

The committee considered desserts first, of course, which is the Christian tradition. Desserts would fit right in with the suggestions for a common meal at the end of communion. But more important, the committee proposed to let those who attended be the ones who wrote the sermon that night, responding to the setting of the garden and the ways that being there connected them with God. But even more important than that, they decided to share the communion elements with each other, rather than the ministers distributing the bread and wine.

"But what about You Know Who?" someone asked.

"Well, what about her?" I wanted to know.

"She won't take communion from anyone but someone ordained."

"Doesn't she know," I bristled, "that in her anointing at baptism she herself was sealed into the royal priesthood of Jesus?" *O my legalistic heart.*

One of the committee, who is full of wisdom and fairness, reminded us that when we don't believe what others believe, it is best to err on the side of compassion. In choosing compassion, then, from the long list of options such as shunning, telling her the celebration was on a different night, giving her the wrong street address, sitting her down and explaining the baptismal covenant, we decided that Pastor Bill would serve her first, serve the one next in line, and ask then that the elements be passed and shared further with one another. We were in one compassionate accord that this was a good plan. We closed the meeting with a fervent prayer for clear skies on that special evening.

Ascension Thursday dawned foggy but turned into an almost summery coastal day, warm and very windy, with the heat in the valley to the east pulling in hearty offshore winds. A phone call to the hostess assured us it was perfectly beautiful in the garden that night. Their tall pines to the west always protected them on days like this. Off we went, carpooling and caravanning, as parking was tight and some did not know the way. The sense of mutual love, fellowship, and community, so strongly present in a worship service, had begun to take hold. And with the great plan of the worship committee, not to be confused with the great commandment, "Love one another as I have loved you," the evening held the promise of glory.

There was a good-sized congregation that night, much to the delight of the pastor, who couldn't have looked more pleased as he welcomed people bearing smiles and desserts through the metal yard gate into the newly formed sanctuary. There were almost chairs enough and we all took a place to sit or stand, cautioning each other to the possible peaks and valleys hidden in the uneven turf. You Know Who chose the first seat near the altar table. It couldn't have been a more compassionate seating if the good Lord had seated her himself. *Be still, my legalistic heart.*

The informality of the evening was evident. We all wore our outdoor "yard" clothes, the priest didn't vest or even wear a stole, and he started the service with a joke. You know the one. The kindergartners are asked to draw a picture of the ascension and one little boy drew a picture of a pair of shoes at the bottom of a big white, puffy cloud. "What's this, Johnny? What are these shoes?"

"That's the last thing you see of Jesus," says Johnny, "as he goes up into heaven."

We laughed and knew what we were to celebrate—the Jesus of earth finally becomes the Christ of heaven.

We spoke no formal creed that night, the one that affirms our belief that "he ascended into heaven and is seated at the right hand of God." Instead we recited, in and because of the garden, "A Creed for the Sowing of Seeds" by Joyce Rupp, from her book *Fresh Bread*, based on Mark 4:26–28. "A man scatters seed on the land; he goes to bed at night and gets up in the morning, and the seed sprouts and grows—how, he does not know" (NEB). That pushed some botanical buttons, and the sermon time had no one without comment.

A high school senior made the opening homiletic, noticing how close he felt to God, the nature of God, and all of creation when he was in a garden. Someone else spoke about the work involved in a garden, lightened by praising God at the time of labor. The host remarked how the yard had always seemed so linear to him before, but now with the altar table and chairs set up as they were, he could see the possibilities and connections with circles as the Alpha and the Omega present in a garden setting. I could see the individual grass blades as the church members: when we are compressed, in crisis or disappointment or misunderstanding, we spring back to life by prayer for one another and mutual care. Someone else could see the vine and branches story.

Everyone seemed to understand where we were. It was a garden, but not just any garden; it was The Garden. We were in relationship with God, and with each other. He had created us, called us man and woman, we were in his image, and it was good (Gen. 1:27). It was as if we heard Jesus say, "Truly I tell you, today you will be with me in Paradise" (Luke 23:43). Even You Know Who commented on what a delightful evening it was, delight being a characteristic of Paradise, the garden of delight, Eden. We all knew we were home and knowing that, ready to give thanks through the communion.

What about You Know Who? Well, what about her? It started off okay at the communion time. She was served first. Step one of the great plan accomplished. But then, for some unknown reason, the bread restarted on the other side of the altar table and came back around to her again. She refused the bread, as she had already received, and kept pushing it back to the one serving her.

The deacon was stage-whispered into rescue: "Get the bread." My compassion withered, like the grass in Isaiah's prophecy (40:7–8), and I felt the blast of Isaiah's Lord.

But this bristling I had felt over the refusal of shared communion had nothing to do with the worship committee; it had nothing to do with You Know Who's understanding of the baptismal anointing. It had everything to do with me, my legalistic heart, my critical spirit, my understanding of the baptism, and my understanding of a garden, The Garden.

We have a yellowed cartoon on the refrigerator door. It pictures the king and queen, throneside, with the king holding a haughty pose off into the future, hoping to see who is seeing him, and the queen saying, "You think it's all about you, don't you?" It was all about me and what I wanted for someone else. I wanted You Know Who to feel the freedom she has through the blood of Christ, not the restrictions of a system of "shoulds" or "shouldn'ts." And how will I know if she's bound to a system, unless I talk to her?

Father, forgive me.

Until I understand the great commandment a little better, the one that we love one another as Jesus loved us, until I understand that love at its true heart is about willing good for someone else, not me, I wouldn't want to see myself as a garden. No telling what weed might grow there.

A garden can tell you a little bit about who you are right now, not so much how you look, but how you interact in it, feel in it, behave in it, change in it, about growing over time in it. Recognizing that there are lots of things going on under the soil as well as above ground, you are waiting for full harvest but grateful for the flowers already seen. A friend has told me we go to church not so much to worship God but to find out who we are. I think that's what happened that glorious Ascension Feast Thursday in the garden.

> The LORD has indeed comforted Zion,
> comforted all her ruined homes,
> turning her wilderness into an Eden,
> her thirsty plains into a garden of the LORD.
> Joy and gladness shall be found in her,
> thanksgiving and melody.
>
> Isaiah 51:3 NEB

Gladness and joy, thanksgiving and melody, a living church, a living God, a Jesus, here, there, and everywhere that night. We were causally connected on that evening, mutually interested in worshiping God. We were the garden in The Garden, comforted, interconnected, living harmoniously, in his own image.

Begging the Question

I hear the word *justice* on the TV news a lot: a late bulletin from the Department of *Justice*, or someone's being brought to *justice*, or *justice* at last for a murder victim. But what God calls justice has nothing to do with courts or juries; in the Bible, *justice* means what people today call "charity."

God doesn't say, "Bring terrorists to justice," "Avenge your children," or "Create a Three Strikes policy." What God *does* say is, "For the LORD your God is God of gods and Lord of lords, the great God, mighty and awesome . . . who executes justice for the orphan and the widow, and who loves the strangers, providing them food and clothing" (Deut. 10:17–18). God hears the voice of poverty, and even David, who liked to beg God to kill his enemies, said, "I know that the LORD maintains the cause of the needy, and executes justice for the poor" (Ps. 140:12).

I try to give money every Sunday morning to a woman who stands in the median strip where I turn to go to church. Her sign reads, "Hungry, Disabled, God Bless." She used to limp to my car window every week, gripping her cane with misshapen fingers, and thanking me graciously, and I always felt happy to have handed her a little cash. But then one Sunday, after I had been out of town for several weeks, I stopped at the supermarket to use an ATM and then walked out to the median strip where she held her sign. Before I could get there, she hobbled out and hugged me, saying she was glad to see me; she'd been worried—had I been sick?

On that Sunday morning God told me I couldn't sanitize my relationship with the poor. I had to be present to that woman, so I hugged her back and asked if I could pick her up after church for lunch.

We are friends now. Her name is Ann. She finally got into an apartment a year later—a good thing, because she wrecked the miserable car in which she lived. The low-income housing will subsidize at least half her rent. She was formerly a centrifuge specialist in a hospital, but rheumatoid arthritis has gnarled her fingers. And her knees and spine. Yes, she gets disability payments, but that isn't enough to pay her nonsubsidized rent and buy food and pay for the car accident she had, with no insurance.

Paul said, "Anyone unwilling to work should not eat" (2 Thess. 3:10), but Ann works. She's on the street eight or nine hours every day, in the relentless winter rain or summer sun, holding up her sign. A hard way to make a living. She works, and her main work is hoping: she has to hope for God's kind of justice coming from God's children.

God says, "I command you to do this. When you reap your harvest in your field and forget a sheaf in the field, you shall not go back to get it; it shall be left for the alien, the orphan, and the widow, so that the LORD your God may bless you in all your undertakings. When you beat your olive trees, do not strip what is left; it shall be for the alien, the orphan, and the widow. When you gather the grapes of your vineyard, do not glean what is left; it shall be for the alien, the orphan, and the widow" (Deut. 24:17–21).

I don't harvest fields; I write and get some kind of payment instead. So that means I have to open my heart and purse to the gleaner, including the impoverished and abandoned and old people who stay in bed late on winter mornings because they can't afford to turn on the expensive heater.

Those poor and downtrodden need a second gift from me: *presence*. I know that many pastors and other Christians believe I shouldn't give money to street people or those who hold signs up near the freeway entrance, that I should give it instead to charitable agencies because beggars might misuse my money. They might buy wine or cocaine or heroin with the dollars I hand out.

But that is not what the Bible says. Jesus told his listeners in Luke 6:30, "Give to everyone who begs from you." That means a beggar who's holding up a sign or standing on the sidewalk with a grocery cart filled with what I might call trash. That means anyone who begs from me with their eyes, maybe wearing schizophrenia or drug use or alcoholism like a tattered sweater. They beg for spare change and hope maybe I'll look them straight in the eye when I say, "God bless you." And I no longer assume there are places for the mentally ill or the addicted to get well because most of those places are long gone, swept away in the flood of budget balancing.

To deprive anyone who asks because I think he or she will use the money for drink or drugs is to offer conditional justice, to put people on probation before I give. What they do with what I give is between *them* and God; "Give to everyone who begs from you" is between *me* and God. It is none of my business what they do with the money.

Someone suggests that I would then enable them to drink, but maybe I enable them more, drive them to it, when I don't even offer them a glimpse of good Old Testament justice. They're poor, they're desperate, and they don't qualify at charitable agencies that still exist, and my aloofness just makes them more depressed.

One day I saw a man in his late fifties or early sixties, sitting on a folding chair outside our supermarket. His sign said he had four teenagers at home, living on his disability payments. While my husband sat in the car, I approached the man, digging in that black hole of Calcutta I call a handbag. He probably thought I was trying to put him on trial because while I pawed my bag for my little money purse, I asked if he was raising his grandkids; he said one of them. I wondered if he needed help getting food stamps, and he said they got them, but they didn't last all month. When I finally found my money and prayed for guidance, God turned a hundred-dollar bill up first, so I handed it out.

His chin trembled and tears spilled out of his eyes; in fact his whole face crumpled. "O ma'am," he said. "O ma'am, ma'am." By then he was sobbing.

"Now you can go home," I said, and I touched his wrist and went back to my car. Before we left the parking lot I saw him fold up his chair and put it in a twenty-year-old automobile. I'm sure that hundred dollars didn't last long for him, his wife, his four teenagers, and a grandbaby. But I hope that besides oatmeal and ground meat it gave them a candy bar or some Pepsi or a little hope. Because hope is what the beggars need most.

Here is God's message: Give. Here's how God says it: "In everything do to others as you would have them do to you; for this is the law and the prophets" (Matt. 7:12).

Kristen Johnson Ingram

Miriam, Builder of a Women's Community

A Reflection on Exodus 15:20—21

The prophet Miriam, Aaron's sister, took a tambourine in her hand; and all the women went out after her with tambourines and with dancing. And Miriam sang to them: "Sing to the LORD, for he has triumphed gloriously; horse and rider he has thrown into the sea."

Exodus 15:20–21

When everyone had passed across the sea with "unmoistened foot," as the old Easter hymn[5] says, Moses and the Israelites sang to God, "I will sing to the LORD, for he has triumphed gloriously; horse and rider he has thrown into the sea" (Exod. 15:1).

They were grateful and worshipful. Their voices were undoubtedly hoarse with amazement. But wherever the Bible says "Israelites," it probably means men. Women and girl children were rarely counted in the congregation.

But then the prophet Miriam, sister to Moses and Aaron, picked up a tambourine and led all the women in their own celebration. They

167

danced to show their delight and gratitude. And Scripture says Miriam sang to them, *the women*: "Sing to the LORD, for he has triumphed gloriously. . ." By so doing, she brought the women of the nation into community. They danced and shook their tambourines and laughed, turning and swooping in the sand, shaking little bells and hitting smooth sticks together. Later, they would go to their husbands' tents and shelters, perhaps sleeping under the moon and stars, but for now, they did what women do best: they celebrated together.

Much of women's spirituality has always included celebration. They come together in excitement, rejoicing over a wedding, a pregnancy, or a new baby. Their information networks happen all the time (and now we even have cellular phones!). Just as in the days when Mary and Joseph took their son to Jerusalem for Passover, where Mary could mingle with women from all over Judea, women still take their children and grandchildren, their new clothes and their new ideas, and congregate in the celebration community to give thanks and praise the Lord.

As the story of Israel continued to grow into present time, women became managers of the Sabbath and of holy times such as Succoth and Passover. Men fast and stand in the presence of God on Yom Kippur; women fast too, but before the holy day begins, they have roasted a chicken and boiled some fruit to feed their families when the fast is over. Food is made by women, and food is at the center of almost every Jewish celebration. Who do you think decided how to prepare all that manna and roast those quails?

One celebratory fact about Miriam's song is that it's the oldest scrap of Scripture we possess. Yes, we have the Dead Sea Scrolls and other amazing portions of the Bible, but Miriam's song is the very oldest fragment of vellum. Perhaps that's the first Scripture every little girl needs to learn, so each of us can supply the "something" that only a woman's song can complete.

Grab your tambourine, my sister, because God wants us to sing and dance and round out the story, not only about the Red Sea, but about the resurrection of Jesus Christ.

Something to Try On

- Get serious about learning to love as God does someone that you dislike. On an index card write the initials of someone you're having trouble being around these days. On one side, write down the three things that irritate you most about this person. On the other side of the card, write down how each of those qualities could be positives. For example, if this person is talkative to the point of dominating conversation (and making your eyeballs roll back in your head) you could truthfully say, "He's expressive." Now tear up the card and pray relinquishment to God of your issues with this person. Do this as many times over as long a period as you need to feel your heart change.

- Read John 13:1–30, where Jesus dines at a last supper with his disciples. Notice his behavior toward each disciple. Note special treatment given to any individuals. Does Jesus wash the feet of only "the disciple whom he loved" (verse 23) or the one (verses 24–25) who proclaims fighting love for him? Based on this example, write down some thoughts about how you can be like Jesus at your next meeting or gathering where someone you dislike is present. Now pray as Jesus did in Luke 11:2–4.

- In the next few weeks ask other women you know who love God to meet for lunch or even a coffee break. Celebrate this company of women God has given you. Before meeting, ask each one to read Exodus 15:1–21 (the song of Moses, the children of Israel, and then the song of Miriam). Then take turns reading this passage once together. Could you write a

169

few lines of a song about what God has done for you? What would your song be? Even if you get silly, try this exercise. Ask everyone to jot down a few lines of a song. Let this be something silly and sacred—a joy—for you as a group and as individuals.

8

You at the Reflecting Pool

Deeper Relationships

For one human being to love another: that is perhaps the most difficult of our tasks; the ultimate, the last test and proof, the work for which all other work is but preparation.

Ranier Maria Rilke

O Perfect Love

Kris: I can't tell you how many weddings I've played the organ for: big, fancy weddings. Caterers. Thousand-dollar dresses. And sometime later, I see divorce notices for some of those couples. Do you think they wanted a big wedding to ensure their love?

Linda: Some of them have the big weddings their parents want. Maybe others have huge events to force themselves into commitment. All I know is, weddings have nothing to do with how long the marriage lasts.

Kris: Well, we can't discuss deep relationships without including marriage, and what marriage has become: in more than half of all cases, couples divorce. I wonder if our friendships and families are going downhill too. Don't people know how to be committed?

Linda: I occasionally see younger people staying in friendships just so long as it benefits *them*. Some people make friends that are advantageous to their careers, their social standing, or their politics. As long as those things are the basis for friendship, then it's dangerous to have a deep relationship. When is it worthwhile to risk yourself for a relationship?

Kris: My son Frank's brother-in-law was dying last year. Frank wept and sobbed for several days, then pulled himself together to make his last visit. "I loved him," he told me after the funeral. "He was my brother." I don't hear that kind of emotion from

173

many people, maybe because, as you suggest, they're not willing to take the risk. But Frank says that no matter how short Jon's life was, it was worth the risk to know him.

Linda: I felt the same way about my girlfriend Patti. And sometimes I feel the same way about pets I love. The relationships we have with our pets are sometimes deeper than the ones we have with people.

Kris: That's because we're God to our pets, and they trust us.

Linda: Not everybody agrees with that, but one thing is true: although we risk the pain and grief that go along with a deep and lasting relationship, we know God won't die or leave or divorce us.

Kris: The words to the hymn I've always played at weddings say, "We kneel in prayer before Thy throne, / That theirs may be the love which knows no ending."[1] I think we might pray for every relationship, whether it's marriage partners or friendships or parent-child or even our doggies. To make our love a sign to a sad and broken world.

At the Reflecting Pool

Linda Clare

Eyes of the Beloved

In the seventh chapter of Song of Solomon, the beloved's eyes are "pools in Heshbon, by the gate of Bath-rabbim" (7:4). Poets over the centuries have spoken of "limpid pools" in describing a loved one's eyes, and many a fair maiden has met her prince as she sat next to a lake or pond. You've arrived at the Reflecting Pool, where God stirs the waters of our deeper relationships.

Spouses, significant others, relatives, and friends make up a precious inner circle of those closest to us. These are the persons we'll do just about anything for: keep a vigil with a sick or dying loved one; sacrifice our time, money, or other resources for their happiness or well-being; invest more than 100 percent of ourselves to maintain the relationship. These people are more than valued—we feel they are essential to our lives.

Yesterday, my first cousin Chuck, in his midforties, died after a long illness. His mom, my Aunt Shirlee, had slept on a sofa next to him for months, in case her only son needed her in the night. From the outside, it appeared that my aunt neglected her own life in order to meet her son's financial, emotional, health, and daily living needs. She gave everything, and then he died anyway.

I can't imagine what her experience was like, but if I reflect on my own loved ones, I can begin to understand my aunt's decisions. In 1 John 3:16 we're told that Jesus laid down his life for us, and we ought to do the same for one another. If one of my children were terminally ill, I know I wouldn't hesitate to sleep next to or even change places with him or her if I could.

And what about loved ones who cause you to tear out your hair and gnash your teeth? You love them, but you can't stand being around them, a fact that produces guilt and the urge not to answer the phone when they call. Maybe you had a falling-out with Great-Aunt Gert, and now she won't speak to you. Or your in-law nettles you every time she gives you unwanted child-rearing advice. Or you and your spouse seem to argue over every little thing. What does God want you to do about that?

My own twenty-seven-year marriage has been rockier than all the gravel in the bottom of this Reflecting Pool. I know something about getting along with somebody whom I love completely, but couldn't he give a compliment or a hug now and then? If you have the kind of spouse who says, "I told you I loved you when we got married. If anything changes, I'll let you know," then maybe you can relate.

I also know about wayward sons, wayward sons' wacky girlfriends, in-laws, and step-relations that drive me nuts. I actually did get one of my elderly in-laws so mad at me that he hasn't contacted me for ten years. I'm sorry for what I did, but he doesn't want to hear that from me. I love them all, but sometimes it's so hard.

So what does God offer our deeper relationships? The Reflecting Pool is about much more than watching koi swim while you tell yourself your loved ones aren't that bad. God invites you and me to sit by the water and listen again, in the laughter of the ripples, for that small, still voice. See your inner circle of loved ones in the way God sees them. Dare to reach out a hand to mend relationships on the rocks. Allow God to change the way you see those around you. Most of all, see God's love reflecting back at you.

Scripture Salon

Kristen Johnson Ingram

The Mandrake Mother

A Reflection on Leah in Genesis 29–30

Leah conceived and bore a son, and she named him Reuben; for she said, "Because the LORD has looked on my affliction; surely now my husband will love me."

Genesis 29:32

You don't choose your family. They are God's gift to you, as you are to them.

Archbishop Desmond Tutu

176

No woman ever spent more energy on a relationship than Leah, daughter of Laban. She appears never to have had a life apart from her husband, from the night she was thrust into the wedding tent where Jacob expected her sister, to the day Jacob buried her in the cave at Machpelah. Nowadays, we'd call the marriage "dysfunctional."

In her day, however, living unloved was not unusual. A couple didn't make verbal vows or exchange a nuptial kiss before the altar: a wedding in patriarchal times was an exchange of property or services, followed by a men's feast that was probably more like a bachelor party than a marriage rite. Attendants led the bride, perfumed and still covered with a veil, into the dark chamber where the marriage was consummated by a bridegroom, who may have been drunk.

In the light of morning, Jacob's rage must have sent his bride's self-esteem even lower than it was in that society where women had status below that of sheep and goats. Newlyweds in those days spent at least a week in seclusion, making love and getting acquainted, since most of them met face-to-face for the first time after the wedding. When Jacob discovered he had worked for seven years only to win the wrong wife, he demanded to know why he had been hoodwinked. Laban, Leah's father, claimed custom and persuaded Jacob to grant Leah her wedding week; *then* he could have Rachel. The woman he'd always really wanted.

What a blow! Leah had no worth of her own but was only part of the bride-price Jacob paid for Rachel. He had labored in the sheep barns and goat pens for seven years, and now he had to work for seven more. But Jacob's years of toil in the fields weren't the whole story: He first had to take on Leah.

And did Leah turn up her nose and say, "So have Rachel if you want her, and forget about me. I can keep busy"? No; she began to strive for Jacob's affection, and her value to him would have been based on her ability to produce sons. Even today, in such countries as Jordan, Syria, or Iraq, a man—a king, even—can divorce a woman who has no male children. And according to Genesis, "When the Lord saw that Leah was unloved, he opened her womb; but Rachel was barren" (29:31).

Yet Jacob still loved Rachel best.

Leah produced a son, Reuben, and said that God had seen her unhappy state and given her a son; she said, "Surely, my husband will love me." But apparently he did not, and when she bore her second child, Simeon, she cried, "Because the LORD has heard that I am hated, he has given me this son also." And at the birth of Levi, she whispered, "Now this time my husband will be joined to me, because I have borne him three sons." Judah was born, and Leah said sadly, "This time I will praise the LORD" (29:33–35). Having children to please Jacob wasn't working, so she threw herself at God, hoping for God's interference.

A modern American woman might wonder how, if Jacob hated Leah, she kept getting pregnant; but a woman's life was different in those days. She was a baby factory, and children were an absolute necessity to a herdsman's work.

After Judah, Leah had no more babies. Maybe Jacob abandoned her bed, devoting himself more than ever to the childless Rachel. And Rachel took advantage of the situation. She handed over her maid, Bilhah, to be the surrogate mother of her sons. Bilhah had two, and Rachel crowed, "With mighty wrestlings I have wrestled with my sister, and have prevailed" (30:8). *I win, Leah! Not only does Jacob love me best, but I have two boys of my own to honor him.*

Erich Fromm, in *Art of Loving*, says, "If a person loves only one other person and is indifferent to the rest of his fellow men, his love is not love but a symbiotic attachment, or an enlarged egotism."[2] Leah projected her longing for *value* onto Jacob and earned esteem only when he was with her, paying attention and probably engaging in physical affection. Her attachment wasn't what a psychologist or pastor would call a healthy relationship: Leah was almost hypnotically fixed on Jacob, trying to earn his favor and knowing she never would.

The competition was on: Leah gave *her* maid to Jacob and gained two more children. "Happy am I! For the women will call me happy," she said (30:13). *At least other women will respect me and think I'm happy in this sham of a marriage.* Leah named her new sons Gad and Asher. And then came the affair of the mandrakes.

In the days of wheat harvest Reuben went and found mandrakes [Hebrew *dudaim*] in the field, and brought them to his mother Leah. Then Rachel said to Leah, "Please give me some of your son's mandrakes." But she said to her, "Is it a small matter that you have taken away my husband? Would you take away my son's mandrakes also?" Rachel said, "Then he may lie with you tonight for your son's mandrakes." When Jacob came from the field in the evening, Leah went out to meet him, and said, "You must come in to me; for I have hired you with my son's mandrakes." So he lay with her that night. And God heeded Leah, and she conceived and bore Jacob a fifth son.

30:14–17

Dudaim has been also translated as "violets," "mushrooms," or several other plants. The weight of authority and tradition, however, points to its being *Mandragora officinalis*, which botanists say is "a near relative of the night-shades, the 'apple of Sodom' and the potato plant."[3] Its roots look like a little man and are said to scream when pulled from the ground. Mandrake roots are dried and ground in Asian countries for their narcotic properties and were probably used as both a fertility drug and an aphrodisiac. The fruit of this plant has been called the "love-apple"; Arabs call it "Satan's apple." Mandrakes still grow near Jerusalem and in other parts of the Holy Land but are rare.

When Rachel asks for the magical mandrakes, Leah is properly enraged. In fact, for a moment we see a woman with some spirit. Imagine her with her hands on her hips. Reuben, by then probably about twelve, stands beside her. She screeches, "You already have my husband! Now you want my son's mandrakes too?"

Rachel probably wasn't friends with her sister, but she knew her well, knew that Leah would sacrifice anything for Jacob.

"Give me your son's mandrakes, and I'll let you have Jacob for tonight," she says, and then we see an astonishing scene: Jacob comes in from the fields, perhaps rinses his face and hands with a gourd of water, then realizes Leah is standing in front of him.

"You're mine for the night," she says.

179

"What?"

"I've bought a night with you for a clutch of mandrakes."

He probably glances past her at Rachel, who is penning up the lambs or stirring a pot. She nods and points to Leah's end of the tent, and Jacob once more has relations with the woman he doesn't love.

Leah was probably dressed up, with a band of coins on her forehead and maybe even a provocative veil. She had borne four children, so her figure was thicker than it had been once, but her addiction to Jacob was unchanged. No matter how many times he pushed her aside and turned to Rachel, no matter how roughly he treated her or how much he neglected her, Leah was one of millions of women who have made fools of themselves over a man.

In his book *Love and Addiction*, Stanton Peele says, "Addiction to a person is just an extension of the social side of all addictions. People who share an addiction form a private world for themselves. For example, a group of people who are addicted to the same drug tend to give their experience a collective interpretation which is incomprehensible to those outside the group. They are not concerned with this discrepancy because only the approval of other group members matters to them."[4]

Peele suggests that the same is true for people whose exclusive concern is to please each other, and their inflated estimation of themselves. Although we don't think of Leah's ego as inflated, she does overestimate her power over Jacob, believing that somehow—through having children, or sex, or cooking, or something, he will come to care for her even more than he does for Rachel or the maids.

"Wait!" a reader cries. "I've always been taught that Leah was faithful in the face of adversity, and devoted to Jacob the same way God is devoted to worthless humanity." Okay. Leah is, indeed, an example of long-suffering love, but look at her own statements about herself and her children: "Surely now my husband will love me. God sees that I am hated, now will my husband be joined to me"—and we see her utter fixation on not God, but Jacob. Her only mention of God is as her champion, the one who could *make* Jacob feel differently about her. Neither she nor anybody else in this story apparently ever trusted God to heal her situation.

Had Jacob's mother, Rebekah, consulted God before she dressed Jacob like Esau and sent him in to fool his father? She was so determined to get the patriarchal blessing for her favorite son that she left God out of the process. And what about Laban? Did he go before the Lord and plead for wisdom about his daughters? According to the Scriptures, he thrust Leah into the wedding tent without prayer or meditation. We have no record of his saying. "Oh, God, tell me what to do." No, he wanted to get his older daughter off his hands and into marriage with Jacob, whom he thought he could push around.

According to Scripture, neither Leah nor Rachel asked God whether they should send their maids to Jacob, and they certainly didn't consult the Almighty about the mandrakes! Besides, Leah—poor, unloved Leah—had no time for God; she was addicted to Jacob. Perhaps if she had been able to tear herself away from plotting to win her husband's love, her neglected sons (who probably took their duplicitous father as a role model) wouldn't have thrown their arrogant young half-brother, Joseph, into a pit and sold him as a slave. Perhaps her oldest wouldn't have lain with Bilhah, his father's concubine; perhaps Dinah would have been home with her mother, weaving and spinning, instead of visiting the Hivite women and being raped and then wooed by Shechem, an event that brought her brothers to unbelievable cruelty.

Leah was unloved, and she spent too much of her life trying to overcome that fact. When she shrieked at Rachel, "You already have my husband! Now you want my son's mandrakes too?" she said "husband." Leah behaved as if Rachel were a thief or concubine or woman of the night, even though she, Leah, had been the original interloper and Rachel had the same marital rights she did. For Jacob's sake, Leah even risked the relationship with her only sister.

One support system was available to Leah, but we have no record of her having used it. Women of that time had tradition networks, exchanges of folklore and medical advice in the menstrual tent, and support in childbearing from one another. Women of that day worked together in the cooking hut and created the first day-care centers for all the children of the tribe. But unless the Bible leaves out a good deal, Leah never took part in these relationships. Her jealousy of Jacob took her out of the traditional female role.

The fellowship of women of faith is still of the greatest importance. Nowadays we rarely deliver each other's babies or prepare a communal meal (unless you count potlucks). But Christian women derive great strength from Bible studies, prayer groups, and friendships within the faith. These same-gender relationships are an important part of maturity. If Leah lost the closeness of her female community, she was alone and miserable in her desperate desire for Jacob's love.

God did not leave Leah's name to be scorned by history. Her son Judah, the fourth-born, founded the house that brought forth the Messiah. The unloved wife became the ancestral mother of Christ. Would knowing that bring her joy today? Or would she still be watching for Jacob?

Reflecting Inspiration

Kristen Johnson Ingram

When Love Becomes Addictive

Many waters cannot quench love, neither can floods drown it. If one offered for love all the wealth of his house, it would be utterly scorned.

Song of Songs 8:7

Don't compromise yourself. You are all you've got.

Janis Joplin

Leta has been going with Josh for five years, and now she's talking about moving in with him. Her two older sisters and several of her friends say she needs to break it off, because he won't settle on a wedding date, or even a formal engagement. Leta is thirty-two and longs for children, but Josh can't commit. He says his father was married three times, and he doesn't want to make the same mistakes; but the sisters say he's passive aggressive, getting all the benefits of Leta's companionship but bearing no responsibility, achieving what he wants by doing nothing at all. They've urged Leta to go out with several men who have tried to date her, but she says she can't think of anyone but Josh.

Cissy's situation is different. Her boyfriend, Todd, is a habitual liar, whose prevarication stopped their wedding two years ago. That time he told Cissy his father was coming into town for the nuptials, was going to finance the honeymoon, and had asked Todd to schedule the rehearsal dinner at a fashionable restaurant. When the wedding invitations went out, Cissy's mother got a call from Todd's father. He'd never heard of Cissy and had no plans to bankroll any part of a wedding. Although she cancelled the nuptials, Cissy later forgave Todd, who made up more lies to cover his lies. Now she's about to plan another wedding even though his own sister says, "He'd lie about what he ate for lunch."

Rita's husband, Mike, cracked her cheekbone, chipped her teeth, and keeps her arms and legs so bruised she wears long sleeves and slacks on hot summer days. Later, he is always remorseful and loving, bringing her gifts or taking her out to dinner. He's never going to punch her again; from then on, everything is going to be beautiful. His resolve usually lasts less than a week, and then he starts the cycle over again. But she's still with him. She's never called the police, and they sit together in church every single Sunday, after Mike teaches the Bible class for men.

Selma lives a financial nightmare. Her pleasant, affectionate husband gambles away everything he earns, even some of her small salary as a veterinarian's assistant. Three years ago, they declared bankruptcy and he swore he was a changed man; but a few months later, when a Native American casino appeared only thirty miles from home, his vow disappeared. Now she's afraid he'll lose the roof over his children's heads. Selma's parents have helped out over and over, but they've decided that unless she does something drastic to change her status, they're not going to throw any more money at a bad situation.

When Fiona got engaged to a man she met at church, two of her friends invited her to lunch, where they informed her that her intended bridegroom was a convicted, paroled child molester. She said, "Yes, I know about it, and I don't care." They were horrified. Now Fiona is married to the man and bewildered because those close friends—who both have young children—have forbidden her to come with her husband to their homes.

The country is full of alcoholics, drug addicts, cross-dressers, and other men who can wreck lives. And the worst part is that women love them.

How can a woman continue not only to love, but to live with a man who would almost certainly hurt or degrade her, over and over? A man she can't trust?

Once, psychologists suggested that women who stayed with violent or adulterous or alcoholic husbands were masochistic and felt fulfilled by pain. Now they know better: a battered woman isn't addicted to pain, but to the batterer. And the addiction frequently has a powerful physical component.

Because addiction involves the body, the center of an addictive relationship is often a powerful physical attraction. Rita said that when she and Mike were first married, the very scent of his skin made her long for him. She is almost hypnotized in his presence. When she tried to describe her feelings to her pastor, he said gently, "This is what the Bible calls 'lust.' The physiological has taken over."

One of the most difficult personalities to deal with is the narcissist, the kind of man a lot of women love. According to Greek myth, a beautiful young man named Narcissus fell in love with his own reflection in a pond. He stood there so long, gazing at his own gorgeous image, that he turned into the white springtime flower that grows from a bulb. He was lost to everyone except one young woman. Called Echo, she felt she was nothing alone and knew only how to repeat and support Narcissus's feelings of self-love.

Echo people like Cissy are attracted to narcissists. Echo women want to become the be-all-and end-all of another person's life, which is exactly what the narcissist wants them to be. Love between these people is symbiotic at best, each feeding off the other's weakness; their love is destructive from the beginning because it is based on need, not want; and at worst, the man slowly drains the life out of his wife or girlfriend until she's as faint and invisible as the sound of "hello" in the mountains.

After a man has become a woman's whole reason for being, she talks about him whenever she speaks. When she dreams, the man is the main player in the drama. When she prays, she prays about him, begging God to restore a relationship that is probably doomed. Such women spend all their time and money for their husbands or boyfriends and hand them their peace of soul as surely as a cocaine addict hands over her sanity and money to the drug dealer.

Whatever made the relationship fulfilling? How could a bright professional woman not only love an abuser but also believe that he loves her? Perhaps one of the most powerful needs is to re-create her childhood, to live according to her role models. Rita "lost" her father to her despotic mother, so having her fiancé lie to her is somehow like the lesson she learned as a child: if her father paid any attention to Cissy, her mother would kidnap him and turn her anger on the child. She keeps resurrecting a little girl's longing for love but, of course, also resurrecting the consequences.

Stanton Peele, author of *Love and Addiction*, says, "Addictive love is even more directly linked to what are recognized to be the sources of addiction than is drug dependency."[5] In other words, if a girl's needs were not met in childhood, she could grow up with fixations on drugs or alcohol—or men. Or love. Instead of turning to heroin or wine, Christians too often take, as their drug of choice, men whose own backgrounds are shaky and dysfunctional and who don't have firm commitments to their partners. And unfortunately, they think what they're offering the man is pure, selfless love.

There *is* such a thing as selfless love. The late Mother Teresa of Calcutta is an example of one who gave her life over to serving God through others. Small and frail, she carried lepers off the street, built homes for abandoned children, and used the money she received from the Nobel Peace Prize and other awards to help the "poorest of the poor." But Mother Teresa did what she did for God, not so that someone would love her in return. The love-addicted woman isn't burning up with love for God; she's destroying herself, and her children if she has any, for the sake of a human being.

And that's the mystery, the turning point—and the hardest part. If a woman can fix her hopes not on relationship with a man but on the God who loves her, she can *then* decide what to do. But of course, that's a huge order because most Christian women *believe* God comes first in their lives when in fact, it's the man who takes precedence.

The woman who married a convicted child molester certainly isn't showing the world that God comes first. She rationalizes, saying God led her to the man and God wants her to show him love. But he was recently arrested again, and she's not sure whether he's guilty or innocent. Unconditional love would change him, wouldn't it? *Wouldn't it?*

No. That man needs a lot more than the love of an addicted woman, and she can't be his therapist. Nobody with even modest self-esteem would marry a pervert or a rapist or a man on death row, but some women do, and they ignore God's warnings in the mouths of their friends, in the Bible, and even in the knots in their stomachs.

The cure is, as C. S. Lewis called it, a "severe mercy." "One way or another, the thing had to stop," he wrote to his friend Sheldon Vanauken, whose beloved wife of only a few years—in what he later called "a pagan marriage"—had died.[6]

The woman who is love-addicted, man-addicted, in a relationship with a man who hits or cheats or drinks or gambles, needs to get completely away from him for a few days in order to think through the relationship and reassess her connections to God. That's as hard as telling a heroin junkie to quit cold turkey, but nobody can quit drinking while holding a glass to her lips. Separation, at least a temporary one, is absolutely necessary in order to get her attention off the man and onto God.

But here's part two of the severe mercy: she shouldn't talk to *anyone* about it until she feels free and separate from the man's presence.

What? she shouldn't go right into counseling?

Not at first, because she's got to get her eyes on Christ, not on how to fix her husband. Counseling, therapy, and even grief support may come later. This is the severest part of the mercy: she has to confess her marriage or relationship as sin. *Sin.* Not because it's sexual or because they yelled at each other or because they didn't tithe. The relationship is sin because it comes between the woman and God. If a man and her relationship with him is what a woman centers her life on, she is in a state of sin. The amount of energy and contemplation she put into thinking and praying about him is the level any woman should have put into her link to God.

In 1979, the rock group Earth, Wind and Fire recorded a song called "After the Love Has Gone." The words say what many women have experienced: they had something beautiful that didn't last, and what was once happy is now sorrowful. But love-addicted women can't admit to themselves that the love they thought was gone never really existed outside their minds. Christ alone offers real love, honest love that doesn't break bones or destroy a woman's self-esteem or wreck her finances.

How different would life be for the addicted woman to find him?

Reflecting Inspiration
Linda Clare

Girlfriends

I have learned that to have a good friend is the purest of all God's gifts, for it is a love that has no exchange of payment.

Frances Farmer

I'd walked to Sunday services at Calvary Chapel that morning, pushing my infant son in a fold-up stroller. The meeting was held at El Cajon High School; somewhere on the grounds there had to be a church. I felt alone and vulnerable—no car, little money, and no friends. My husband was a thousand miles away, working in Oklahoma. My family also lived elsewhere. And where was God when I needed him? I stopped in the parking lot, determined not to cry.

Then a tall, Scandinavian-looking blonde asked if I needed help. Patti. She directed me to the church nursery, but she didn't melt back into the crowd. She took me by the arm and sat next to me in the service. I'm not sure why, but Patti went beyond the shallow greetings and hugs you expect from a congregation. That Sunday, Patti made sure I had a friend.

We chatted, and before I knew it, she'd invited my little boy and me to lunch that afternoon. She had a beautiful smile, and we hit it off immediately. Although she was only two months older than I was, her two sons were already in first and second grades. Patti seemed to know everything about homemaking and child care, areas in which I'd never been competent. She made a mean batch of Rice Krispy Treats, and we shared an interest in sewing. She listened for hours as I spilled my guts about the trials and troubles of my married life. She was the one I called if the baby was spitting up or I needed to know how to cook a turkey. She became both a friend and proof for me that God had been there all along.

I've been lucky enough to have several best girlfriends like Patti. Over the years, I've known women who were kindred spirits in some way, women such as Nancy and Kris, who've enriched my life in ways that lead me to believe I'm blessed. Each has played an integral part in my daily life and my artistic endeavors, whether it was through drama or aerobic dance, poetry or potty training. The whole idea of girlfriends can sound smarmy and commercial, but I think there's truth there too. My friendships with other women go far beyond greeting-card verse or syrupy sentiment. At times we've laughed or even spontaneously broken into song. In crisis they've wept with me. My friends have sometimes quite literally kept me alive.

I used to long to find a soul mate—the perfect match that would spell wedded bliss for my mate and me. I thought a soul mate was the one person in the universe who was preordained to make my life complete. Together we would finish each other's sentences and build a life so harmonious we'd never raise an eyebrow to the other. Yes, it was the sixties, and no, I didn't know yet that God was supposed to make life complete.

Then I got married and came back to earth. My soul mate not only left the cap off the toothpaste tube, he had a serious alcohol problem. We argued about money and the kids. On his way to work in the morning, he'd say, "See you for dinner," and I'd get a distinct feeling that he wouldn't be home until very late. I was almost always right. A good deal of the time I was terrified his drinking would kill one of us. The only refuge I found in those stormy early days of marriage were my sisters in Christ.

Every time my husband and I got to the brink of splitting up, I ran to Patti's house on the other side of town. She prayed with me and let the kids and me stay as long as we needed to, no questions asked. When I was wrong, she held her tongue. When I thought I couldn't take anymore, she talked me down from whatever scrawny limb I'd climbed out on. No matter how tumultuous life became for me, Patti was there.

I tried to be there for her too. A friendship, I learned, has to be a two-way relationship. I can't be the sole giver or taker. Unlike married people or family, friends rarely suffer in silence or thrive without positive input. Refuse to keep up a friendship, and you may drift apart. Proverbs tells us that a friend forgives much, loves at all times.

Jesus had friends while on earth—people he trusted with his very life. He kept a close-knit entourage with him almost all the time, and he himself is the perfect model of friendship. Loyal, yet unafraid to tell the truth, even when it hurts, Christ is the companion I can count on. Whether I'm floating some of my crazy ideas or just want to opine on a subject that interests me, Jesus never says he'll have to let me go now but he'll call back later. He listens as long as I talk. I try to be there for him, even if all I'm doing is praying. He usually lets me wander around a while before I admit I'm lost. Most of the time, though, God keeps sending me women pals who help me find my way.

What kind of person makes a friend? Is she someone with a shoulder to cry on? A place to seek advice? Someone who appreciates you for what you are? Marlene Dietrich once said it is the friend you can call up at 4 a.m. that matters. Or maybe a friend is simply, as Joan Walsh Anglund wrote, "someone who likes you."[7]

Many married couples say they're best buddies with their spouses. While I count my own husband as lover as well as confidante, the older I get the more I rely on my associations with other women. Only another woman understands PMS, or now, at my advanced age, hot flashes and night sweats. Hubby looks at me blankly. My girlfriend and I can shop—my husband would rather wait in the car. Girlfriends can meet for coffee or during lunch hour and discuss anything from child rearing to quantum mechanics. I'm not saying I never discuss physics with my husband, but my girl friendships are different and more precious than any other relationships in my life.

If I count my friends as jewels in my crown, I'm instantly queen for a day. Like those mother's rings, with a gem for each child, most of us keep an array of friends for various seasons of life. Your maid of honor might live three thousand miles away by now. The girl you whispered secrets to when you were six might not be around when you're going into labor. The kind of friend you need when you are seventeen might not be the same when you're past fifty.

And what about the friends you wish you knew better or dream about meeting? Besides fantasizing that someone famous named Anne Lamott will ring me up and want to have coffee, I often pass by valuable opportunities to connect with women I know but seldom see. Perhaps, like Heather, Mel, Kathy, and Linda, they live far away or have as many kids and obligations as I do. I try to stay connected, but they know how it is. Still, just in case someone famous named Anne is reading this, I'm available for latte anytime. But I'd be even more thrilled to get together with some of those "gold" girls, those friends I haven't seen in years.

I still keep in touch with my childhood friend Nancy, although we live far from each other. Our lives have taken us in very different directions: I'm a writer in the Northwest, she owns her own puppet theater and company in my home state of Arizona. Yet the moment we see each other, we pick up wherever we left off and talk as if we just went home for a few minutes to get something.

Likewise, Patti and I still tell each other about our kitchens and our gardens, even though she now lives in Oklahoma and has battled cancer for the past few years. The aggressive form of breast cancer she's fighting has spread, and only God knows how long she'll be around. Some days I want to hop on the plane to see her again, and other days I can't bear to think of what she must endure. Mostly I'm stuck between my memories of her that day at church and fearing her death. In her letters, Patti is always cheerful and has a purely Scandinavian stoicism about her chances of survival. (Postscript: Patti did not live to see this book. She passed away in 2004.)

Lately I pal around with another Scandinavian, a dear friend who's a generation older. I knew Kris was friendship material when I found out she and I both adore an obscure old movie called *The Twelve Chairs*. I'm convinced God brought us together for a slightly more important reason: she is very wise and teaches me things I never knew. She says I occasionally get a good idea. We have a blast writing, traveling, and just bumming around together.

And although I'm rather introverted, I've even begun making friends right in my neighborhood. For many years I limited my associations to other Christians who thought and acted much as I did. But lately I've branched out. My neighbor and walking partner had an unfortunate Christian experience as a child, so she wasn't thrilled to learn I was a believer. She practices meditation and follows a more Eastern spiritual practice. We walk through our streets and comment on the beauty of shadows from a plum tree or the raw happiness from a bed of red poppies. At one time I might have thought it my duty to convince her to become born again, and I do pray for her. But I'm able to enjoy her company without proselytizing. I'm learning tolerance and discovering that while we disagree on religion, we can still be friends.

Whether it's Nancy, Patti, Kris, or the next-door neighbor, I think God uses these relationships to teach me more about myself. We are all traveling down a similar road, a bumpy concourse full of heartbreak and disappointment, yet bursting with laughter and the crazy urge to break out in song.

When I go to church, I remind myself to look for someone who seems lost or alone, the way Patti did more than twenty years ago. I often ask myself, *Where would I be without my friends?*

The answer I think is always going to be the same: I wouldn't be anywhere that matters, for God sends friends to help us find our way.

Reflecting Inspiration
Joyce Carlson

To Honor a Woman

Along the road to the mailbox, my husband and I encountered three women coming toward us in single file. The first old woman had a black pot on her head. The second had a plastic bucket with water, and a calabash floating in it. The third old woman had a bundle of straw.

A little procession like this at the end of a day, heading away from the center of town, should excite some comment, so I commented and wondered. After all, for five days, the whole population of two villages had been giving themselves over to a big funeral celebration, and if these women were going somewhere in procession, it must have had something to do with those ongoing festivities. In the interest of research, I fell in behind them while Bob continued toward the mail.

We four, three fully aware of what they were doing and one entirely clueless, walked along the gravel path toward my house. I wondered if we were going all the way to the graveyard, but this was not the case. We turned aside from the path into a place that, in the rainy season, becomes a meadow of shoulder-high grass. But now before the rains came, it was hard bare ground with scattered bushes and wind-blown leaves. We stopped twenty yards off the path where the ground had

192

been completely swept by the wind, and the first woman flung her pot, blackened by years of cooking fires, down on the ground where it broke into shards. Why did she do that, I wondered. From somewhere a piece of heavy homespun cotton cloth appeared—a remnant from some larger piece of cloth. The younger woman removed the black plastic bucket from her head and set it on the ground, where the calabash bobbed around in the water.

I love African funerals. Around here, a funeral is the one event in a lifetime that pulls all the threads of women's relationships and experience together. For a moment, the structure of a person's life hangs in space like an intricate web before it disintegrates and disappears. When an old woman dies full of days and rich in descendants, the party just goes on and on. So for days the musicians had been wearing themselves out on the drums and *balafons*, the cooks had been cooking, and the children of Old Nampuno had been receiving gifts and greetings from hundreds of people. If there was anything the living might have to complain of, it's that Nampuno had a lot to say in advance about her funeral, and didn't want to leave the village too soon.

Three days of lying in state under bright cloths outside her sleeping house was what she ordered. But times are changing, and the old way of holding a really dead body over for days and days before burial has given way to the new idea that twenty-four hours are quite enough, thank you, for anyone dead to stay above ground. Nampuno, standing by tradition, would have none of it. Her children begged—in fact prayed—for her to relent, but she insisted on hanging around. It got to be a strain on everyone. By the morning of Day Three, some overwrought members of her family came by our place to greet and ask if we had any disinfectant to pour on the body. Our household search turned up only a lightly scented bathroom disinfectant, which didn't clear the air at all.

But when the processional music started playing in earnest, and the people started dancing to the sound of the big drums and the flying fingers of the *balafon* players, the air though charged and heavy and hard to wade through carried everyone along down the road to the grave dug that morning. Nampuno, ninety-five years old when she died and thin as a twig, was an enthusiastic supporter of the local village soccer team. She went to all the games. So when she made her last journey out of town three days ago, the team carried her and buried her six feet under in a grave decorated with drawings of two footballs.

Now, the woman who had carried the pot on her head produced a packet of matches, and the other old woman set the straw alight. When it was going well, they began to burn the cloth. They should be careful, I thought, because the wind is picking up, and they might hurt themselves if the fire takes off. But these women know fire. They've been handling it all their lives. They know how to regulate the temperature under a cooking pot, and how to carry coals around town. They know all about the way fire behaves in the wind and what direction it will take. I needn't have worried. With a small bundle of straw and a single match, they reduced that thick piece of homespun cotton to nothing but ash in ten minutes of carefully controlled burning. I watched in silence while they kept turning the cloth, lifting it to catch the wind and flame, balancing it on the straw brand and adding more straw when necessary. One old woman took a stick to stir the fire and keep the flames jumping. They were not going to have a thread left when they were through. That was clear.

When nothing remained but smoldering, fluttering ash, the younger woman standing by threw water by handfuls over the dying fire, and the two oldest women began to scoop the damp earth together into a pile. Every bit of the burned earth they threw away among the scattered leaves at the edge of the clearing so no one would ever be able to find it and gather it together again. Finally the rest of the water was thrown over the place where the fire had burned, and in silence we all turned and left again in single file. What had they done all that for?

The woman who had carried the straw was a sister to Old Nampuno, who died five days ago and was finally buried two and a half days later. Now everything was "finished," she said. The pot, carried and broken by another of Nampuno's sisters, had been used to heat the water that the newly dead body was washed with.

The cloth? Why the cloth? Where did it come from? The old woman said it was the rags of the dead woman, but it seemed pretty solid a piece of cloth to me. I'm speculating that stands for something that hasn't quite been articulated. Bintou had said everything was "finished," but that was not strictly true. Finished for her, perhaps, but I knew good and well that in a couple more weeks, another group of women would get together and throw away Nampuno's hearthstones. Then the funeral would really be finished, and Nampuno, in the Village of the Dead, should have nothing to complain of.

"It ain't over till it's over," is one of the most apt things you can say about these funerals. Just when you think you've gotten to the end, there's more. So getting the body buried, while an important and necessary step for which we are all profoundly grateful, is only the prelude to the real *funerailles*. After years of living here, I still don't really understand deep down why the burial doesn't count as the funeral itself. But until the daughters of the village have come back with their friends and danced and sung to the beating of the calabash drum, and until the belongings of the deceased are given back to the patrilineage, and until everyone imaginable has received some kind of gift in recognition, it's not over.

Later I was hanging out with the women married into this village. They were getting down and dirty by throwing red mud at each other. Why mud? Very good question. I understood why the Daughters of the Village would, in two weeks throw away Nampuno's hearthstones. Once that was done, she'd be able to cook in the Village of the Dead and wouldn't have to borrow anyone else's kitchen.

But why should women who married here, who are all strangers, like me, to the patrilineage, be responsible to smear each other with mud? They might not be able to articulate a reason that made sense to a real stranger like me, but for sure they knew what was going to happen and wore their oldest clothes. Like the innocent I am, in search of answers to some of life's deepest questions, with notebook and camera in hand, I trotted down to the stream wearing a white skirt, and my skirt will never look the same again. If a moment ever comes when some of my rags have to be burned, I'll have some.

What God Says about Relationships

A Reflection on John 15:12–14

> This is my commandment, that you love one another as I
> have loved you. No one has greater love than this, to lay
> down one's life for one's friends. You are my friends if you
> do what I command you.
>
> John 15:12–14

Nobody has too much trouble with Jesus's commanding us to love one another. But add on "as I have loved you," which means his death on the cross, and the context verses—"No one has greater love than this" and "You are my friends *if* you do what I command you"—a person can start to squirm. And start to rationalize: *Surely this was for the disciples, wasn't it? They* should risk their lives for one another, but nobody has to be willing to die. We don't think Jesus meant that for the rest of us.

But what if he did? Do we have to die for a woman in Red China or one who wears a *burqa*? After all, they're not our friends. Are they? *Are they?*

I hear a whisper. I think it comes from a woman who is a lawyer, and she's asking Jesus, "Who is my friend?" just as her male counterpart asked two thousand years ago, "Who is my neighbor?"

Throughout Scripture, the words *friend* and *neighbor* often occur together. Neighbors become friends sometimes, and, if we're lucky, our friends buy the house next door and become neighbors. So if everyone on earth is my neighbor, then everyone is at least a potential friend. Someone for whom I'm supposed to be willing to die.

Well, that's a laugh. Not only am I unwilling to die for someone like Saddam Hussein, I'm not even ready to die for the nice young woman across the street or her baby. Or even for Linda, my best friend, with whom I wrote this book. As Lily Tomlin used to say on *Laugh In*, "And *that's* the truth" (followed by blowing over her tongue).

Can I call myself a follower of Jesus if I won't risk my life for a friend? (I originally wrote "can't risk," but I can. My steps would falter and they'd probably have to drag me to the gallows to take my friend's place, but I am at least physically, if not emotionally, capable.) Fortunately, God rarely asks me even to *risk* my life for another. I've never been in a position to run into a burning house to rescue someone's child or doggy or gerbil, and I haven't had to jump into a lake to save a drowning person. In fact, I can't think of a time when, for the sake of a friend or one of my children or grandchildren, my life was in danger. I've been lucky. Or God knows what cowardice I hide beneath my brave countenance.

But as I write this, another soldier was just killed in Iraq. A mother *did* run into the flames to rescue her daughter. A man went out on a building ledge to talk a friend out of suicide. All around me, people are laying down their lives, showing their love. Jesus's kind of love.

So how am I going to keep Jesus's commandment to love others as he has loved me? Behold, as Saint Paul said, I tell you a mystery, one I am both proud and ashamed of: every time I fail to love, Jesus does it for me. Does it again, or still, however eternity works.

Just as Jesus died for Jews who could not keep the Law and died for the sins of the world, so he dies in my place when I fail my friend. Jesus is in Iraq and on window ledges and diving into the waves to expire in place of the dying swimmer I was unaware of or too afraid to rescue.

I'm ashamed because I keep sending Jesus to the cross for my infirmity of spirit, but I'm proud that Jesus loves me enough to accept me as his sister. And I *can* redeem my time; I *can* start the process of becoming the full, perfect, and sufficient sacrifice and oblation that Jesus Christ himself has asked me to be. Because while most people don't die in their friends' places, there *is* another way they can give their lives: by living for their friends and neighbors. Every small sacrifice I make for another person—"for the least of these"—is an opportunity to die to self, to offer my time or treasure.

And sometimes we get a chance to make big sacrifices. For instance, I read about the dean of a seminary whose fifty-year-old spouse had early Alzheimer's disease, and he *resigned his job* to care for her, saying, "She took care of me for thirty years. Now it's my turn." He was at the peak of his career, but he was willing to lay down his professional and personal life for his wife, his best friend.

Jesus is the friend for whom I'm going to lay down my life. I'll give him my days, because he's given me so many of his. And in the meantime, I'm at least working on being a woman who would jump into a lake to rescue someone.

Ideas for Reflection & Application

Something to Try On

- Invite a girlfriend to take a walk with you to a nearby park or just around the neighborhood. Focus on your senses in God's glorious world as you walk and talk.
- Send a greeting card to someone you've drifted apart from or disagreed with. If you get along with everyone, send a card to someone who will be surprised to receive a greeting from you.
- Next time you have a disagreement with your spouse or loved one, take responsibility for your feelings to avoid blaming others. Notice when "blame shifting" begins to leak into your speech. "I feel angry when you are twenty minutes late and you don't call me" is much better than "You make me so mad by being late."
- Talk back to your inner critic. Tell God you'll replace each of your put-downs with a self-affirming statement or uplifting Scripture.

9

You at the
Luncheon

Nourished by Grace

In life as in dance: Grace glides on blistered feet.

Alice Abrams

Phantom Guilt

Kris: Why do so many of us feel guilty so much of the time?

Linda: When I shift between the Old Testament and the New, I feel guilty.

Kris: Guilty about what? Why does going between the two sets of Scriptures make you feel that way?

Linda: The God of the Old Testament sounds more concerned with the rule of law, which I constantly break. For grace, I have to go to the New Testament.

Kris: You think those are two different versions of God? How about *hesed*, the Hebrew word for "mercy" or "loving-kindness" that shows up all through the Old Testament?

Linda: All right, go ahead, show off your Bible studies. Anyhow, mercy doesn't show up in the parts I read most, and our culture's way of dealing with wrongdoing always seeks punishment.

Kris: And we ascribe that punishment to God's way, don't we? We chant "An eye for an eye" and scream for tougher prison sentences. But does God do that, in either testament? The "eye for an eye" was really given as the limit of punishment, not the requirement.

Linda: The bottom line is, people don't want grace to be easy. Isaiah says if we confess, God will wash our sins white as snow; but we want to suffer first, before forgiveness. And guilt is part of that suffering.

201

Kris: That philosophy comes straight from the pit too. God tells you immediately when you are guilty and helps you fix it. The enemy wants you to *feel* guilty—for a long time. So we're looking into a phantom curse, the way an amputee feels phantom pain. Phantom guilt.

Linda: Phantom guilt has another accomplice in the American need to be more, do more, have more. As long as I never think I am quite enough, guilt will be my companion.

Kris: Okay. Then let's explore the answer.

Bon Appétit

The tables are draped in white linen. Next to your carefully folded napkin, a crystal goblet of mineral water sparkles in the filtered sunlight. Soft music plays. You sink into a comfortable chair, ready for a break from your spa day activities. You spread your napkin on your lap and study the menu.

At this point, you've been to the Salon, worked out, and alternated contemplation and bodywork. You're famished. All the offerings, from the lightest aperitif to the full course, sound scrumptious. Maybe you'll have one of everything. You look around for the waiter. Someone approaches your table and says, "Hi, my name is God, and I'll be your waitperson today."

God, waiting on you? If you're like me, you nearly fall out of your chair. But when your soul screams for nourishment, isn't God the only one who can supply it?

God feeds us grace when we know we've blown it, when we're not sure what we want or need, and when we're too tired or weak or sick to get up and make our own lunch. Grace is a gift of spiritual food that's often misunderstood by even the most knowledgeable Christians, but that doesn't seem to stop God from trying to serve it.

When Jesus was alive, cleanness or uncleanness in food was a big issue for Jews. They performed ritual washings and had strict codes for animals that God said were fit to eat. This cleanliness idea extended to Jews themselves, and animal sacrifices bridged the gap so a person could maintain a relationship with God. Until Jesus arrived, there had never been a way to come to God by faith through grace. Grace hadn't been invented yet.

All through his ministry, Jesus emphasized that grace was free. Yet then as now, people have trouble receiving the gift. "I'm not good enough," you say, "for a plateful of free grace." And you're right.

As Philip Yancey has written, we must escape the force of spiritual gravity by seeing ourselves as sinners who can never please God through self-improvement or self-enlargement.[1] When you acknowledge your imperfection, suddenly God cooks up a grace entrée and invites you to eat your fill.

Some of us have more trouble accepting grace than do others. I'm the sort who, no matter how many times I hear about the feast of God's grace, still thinks I'll have to wash dishes in order to pay for my meal. Kris hasn't bought the idea of working for grace, but I think even she'd admit that you never know how or when your next grace lunch will come.

And when you belly up to the table, where will you sit? Next to someone more accomplished than you, or richer or more famous? Are you seated next to a person who gets away with doing bad things, or is your place card set beside a "deserving" Christian woman?

Just as you're trying to figure things out, God strides over, towel over his arm, bearing a large tray full of delicious sustenance. He sets your luncheon in front of you and says, "Would you like some fresh-ground grace with that?" You nod dumbly and God whispers, "I'm no respecter of persons, you know."

Suddenly a light comes on. That's it—there *is* such a thing as a free lunch. You'll never deserve it, but when you open yourself to God, grace comes as the extra you weren't expecting, to nurture body, soul, and spirit. *Bon appétit.*

Kristen Johnson Ingram

The Forgiven Woman

A Reflection on Psalm 65:2–3

O you who answer prayer! To you all flesh shall come. When deeds of iniquity overwhelm us, you forgive our transgressions.

Psalm 65:2–3

The big question after Christ's resurrection was whether salvation was retroactive. Could Jesus be glorified through someone who died, say, a thousand or more years before his incarnation?

In the third chapter of Peter's first epistle, he says, "For Christ also suffered for sins once for all, the righteous for the unrighteous, in order to bring you to God. He was put to death in the flesh, but made alive in the spirit, in which also he went and made a proclamation to the spirits in prison, who in former times did not obey, when God waited patiently in the days of Noah, during the building of the ark, in which a few, that is, eight persons, were saved through water" (vv. 18–20).

Well, then, Christ went to hell and decreed that the disobedient were now free to enter heaven. A proclamation *once for all.* Then and before and forever. And so, without any systematic theologians present to fight with me about the meaning, I hereby announce that Eve was forgiven.

I once read in *Christianity Today* an interview with the brilliant writer Annie Dillard. The questioner asked if she didn't think that human beings were depraved and worthless and ugly and vile in God's sight, and she answered, "Well, we deserved the incarnation, didn't we?"

And the "we" she's talking about are Eve's descendants. If God was willing to send prophets and lawgivers and reformers, if God would kill one of his animals for its skin as clothing for Adam and Eve, if God was willing to become the fetus in a woman's womb, and then a little baby, and finally a man who was tortured and killed, then the human race must be important to God. We deserved the incarnation. And Eve is not only among the humans, she is their mother.

Eve committed the first sin, was the first to miss the mark: she allowed herself to be hoodwinked by a snake. I don't know if all animals talked in the Garden of Eden or just the serpent. Apparently the serpent looked more like a lizard in those days, because after the ruckus, God cursed the snake and told him that from then on, he had to crawl on his belly and eat dust. I once attended a terrible vacation Bible school at a new little church in our town, and the teacher, who was full of awful tales about the mark of the Beast in people's hands and foreheads, who made me cry by saying in 1942 to get ready because the world was going to end within a few weeks, also said that if you lifted up any kind of snake to look underneath, you could see the little scars where their front and back legs had been. I believed her and fell to catching bull snakes and king snakes, holding them up and looking for the scars.

But whatever you believe about the Eden adventure, whether you think it's the word-for-word account of what happened, or an important allegory that describes the wound between God and humanity that only God could heal, somehow or other Eve is at its center. She talked to the serpent, who asked with false innocence whether they were forbidden any foods in the garden. A snake just walked up on its then legs and said, "Nice place you have here . . . Say, can you eat all the fruits?"

205

Eve wasn't apparently as startled as Mary was when the angel showed up; she answered, and one thing led to another, and the next thing you know, Adam was saying, "The woman did give to me, and I did eat." Then they're out on the desert, wearing the skins of a dead animal, and Adam "knew" his wife. *Yada*, the word we translate as "knew," makes some interpreters take this to mean that Adam and Eve before the fall had no intercourse and were not aware of their sexuality; but that makes nonsense of God's command to be fruitful and multiply. And it also suggests that sex is a function of fallenness, and therefore tainted with sin and shame.

What happened on the outside was that the tenor of their intimacy changed. In the garden, they were innocent and joyful and in love. The fragrance of Eve's skin must have called up Adam's yearning, and the straight line of his back and legs surely delighted her. They walked through the trees, they picked fruits for meals, they made love with innocence and honesty. Until the fall, Eve was equal to Adam; only when their sin was out in the open did God say that Eve's husband would rule over her. And that's when intimacy and love became plain old sex.

Adam *yada* his wife, it says, after the expulsion. He didn't make love to her or caress her or whisper that he'd like to have a son, whatever that was. Though *yada* is often translated as "know," the sweep of the word is wider and sometimes worse than that. The word also means "to take down." The love they experienced in the garden was gone, and this was the very thing God tried to prevent, knowing if they ate from the tree, they'd lose their innocence and learn spousal anger and hate. Adam blamed Eve, and Eve blamed the serpent, and the serpent blamed God for banning the Tree of the Knowledge of Good and Evil in the first place.

Now they needed each other. They had nobody but their children, who didn't all turn out well.

Love? Well, love is fine if you aren't having to earn your bread by the sweat of your face or bearing your children in agony.

And if God didn't want them to eat, why did he let the serpent enter the garden? Did God *have* to test free will when the first humans were only a week old? An awful lot of questions about the Eden story have never been answered.

I vote for forgiveness. God could have struck her dead, killed both of them, in fact, on the spot. The earth still produced plenty of clay and man-making could start over, but God had too great an investment in the beautiful young couple that Michelangelo portrayed so perfectly on the ceiling of the Sistine Chapel. This woman wasn't a figment of God's imagination, or a demon spirit like Lilith; this was *Eve*, for crying out loud, the woman God had designated to be the mother of the human race.

In the ancient Church of Our Saviour at Karye, outside Istanbul, Turkey, I discovered the original fresco of *Anastasis*, or "resurrection." You've seen it in a hundred art books: Jesus is pulling Adam and Eve out of their tombs; Jesus is in gleaming white raiment, the tombs are stylized, and Adam and Eve bear looks of shame that barely hide their secret surprise and delight. They'd dwelt for thousands of years in Sheol, where other souls were shadows and nothing moved; suddenly like the trumpet sounding, they heard the foundation of hell crack, then someone grabbed their hands and pulled.

I had never engaged in any kind of icon meditation, but the Byzantine faces and colors and formal rhythm of that fresco caught and held me for at least twenty minutes, in fact until my husband touched my shoulder and said our tour bus was leaving. After I gazed at the fresco I knew something about God I hadn't known before. I knew grace and celebration and hope.

Hope for Eve and, by George, hope for myself.

Nothing but Grace

> If you notice anything, it leads you to notice more and
> more.
>
> Mary Oliver

Bobby Martinez had a mean streak. When I was six, he was the boy
next door, and one day he bet me he could catch more tadpoles from
the canal than I could. "Nothing will happen to you," he said when I
told him my babysitter wouldn't allow me near the canal. He smiled.
"*Nada*."

I wasn't so sure. He and his not-so-mean younger brother, Peterbone,
were my friends, but they were also Catholics of Mexican descent.
Carmelita, my babysitter, was Mexican and Catholic, and I thought
she had a mean streak too. I was convinced she hated me, so I hated
her.

I'd somehow gotten the idea that other races weren't exactly equal
to us whites, especially if they went to Mass instead of Sunday school.
But when you're six and there aren't any other playmates, you just want
to play. Mean Carmelita was there to make sure I didn't have any fun.
When Bobby dared me to the tadpole-catching contest, he knew he
had me: white girls like me weren't permitted near that canal.

It may as well have been the Panama Canal. Little more than a
drainage conduit that ran beside our house, the three-foot-deep ir-
rigation ditch was my favorite off-limits spot. The water teemed with
tadpoles and silvery minnows, a few crawdads, and the occasional old
shoe. Instead of the usual Arizona cacti and tumbleweeds, the bank
was overgrown with Egyptian grass, tules, and wild mustard. To me it
was a magical oasis. I couldn't wait to get there, and I didn't care if I
broke the rules.

The day was hot as a pistol, as Mom liked to say. Bobby and Peterbone were no doubt waiting for me, getting a head start. They'd
probably already jumped in the muddy pool where the floodgate was,
a square reservoir with a giant steering wheel at one end to control
the water level. Mom thought the canal was dangerous, especially the
deeper pool. She thought I might step on broken glass or come down
with some awful disease if I played there. Besides, nice girls went to
the public swimming pool, not a putrid ditch.

The floodgate did smell pretty rank—a cross between dirty socks and
moldy bread. There *was* a little broken glass, but you just watched your
step. I loved the mud in the pool squishing up through my toes and the
reeds swishing in the slight breeze. The cool water and the thought of
Bobby losing the dare made the place that much more attractive.

So that's exactly where I went. Mom worked full-time and I was
used to taking care of myself. The babysitter, Carmelita, was inside
with my younger sister, Leslie Kay. Carmelita spoke almost no English,
so I'd blame the language barrier or her inferior race if I got caught.
I grabbed the biggest empty jar I could find and headed out to find
Peterbone and Bobby.

I made it as far as the door. Nosy Carmelita asked, "*Por que*, Linda?"
Since the babysitter wasn't Anglo, I figured lying to her wasn't a big
deal. She wasn't the same as you and me. I held the jar behind my
back to prevent more questions.

Carmelita mostly ironed clothes and flipped through magazines
when she came to sit. Her hair was always wrapped in a coil that went
around her head several times—I used to imagine if she let it down
her hair would go on forever. She had this habit of snapping gum like
a gunshot, sometimes so loud I jumped. One time she'd taken away
my favorite Jesus Loves Me bookmark with the purple tassel when I
wouldn't stop teasing my sister with it. I really couldn't stand Carmelita.
Truth was, I was scared of her.

Now she stood in the doorway with Leslie Kay in her arms. The
woman's ample hips left little space for me to squeeze past. My kid
sister rubbed her eyes and whined to get down, but Carmelita held
her firmly. "*Adonde vas?*" Carmelita's black eyes flashed suspicion.
Where are you going?

A fib to someone like Carmelita wouldn't count. She was just a Mexican, like the old woman who came down our street with her tamale cart and those dirty children from the melon fields who sometimes came to school. My bigoted attitude didn't come from Mom or Dad, who carefully taught me that I should say "catch a *tiger* by the toe" instead of the racist alternative. I honestly don't know how I ended up thinking the Mexicans counted less than whites, but I did. So a small stretching of the truth was not going to get me in trouble with God or my folks. I thought.

"Where you going?" Again Carmelita grilled me. I couldn't look at her, so I picked a spot above her breasts, where a crucifix hung. She wasn't even a proper Christian—rosary beads and crucifixes were not allowed at my church. I smirked and said, "Just playing with Bobby and Peterbone." I shrugged. "Maybe we'll run in their sprinkler." I sidled past Carmelita and Leslie Kay, who thankfully was still too young to rat on me. The door slammed, muffling Carmelita's "Stay away from *la canal, chica.*"

I raced to the bank where Peterbone stood, watching Bobby take giant steps through the murky water of the floodgate. Peter had rolled up his pants and discarded his scuffed church shoes. I held up the large pickle jar. "See?" I announced in an important voice. "To get the most tadpoles you need the biggest jar." I tossed my head back and eyed Bobby, who held only a small, empty coffee can. I sloughed off my flip-flop sandals and thought of sticking out my tongue at those sorry boys. Then something in the water caught my eye.

I squinted to get a better look. The pool was so brackish that you couldn't see much, especially after Bobby stirred up the mud on the bottom. But there was something there, waving silently underwater.

"What's that?" I asked. Peterbone kept quiet. I repeated the question, but Bobby only laughed that mean laugh he had. Bobby strode to the opposite end and scooped up a can full of tadpoles. He grinned, but his eyes were narrow slits of black. I would have to see for myself.

I jumped in, shocked at first that the water was much deeper than it had looked. Was Bobby that much taller than I was? My feet sank into the silty mud until only my neck and head were above water. The pickle jar still sat on the bank, but I didn't know how I'd catch a tadpole if I was busy dog-paddling. Bobby had hauled himself out and now stood dripping above me, smirking and calling me "*Estupido.*" Peterbone looked terrified, and he put his shoes back on.

I paddled toward the bank, but something brushed against my leg. I stared down into the water and then screamed: the strange object I'd seen was a cat, a dead cat. Its tail was anchored to a rock so it floated upright, its mouth open in a kind of cat screech. It was black except for four white paws.

I kept screaming. I swallowed a mouthful of canal water and choked and cried and confessed my sins to God if he'd get me out of that hole. I'd never lie again. I was sorry I had disobeyed Carmelita. Could I have one more chance? Please?

Bobby and Peterbone hightailed it out of there. I was going to throw up or pass out any minute. If somebody tied a rock to my leg I'd look just like the poor kitty. I was doomed, but the worst part was, I deserved what I was getting. I was a liar and a bad, bad girl.

I thought of Leslie getting my stuff after they found me and wished I'd made out my last will and testament the way I'd seen on TV. I am sure my six years of life passed before my eyes as I treaded water. My arms and legs ached, and I kept bumping into the cat. I was going down. Then I heard a familiar popping noise.

"*Socorro,*" someone yelled. Help! Before I knew it, Carmelita splashed into the water, shoes and all. Her strong hands buoyed me and she dragged me onto the bank. I struggled to catch my breath, pointing to the cat still swaying beneath the surface. I shrank back when our babysitter reached for me—I thought she might even slap me for my disobedience. But Carmelita held me gently. I could have been one of her daughters.

She carried me all the way home, murmuring things in Spanish. I didn't know what the words meant, but she didn't sound mean or angry. I wondered if she'd make sure I was okay and then let me have it.

I'd hated Carmelita for being bossy and for being Mexican. And I'd hated her strange religion too. She kept me from doing what I wanted. I'm sure she thought I was the worst spoiled brat alive and one of those better-than-you whites too. I thought she'd enjoy telling Mom and Dad all I'd done.

Revealed

Instead, I got a bath, a freshly ironed shorts outfit, and some milk and cookies. The scolding never came. Carmelita brushed my hair and fussed over me and never once said anything about the canal, except to pray to Saint Francis for the cat and to pray about her crucifix, which had been lost during the rescue. When my parents came home from work, Carmelita didn't squeal.

I ate my cookies that day, glad to be alive, happy to stay inside and play with my sister. After a while I couldn't stand the silence and begged Carmelita to forgive me for lying, for disobeying, and for making her lose her crucifix when she jumped into the water. She snapped her gum with a flourish and smiled. She said, "*De nada.*" It's nothing.

I never went near the canal again, and Bobby and Peterbone found other kids to play with. When I got in over my head, Carmelita rescued me, even though I'd been a naughty pain in the neck. I knew I didn't deserve the break she gave me, but I embraced her kindness. That summer Carmelita became my best friend, the one I presented with a homemade ant farm and my Jesus bookmark. She was more than a babysitter, more than Mexican, more than Catholic. She was Carmelita, whom I loved.

I didn't understand the word *grace* then and probably thought it was only a girl's name. Yet from then on, Carmelita and I lived out a version of grace that I often forget but so desperately need to remember.

The kind of grace that goes against the grain—not required and riddled with danger—is possible only when you've faced yourself from the bottom of a muddy pit. Death, like a murdered cat, is there as long as you refuse to acknowledge what you've done, as long as your hands are full of excuses or tadpoles of sin.

Grace calls to us when we're tempted to break the rules and head for unknown territory. Grace seeks us out although we're worth less than an empty jar. Grace reminds us that even though we are probably the worst Christians we know, God loves us anyway. And grace isn't black or white or Catholic. It's the color of love.

212

Linda Clare

The Beans of Surrender

> I do not think it helps for modern women to view the past as a kind of male conspiracy to keep women down, because the blindness around the assumptions were so universal, among women as well as men, that almost no one, women or men, saw through them before the Enlightenment brought them into question.
>
> Monica Furlong

The Christian concept of surrender is a wonderful idea. A few years ago I began to think of it in terms of Reinhold Niebuhr's Serenity Prayer—and I started to worry less and pray more. I began to live in the moment and stopped regretting yesterday. I gave myself completely over to God. I thought.

Somewhere along the way I also bought into a more sinister version of letting go. Sure, I released things that held me back in my relationship with God. But somehow I managed to sell myself for a handful of beans—as Jack did in the famous bean-stalk fairy tale. I ended up with beans of misinformation that starved me instead of nourishing my soul. Beans that perpetuated a few ugly myths that, it turns out, weren't really what God had in mind for surrender at all.

The first myth I heard about surrender is that it means never making a conscious decision. If you are surrendered, fully and finally, the story goes, God will communicate with you on every part of your life—what to do, how to think, where to go. Which would be all right except sometimes I admit I've let others tell me what to do, what to think, and where to go, believing I couldn't possibly know what's best for me.

Could I surrender to God without donating my backbone to those around me? At the time, I hung on every word that my Bible-study leader and pastor said. They urged women to be creative counterparts in marriage, patient mothers, and joyful servants of the church. If I had to work outside the home—something my husband was supposed to approve for me first—I ought to make sure I baked a few cookies now and then too. I felt wedged between the pressures of modern life and a bygone era in which women wore aprons and heels to vacuum the carpets. After work I cooked supper, cleaned, and did homework with my four children before I fell into bed. The decision to juggle career and home had been made for me. I surrendered, all right—I didn't have energy left to do anything else.

Another myth I learned about surrender is that what I want doesn't count. Many women, myself included, will respond to the question, "What would you like?" with "Well, that depends on my husband [or the kids]." I placed others' happiness before my own. The nurturer in me whispered, "Don't rock the boat." And, of course, I never took the last one of anything, even if it was a withered old bean.

And what about biblical surrender? I thought of headship in marriage, and there were Scriptures in this area to guide me. The mandate for wives to be subject to their husbands has spilled over into women's careers, equal pay issues, and who's in charge of making decisions. Yet the "husbands, love your wives, just as Christ loved the church" (Eph. 5:25) portion of the Scripture gets neglected in too many relationships. Some wives surrender to husbands who regularly abuse their headship, and then those wives wonder why they feel so empty inside.

The late actress Katharine Hepburn was a trailblazer for women. Her trousers and sassy, intelligent characters opened doors for what later became the women's movement. Yet Kate had a secret—her relationship with Spencer Tracy was as traditional as her characters were progressive. She wrote of toning down her personality to please him, of sitting at Tracy's feet demurely in order to gain his approval.

I have a friend, Barb, who holds several advanced degrees, as does her husband, Max. In many ways the Smiths are wise and knowledgeable. They are known for their progressive ideas in the academic community. Yet when it comes to their marriage, my friends are planted firmly in tradition. Max controls their finances, supervises all purchases, and tells his wife where she can go and what she can do. Barb loves Max and allows him to run things because he's the man. Max thinks he's leading the way God intended. They actually get along very well.

But sometimes Barb has doubts. She privately wonders if surrendering to God must automatically include one's husband. If she feels like going away alone for a weekend, she wishes she didn't have to ask Max. For years she has deferred to his wishes because of his gender. In her career field, her colleagues respect her opinions. But at home Max always has the last word, and at church she's not invited to help make decisions. At times Barb is ashamed to say she resorts to manipulation to get her own way. She's leading a double life.

In the past, she and others like her had been advised to smile and let men go ahead and run things because that's the way we'd always done it. Barb cringed if she dared to reject traditional roles. Church leadership could cite particular Scriptures supporting this idea, leaving out other equally valuable verses. With this proof-text mentality, many women, even educated ones like Barb, often give up. They say it's easier to play dumb.

We could make a case that some women actually enjoy the role of traditional wife. They relish the idea of being taken care of, of letting the burden of finances or careers or even lawn upkeep fall to their husbands. Yet the comforts of remaining free from responsibility are rare in this fast-paced society. Most women end up doing all the traditional things plus holding down a job and mowing the lawn. Confusion about gender roles in marriage often leads to resentment and hurt for both partners.

Things got so tense for me that I sought counseling at my church. My husband wasn't really interested in airing our dirty laundry, he said. But we had serious problems—alcoholism, one of my children was mentally ill, I myself was physically disabled—and I knew I had to seek help.

Yet the first session was shocking: the counselor asked me to promise that no matter what was wrong, I would not entertain divorce as a solution. I felt trapped, as if my situation had somehow fallen through the cracks of doctrine. Although I went for several appointments, the answer to all my problems seemed to lie in my somehow enduring my circumstances with long-suffering and hope of a heavenly reward.

For some, that might be enough. For me, it wasn't. Counseling to redefine expectations and reestablish communication between partners can work wonders when spouses contest their roles. As author and counselor James Kilgore says of those with marital difficulties, "When a couple learns to communicate, they add to that process the ability to negotiate."[2] If a couple works on communicating, the odds of improvement are higher.

But what about marriages like mine, those "unequally yoked" unions in which at times only the wife wants to work on the relationship? The wife sits in church alone each week, hoping to hear a spiritual solution to her loneliness. Sometimes she even considers the church or the pastor her surrogate mate, while her marriage dies a little more each day.

Churches sometimes accommodate that woman and take the idea of "shepherding" to extremes. Pastors and church elders dictate what members may wear, which activities are permitted, and even how children are to be educated. Single women especially may feel they are becoming the bride of Christ as they wed themselves to the church. Yet for these vulnerable women, the first area of surrender is often permission to question authority, to think for one's self.

Church leaders meet a challenge to male authority with censorship or chastisement. While most congregations are not so radical, the mandate that men are always leaders and women are always followers can result in women who start to feel innately inferior to men. They may believe that all gifts of God must be filtered through our male leaders, both in the home and in our churches.

The marriage bed is another area where women wrestle with surrender. We have been told that we should "yield" to husbands who are crude or violent, make them happy for the sake of the union, obey our husbands when they want sex three times a week even if we don't. Women should be responders only, they say, not initiators. One recent Christian book even advises a wife to try to please her husband sexually because his pleasure makes God happy. That kind of surrender breeds anger and the feeling that a woman's needs are nothing compared to a man's. The man-in-charge-of-sex bean is a myth where husbands are burdened with retaining their image of "sex-pert" while women don't have to do anything except lie there.

But is this the surrender that Jesus asks of us? Does the Creator demand you turn over your paycheck to your husband because a woman can't possibly keep her own money? Is Jesus telling us we aren't quite as capable when it comes to those thorny issues of a woman's place? If we are considered "helpmeets," does this mean we can never go our own way? Do we really have sexual needs?

"Ouch," you say. "Let's not talk about surrender anymore. I'd rather keep all my different selves separated: the wife-self, mother-self, daughter-self, sister-self. Even my Jesus-self must stay in its compartment. Artist-self, work-self, and any other selves are to behave and not make trouble."

But Jesus came to set us free, and the truth is, letting go is only about the release of one self—your *false self*. This is the part of you that chafes under the limp assumption that women should be treated as children. *False self* builds barriers that prevent our souls from getting closer to God.

Trading that false self for the True Self, as psychoanalyst C. G. Jung called it, means more than simple attitude adjustment. According to Sue Monk Kidd, this True Self may be what the Scriptures call "the mind of Christ" (1 Cor. 2:16).[3]

Surrender implies casting off all self-centeredness to adopt a God-centeredness. We get in touch with our wants and needs and we make them known. In practical terms, we don't expect others to know what we'd really like for dinner.

You've heard the saying "Jesus came to take your sins, not your mind." Surrender isn't related to becoming mush-brained, nor is it an excuse to be wishy-washy. You are smart and possess God-given talents. Use them.

We become self-directed and, at the same time, God-infused. We don't need to remain children, because we can use our brains. We agree to accept a portion of the responsibility we've abdicated to our husbands. We might mow a lawn, or we might not.

We look beyond traditional gender roles and embrace ourselves as persons who have God-given creativity, wisdom, and opinions. We have meaningful things to say and we can be assertive without being "witchy" or shrill. We are free to pursue God by ourselves and for ourselves. Sue Monk Kidd, in her book *When the Heart Waits*, says, "In Christian language, this is plain, old-fashioned surrender—giving up our conscious will and yielding instead to the inner kingdom."[4]

To some the search for the True Self may feel uncomfortable and even heretical. But the Bible tells us that God's gifts are rained down on "all your sons and daughters" (Joel 2:28). Could God really mean that our gifts are to be weak and watered-down versions of those God bestows on sons? In the quest to replace their wills with the will of God, some women dare to think beyond the traditional definition of surrender. Some dare to open their hearts and minds to God in new and mysterious ways, and in the process they transform themselves.

The voices of Christian women today express a groan of longing, according to Ruth Haley Barton, a profound need to bring impact to their lives and have impact upon the world.[5] Women today, in their search for surrender, are discovering that the Holy Spirit is available to them in the same powerful ways that God affords males who believe.

And surrender, true surrender, is a love affair with God. Surrendering to Jesus means filling myself up with as much of him as I can—whether it's through prayer, Bible study, a sermon, or a beautiful sunset. I don't believe in a formula for this process, because one way to surrender may not fit all.

So I make my own way, imperfectly, toward the Holy City. I pray Niebuhr's prayer—that I change the things I can, accept those I can't, and learn to know the difference—all while asking the Holy Spirit to guide me. This is my True Self, the one that is wed to the Creator and has grown past myths and the brambles of traditions and others' expectations.

How can I soften these dried myths, these beans for which I've sold my True Self? Change, especially cultural change, can be a lengthy and painful process, one in which most will demand that we not rock the boat. A book from the 1970s may hold part of the answer. In *Lord, Change Me!* Evelyn Christenson reminds women that we cannot change anyone but ourselves.[6] I can allow God to direct my thoughts, but it is up to me to do what God is calling me to do.

Dare to imagine a life brimming with God, a life that uses its intelligence to make decisions, chases after its own dreams, and seeks first the kingdom of God. See your false self fade away while your True Self, the woman God made and loves, emerges fresh, mysterious, and ready to surrender to Christ.

Nourishing Inspiration
Melody Carlson

O Holy Night

Looking back I can see it all makes sense, but at the time I felt completely discombobulated. Don't you love that word? Anyway, it seemed that every level of my life had been scrambled and tossed and was landing in places I'd never planned to go.

First of all, my two sons had become teenagers. Talk about some challenges. And it didn't help that my younger son had turned into a real rebel who seemed to thrive on shocking his parents. Think green hair, facial piercing, bizarre clothes . . .

Next I'd completely relocated my life by accepting a new job in a town two hours away from where my husband and I had barely moved into our recently built home. Just the same, we felt it was the right step for our family. It not only gave our younger son a fresh start but also helped us to move to a lovely mountain town that we'd often dreamed about, but never thought possible.

Still, when the time came to cram everything I could into the back of my old Jeep, including my fourteen-year-old son (who left two long sets of heel marks on the highway that took us over the mountains), I wasn't so sure about it.

Besides everything else, I did wonder why I had accepted a job in publishing when I'd barely launched my own writing career by selling my first book. What sense did it make to work on other people's books when what I really wanted was to write books of my own?

But my deepest level of confused upheaval was probably spiritual. I felt as if I'd almost given up. Not on God, but on religion. We'd been hurt and disappointed by the church we'd faithfully attended and served for years. And while I wasn't sorry to be leaving that situation behind me, I just wasn't sure what to expect in the future or how involved I wanted to be in any sort of "organized" religion. Call me jaded or disenchanted or simply church-weary, but I wasn't eager to join a new congregation.

Of course, I'm sure I wasn't consciously thinking about all these things as my reluctant son and I unloaded our piled-high Jeep. We made our way into the little rental cabin that we planned to inhabit until my husband and younger son could join us (after the school year ended and our home sold). It was getting pretty late and I was tired but still trying to maintain a cheerful front as I hauled boxes and bags into the small cabin. I'm sure I hoped that my Pollyanna attitude might somehow convince my son that this really was a good move—thinking he'd see in time and maybe even thank me someday. But, as I recall, he went to bed mad.

I went to bed exhausted. It didn't help to know that I'd need to get up early to fix breakfast (no Egg McMuffins in this tiny tourist town) and then drive my heel-dragging son to his new school, get him registered, then show up to work (hopefully not too late) at my new job where I knew not a single soul (except for my new boss, who'd be gone for two weeks on his honeymoon). To say I was feeling overwhelmed might be an understatement. I'm sure that I was close to tears as I attempted to fall asleep in a strange bed, in a strange house, in a strange town, more than a hundred miles from my husband and older son. What had I done?

Normally I would have turned to God at a time like that. I would have asked him to straighten everything out, fix everything up, and get me back on track again. But that particular night I felt too tired to pray. And so I just lay there, feeling more and more hopeless.

Finally, giving up on sleep, I opened my eyes—and was amazed. In all the hubbub of moving into the cabin and getting us settled in, I'd failed to notice a huge skylight above the bed. And when I looked up I was stunned to see a canopy of brilliant, I mean my-eyes-must-be-kidding-brilliant, stars overhead. If you haven't seen a starry night in the mountains of Central Oregon, you cannot understand what I'm saying. But take my word for it, they are stupendous.

And as I stared up at them I felt a strange sense of connection and timelessness encompassing me. I felt as if I were looking into the face of God. And suddenly I realized how he had a perfect order and timing for everything, and that despite how dazed and confused I'd been feeling, he was still God and the universe was still orbiting under his dominion and control. Not only that, but I sensed more than ever that he was holding me in his hand.

I believe it was in that moment that I really began to let go of the many things I'd been futilely attempting to hold together in my life. Things such as my family, my teenaged sons, my career, where I lived, and even my attitudes toward religion. Oh, I don't believe I consciously thought of all those things exactly in that order. Mostly it was just a great big letting-go-and-letting-God moment. But in the letting go, I think I was beginning to realize that all my hard work and good intentions would never achieve my desired results. Only God was able to do that.

For the first time in days I felt myself begin to relax and actually breathe, as I imagined myself stretched out and peacefully resting in the palm of God's hand. I felt safe and secure, and I was convinced that, just as he had hung stars in such perfect order, so he could arrange and rearrange my life for me. And I could trust him to do so.

Now, nearly nine years later, I am still awed to look back and see what God was doing in my life. I'm amazed at how he executed a plan so above and beyond anything I was able to dream. My writing career took off in unimaginable ways. We got into a rustic home in the woods that we absolutely love. Both of our sons made good friends almost immediately and actually enjoyed the lifestyle here. My husband and I now participate in a spiritual community that we really appreciate.

Oh sure, our lives aren't perfect and we've had our fair share of trials and questionable moments, but that's how life happens. Just the same, I've been blessed to watch God unfolding a plan that never fails to humble and amaze me. And it all seemed to fall into place back when I began to let go.

A friend told me about something he calls "convergence." It's a point in time that can radically alter your life. It happens when the most important areas of your life (your gifts, relationships, spirituality, abilities) all come together and reach their peak at the same time

Looking back, I believe that's exactly what was starting to happen for me on that starry night in that little cabin. Despite how jumbled my circumstances looked and felt, I believe that when I took my hands off and let go, God was able to take all the disparate bits and pieces of my life and miraculously converge them—in the same way that he lines up the dazzling stars.

Scripture Salon

Kristen Johnson Ingram

What God Says about Grace

A Reflection on Jonah 2:7

As my life was ebbing away, I remembered the LORD; and
my prayer came to you, into your holy temple.

A lot of women live in big fish.

God called the prophet Jonah to Nineveh, to preach repentance and revival. But thinking he could escape God or the task by sailing to another country, Jonah headed for Joppa, now Tel Aviv, and got on a ship. When a storm threatened to sink the vessel, Jonah confessed that he was the cause and urged the sailors to pitch him overboard. Which they did. Then a big fish that God had prepared swallowed the prophet right up. Only on the third day, when he remembered God and begged for deliverance, did the fish spew him out on the beach so he could go to Nineveh and save its people.

Jonah was a man, of course, but his story applies to women who flee from God. They run out of fear or self-hate, or feelings of inadequacy or a refusal to sacrifice their comfort. Or they mix up the sounds of their consciences with the voice of God, and they shy away from the nagging and condemnation they hear. So they run, thinking God is mean. Others run because they think they're so sinful God hates them. And still others flee because their lives have made them afraid of intimacy with God. So he puts them in a spiritual fish until they come to themselves and realize that their mission isn't impossible.

The signs of a woman who's running from God are clear: she's swallowed by work or angry at her kids or codependent on her alcoholic husband. The view from inside the whale is so limited she may become a compulsive shopper or bulimic. This woman may look just fine to others because she's usually cheerful and kind, good at hiding the tempest that rages in her heart. A woman who lives in a fish creates her own agony and believes God *can* help her but *won't*.

Once in a while when God summons a woman, it's so she can *do* something. God might invite her to a journey or a job that will make her life harder or at least different. But most of the time, God longs for her to *be*, rather than to do. God is passionate about what people are, about what kind of stuff is crammed into their brains and minds and souls. God is more interested in a woman who gives money to panhandlers than in how much she gives—or even what the panhandler does with it.

God calls not out of a demand for human service, but out of yearning. God yearns for us the same way lovers yearn for one another, the way a mother longs to see her newborn infant, the way people fly across country to see family members who have been away too long. God's longing is not general: God longs for specific human beings, as individually as the way you might pick out tomatoes at a farmer's market: *this one is ready, this is ripe*.

God's ideas are not always religious. God might call a woman to sell plasticware because her personality is so loving that she heals an unhappy woman at the party. Or perhaps God excites her about mathematics or science so she can light up dark places by teaching and experimenting. Perhaps she writes poetry that doesn't talk about God but lifts the heart of anyone who reads her words. A church secretary who answers the parish phone may be the first person who talks to a new widow or a suicidal man or a rape victim. And of course, some denominations believe women are called to be ordained ministers or church workers, nuns or deaconesses.

On Jonah's first day or two in the fish, he might have concentrated on how to avoid being struck by incoming food and water, but eventually he realized he was going to die. And not only would he die, he would do so in a state of disobedience. His sense of panic about his spiritual state won over even his fear of death, and he headed into transformation.

"As my life was ebbing away, I remembered the LORD," Jonah said.

The God of love is not one to throw accusations in the faces of sorrowing women. And God will *never* whisper, "It's too late," because God doesn't impose deadlines or have an "only one chance" philosophy. God never said to Jonah, "I'll give you three days to complete your mission. After that, forget it and stay in the fish." Actually, when Jonah demanded shipboard justice and tried to commit legal suicide, the fish rescued him. God didn't put him in the fish to punish him, but to save him from the waves and the dangerous rocks near the shore, and then to give him time and a place to recover from being a fool—a fool who thought he could run away from God. Then, because God never wastes anything or discards it, the fish quit being Jonah's cell and became his transportation, delivering him right to the beach where he could start the journey to Nineveh and finish his mission.

A woman knows when the time has come for major change because she's restless. She wants something and knows someone is making a demand on her attention. She might make a mistake and project God's call onto a man or a job or alcohol. She might take drugs, thinking, *This will make me feel better*. Nothing does, however; the Reverend Maron Van says that if God wants you, you'll feel completely crazy if you try to run away. Darkness is in the fish, but light shines on the beach, where the woman starts over. She either changes her life completely or changes what she sees. She may look around and recognize the splendor of ordinary days, may know walks are accompanied by angels, and that fiery seraphim hover over her even when she folds laundry or stirs the pinto beans.

In *Descent into Hell*, a religious novel by Charles Williams, one of C. S. Lewis's Inklings, a woman has fulfilled her first calling, which was to give comfort to a dying man. After that she heads to London, where her cousin will find a job for her. Her friend, a Christian poet, says, "Won't it be wonderful? Whatever it is, you'll love it." And she answers, "Under the Mercy."[7]

Under the mercy, a woman can become who God intended her to be, can crawl out on the beach of life, shake the water out of her shoes, and begin her journey toward heaven.

If you feel your life ebbing away, as if all your being is used up and you can find no trace of yourself within yourself, when you can't stand one more day in the belly of the beast, perhaps you'll remember the time when you and God were friends and ask for grace. If being restless and empty drives you hard enough, you can let your prayer, like Jonah's, go all the way to God's heavenly temple. But rather than changing your behavior or appearance or even your job, you have to let God's grace affect you on the inside.

One woman did it. God called, and she assented, without running or hiding or arguing. She was a young girl when she became part of the central act of history. Her name was Miry'm, Mary in modern language, and because she answered God, the world has a Savior.

Find a need and fill it.

Something to Try On

- On the next clear night, spend a few minutes looking at the stars with God. Pick out your own special star or identify some constellations, keeping in mind God's gifts of grace in your life.
- We all make snap judgments now and then. Think of someone about whom you assumed something that turned out to be untrue, and ask God's forgiveness. Did you misjudge that person out of fear they were different? Work on seeing others as God sees them.
- In your journal, write a "what if?" story about your life. Are you interested in learning something new but stuck in a routine? Where do you think God wants you to go? Listen for God's direction in prayer and Scripture, and be courageous enough to take a baby step toward a new opportunity or phase in your life.
- Plant a flower or vegetable from a seed and watch it grow. Take note of the ways God tends to your needs in everyday life. What does spiritual surrender mean to you?

10

You in the Hot Springs

Healing and Revitalization

Healing is embracing what is most feared; healing is opening what has been closed, softening what has hardened
into obstruction; healing is learning to trust life.

Jeanne Achterberg

Does God Heal?

Linda: I feel funny talking about healing, at least the physical kind, because I have to make peace between the real world and what the Bible says about healing. Emotional healing is easier to get my mind around, because it doesn't involve regrowing limbs or causing giant tumors to disappear. What should Christian women expect from God about healing?

Kris: Oh, thanks, Linda. Such an easy question to answer. But maybe we ought to ask what they *do* expect. I keep wanting God to fix my miserable spine, my finances, and my relationships, but to be honest, I don't have a whole lot of faith anymore about my spine. When I read Scripture, I'm not sure what to think.

Linda: Here's what I know: God *does* heal. Broken hearts, loneliness, sinfulness, to name a few. But God isn't going to wave a magic wand over my life.

Kris: I don't know why you and I both live in so much physical pain while we're trying our best to do God's work. But I know God loves me, and his presence is wonderful.

Linda: When I get to heaven, I'll ask God why we had to suffer. But here in the hot springs, God comforts, soothes, and energizes me. And assures me that God will always provide that comfort when I ask.

229

The Way Is Faith

Your beloved mother is dying. She's battled cancer, but now she's losing ground fast. Your favorite sister suffers with debilitating migraine headaches, and doctors can't find the cause. Or maybe your best friend from high school calls you late one night, saying she's thinking about ending it all.

Painful scenarios like these happen to many of us. You can probably think of at least one person you know who isn't healthy. That person may even be you. As we age, the list of friends and family who contend with physical and mental ailments gets longer. And at some point all of us pray for God's help in making them or us well.

When Jesus walked the earth, he healed. Over and over, to those with physical, mental, or emotional disabilities, the Lord restored sight, made cripples whole, and rescued madmen from their demons. The proof that Jesus was God's only Son often came with a healing miracle.

Ever since, Christians have tried to tap into this healing power. The formula proves elusive, even in our technological world. Some say Jesus's miracles were only for his generation, to get those who lived in biblical times to accept him as the Messiah. Others insist that healings—from such things as terminal diseases to hangnails—are available to modern believers. Despite modern medicine's best efforts, some people get well, others die. Sometimes we witness miracles, sometimes we don't. What's going on?

Why God heals on some occasions and other times does not is a mystery, one that theologians and laypersons alike have not defined. The Bible says we can know God, but we won't always understand the reasons things happen as they do. Eugenia Price asks, "What might happen if we stopped restricting the creativity of God by giving up the demand for receiving or giving 'pat answers' which we interpret as being God's own?"[1]

When your loved one suffers or a painful condition tortures you, the first thing you want is for God to explain the situation. Why does God allow it? Why don't you or your loved one receive healing? Why?

"Why?" is a natural question when things go wrong. "In the first throes of tragedy," Price writes, "we rush at God with our questions, and I firmly believe God welcomes them."[2] She adds that it isn't sinful to question God, merely human. Yet God's answers may not be the ones we expect.

If we seek our healing answers in the Bible, we can find comfort. "Pray without ceasing," we're told, and keep "faith, hope and love" no matter what the circumstances. If we pray and a sick person recovers, we rejoice over God's miracle. If things get worse, or healing doesn't come, we often blame our method or ourselves for the failure. We cannot understand a God who can allow pain to continue.

You want your precious mother to survive. You can't stand to watch your sister suffer with migraines, and you can't imagine life without your old friend. So you don't give up. You pray and you keep vigil, begging God to heal them. And sometimes, God does.

Those who've lived through trauma and grief know life can be confusing and disappointing, even with great courage and faith. They know that sometimes the only answer is to stand in the pain and let God stand with them. At some place, survivors of disasters stop praying for miracles and learn to see the miracles in every living thing.

Beyond the pat-answer approach or even a bed of Scriptures to keep you warm, there lies a way to help us leap across the "Why?" gap. The way is our faith, and the vehicle is hope.

The stories in this section travel along that faith road. Some of the writers are miles closer to healing, inward as well as outward, while some are still asking, "Why?" The women who have suffered or watched others deal with sickness don't express any form of self-pity. They don't always understand the whys of life, but they trust the God who allows them to question. They've discovered that healing is a journey, one in which the quest for healing can be a comfort in itself. For at the end of the healing road, Jesus beckons.

"Follow me," he says. "Follow me."

Helping Heal the World

A Reflection on Phoebe in Romans 16:1–2

I commend to you our sister Phoebe, a deacon of the church
at Cenchreae, so that you may welcome her in the Lord as
is fitting for the saints, and help her in whatever she may
require from you, for she has been a benefactor of many
and of myself as well.

Romans 16:1–2

The Bible gives us just this one line. Everything else we know about
Phoebe comes from church tradition, or from correctly translating the
Greek of the Letter to the Romans.

Phoebe was a minister. Paul used the masculine term *diakonos* to
describe her, which means church leaders had consecrated her by the
laying on of hands. The feminine version of the title would have meant
she was just a servant to the congregation. In the ancient church, as
in the liturgical church today, a deacon was not an honorary position:
deacons were ordained and could marry or bury their parishioners.
They could also preach, anoint, and disperse communion.

Paul also calls her *prostatis*. Bible translations render this term "benefactor," as well as "servant," "friend," "patroness," or "helper." This is
appropriate since leadership roles in the church are roles of service.
Yet theologian Mark Mattison writes, "What we may not realize . . .
is that this term is a variation of the term *proistemi*, used to describe
elders 'ruling' or 'managing' in 1 Timothy 3:4–5; 5:17."[3]

Who was Phoebe? And why is she important to modern Christian
women?

The search for Phoebe takes us first to Cenchreae, which is the port city for Corinth, about four miles away. Corinth had long controlled trade; in 46 BC Julius Caesar rebuilt it and made a Roman colony. A mole, which is a massive stone wall constructed in the sea as a break-water, was built in the harbor at Cenchreae and enclosed a temple to Isis or Cybele, goddesses who inspired temple prostitution.

The area was a multicultural: every two years the Panhellenic festivals were held there, an event second only to the Olympics. Cenchreae was a lively, rough city, a boomtown, open and feisty. The church there had not only the problem of Roman oppression, but the temptations of an ancient Sin City: prostitution, gambling, wine and distilled liquor, and gang activity. And out of this rough-and-tumble atmosphere rose a woman of such character and purity that Paul trusted her to take the Letter to the Romans to Christians in Italy.

Chances are that when you think *church*, you imagine a building where people gather for Sunday services. But the early church was not yet gathered under the great dome at Saint Peter's. Christians met in house churches whose congregations ranged from three or four people to perhaps thirty. Their services usually included a common meal and ended with the familiar elements of bread and wine. These meals were called *Eucharist*, which is Greek for "thanksgiving," the "Lord's Supper," or "communion"; Priscilla and Aquila held such a church in their house.

When Paul was looking for a word to describe the groups he was setting up all over the Mediterranean world, he chose the neutral term *ekklesia*, which was not a religious word. An *ekklesia* meant any kind of gathering, and Luke used it in Acts 19:39–41 to describe both an ordered assembly and a near-riot.

As the church evolved in the first centuries, Phoebe acquired the title "deaconess," an office abandoned by the Catholic Church after the eleventh century, continued into the present by the Orthodox Church, and retained as an appointment in many evangelical churches. Until they began to fully ordain women in the last thirty years, Episcopalians and Lutherans had orders of deaconesses.

The early church deaconess ministered to women in their homes and assisted at baptisms of women. Later the deaconess kept order in the church; cared for women who were sick and poor; was present when bishops, priests, or deacons spoke with women; and introduced women candidates for baptism. Their work was full-time in the joyful ferment of the first churches, so most deaconesses were either virgins who chose not to marry or widows without home responsibilities. Phoebe was more than this kind of deaconess, more than a simple servant in the church; she was a leader, because the apostle Paul laid his greatest epistle in her hands and sent her from Corinth on a ship to Rome.

She was much more than a courier. Most Christians in Rome were not literate, and even those who were probably didn't read the *koine* Greek that Paul wrote. So this excited Christian woman probably visited most of the Roman house churches and read the letter to them. She may have carried two or three copies with her, but in the days before photocopies, hand-lettering such an epistle would have been expensive and time-consuming, so she had to read it to groups. Because the entire Epistle to the Romans isn't a document a Christian can grapple with in one evening, she probably stayed for several days with each church, answering questions as well as she could, talking about Paul, and reading more of the letter to the *ekklesia*, the house church.[4]

All this means that Phoebe was literate, something rare for even upper-class women. She had to be careful, because Nero's persecution of the Christians was going on in Rome while she was there. Since we don't hear of her again, she may have ultimately given her life in the Colosseum, or, if she could have proven she was a Roman citizen, she may have been beheaded—that was the "nicer" form of execution, saved only for citizens like Paul himself.

Phoebe's journey was more than taking some letter to Rome. Paul was the great apostle, but he would have been unknown except for ministers and teachers like Phoebe who carried his letters, and she delivered the Word to people afraid in their sins, oppressed by the Roman emperor, and subject to persecution. And for the two thousand years since, the letters that Phoebe carried to Rome have healed the world, because they include these words: "There is therefore now no condemnation for those who are in Christ Jesus" (8:1).

And perhaps along with *diakonos* and *prostatis*, we should call her "angel," or messenger of God.

A Healing Gratitude

Nineteen sixty-two was a bad year, my father said. The Cuban missile crisis had all the grown-ups terrified of World War III. I was terrified too. I was eight years old and I prayed and prayed for God to heal my left arm, paralyzed from childhood polio. I was sure that in order for God to hear that kind of prayer, I had to be grateful.

I'd been stuck for months in a hospital for crippled children, separated from my family, enduring painful surgeries and procedures. I was put on an airplane by myself and reminded to be grateful for the wonderful healing I would be receiving from the doctors at the hospital. I received an awful plaster cast and slept my first night in a giant baby crib. My clothes were placed in a box and I received hospital clothing—cotton dress starched like cardboard. I also received advice: don't mess with the head nurse because if you are a problem, she'll send you to the cast room. I received all this in the first day, and no one mentioned the wonderful healing from the doctors. On the girls' ward, all around me lay other patients who were much more disabled than I was. But somehow I didn't feel all that lucky.

Or grateful. One of the few personal possessions we patients were allowed from home was a Bible. I kept mine, a white-leather, zippered King James Version, under my pillow. If things got so bad at night that I couldn't stop my tears, I kept the trusty red-letter book close, where I could finger it like a talisman. By the way, the nursing staff didn't allow crying. In those days stuff like being scared or homesick only made the nurses decide that you were a problem. And they really did banish weeping children to the cast room for the night.

What did I have to cry about? I could walk around, and only one arm was wrapped up in plaster. Many of the other girls wore heavy body casts that clanged against their bed rails—they couldn't sit up, much less walk. How could I complain? Why wasn't I grateful?

I thought gratefulness meant telling God "Thank you" no matter what. In Sunday school I learned that God loves us and wants us to love him back. Well, I thought I was doing my part. But there I was, still stranded a million miles from home, in pain, and too afraid of needles to take any medicine for it. I missed my mom and my clothes and my bed. Every time I came close to accepting that God loved me so much he had sent me to this hospital, I couldn't even fake gratitude. I waited until the lights were out and squeezed that white Bible as hard as I could. I told God over and over I was sorry that I couldn't say "Thank you." I wanted to sit on Jesus's lap, but I didn't want to be a problem.

If I ran up to Jesus, would he know my name, or would I be just one of "those crippled kids"? I wondered if we "crips" were the "least of these" that Jesus talked about when he walked around on earth. Perhaps I lacked that something that would make Jesus smile, throw wide his arms, and say, "I know you. You're my special one."

My musings about the way God worked, while oddball, only reflected the world I knew. Like most kids, I was pretty literal in my philosophy of life. If you did good deeds, you got a reward, although it might not come right away—kind of like waiting for the cereal-box prize you sent away for. I also had the notion that if you did bad stuff, then you had to, as my father liked to say, "face the music."

I recently attended an event where a famous person stood in the midst of a crowd, and I longed to meet that celebrity. I elbowed my way closer, waiting for the right moment to extend my hand. The famous one suddenly brightened and called out to a familiar face. They hugged each other while I stood there, wishing she would notice me as well. I tried to make eye contact, but too many clamored for attention. The famous person was whisked away. I told myself to be grateful I got as close as I did. Yet I was stung by the fact that I was just another face in the crowd. Did the one hugged by the special person have something I didn't?

Comparison has been one way I have always held myself in check, horrified by the specter of self-pity. I did not survive a death camp or lose my parents in a fiery car crash. My father didn't beat me, and I never went hungry: these facts have set me squarely in the lap of ordinariness.

How I came by my irrational idea that God loves all the little children except one or two of us who are too messed up is not important. I only know that it's rooted in girlhood, in a place where language formed and personality developed in a buck-toothed kid from Yuma, Arizona. And no matter how I try, I am confronted with the truth that this scared little girl is a big part of who I am.

So how does someone with a few spots of misfortune and many islands of opportunity come to believe that God can't possibly love her? I don't know where I got the idea that God was a very famous person and everyone wanted to shake his hand, but I figured I'd never get the Lord's attention. Even Jesus, always shown with kids clambering onto his lap, might have too many charges to think about a girl with big teeth and one arm that didn't work. In church I couldn't even raise my hands in praise when the songs said to.

Kids just add things up in a row. When I prayed for God to get me out of that hospital, I felt selfish and ungrateful. So, of course, when I wasn't magically healed, I knew why. God was either too busy to rescue a crippled kid, or else he was making sure I faced the music. I clutched my Bible and kept praying in case God suddenly changed God's mind.

I doubt God changed at all, but the sad part was, neither did I. I did finally get home and grow up, although I had to return to that awful girls' ward twice more for surgeries that didn't help at all. I did as much good stuff as I could, but I never got comfortable with God. I thought he was like your least-favorite uncle, who once catches you in a fib and never again takes you for ice cream. That uncle writes you off and concentrates on your younger sister, who never lies.

I wasn't good enough, nice enough. I didn't pray enough, read the Word enough, and I still couldn't lift my hands in praise. Inside I was a crippled eight-year-old, scared and guilt-ridden for not being grateful for pain. I was willing to come to God's gatherings, but I thought I was always going to be anonymous to him. God had more important people to think about.

For a time I ran away, much as a kid wraps all her belongings in a scarf and stomps out the front door. I stopped attending church, dropped out of music ministry, and quit the women's study. I contemplated divorce from my family. I got to the edge of my Christian life and sat on the curbside, suddenly afraid to cross the street. The world, I already knew, didn't have much patience for a disabled nobody like me. I was terrified but still hurt and angry with God. Hadn't God left me alone in that hospital years ago? Hadn't I felt abandoned and insignificant? Why did I still feel unloved?

One day I read a story of a woman whose faith was tested as she lay in a hospital following emergency surgery. She told of experiencing God's presence, of God seeming to say, "We are in this together. Hold on to my love. It will see you through anything." As I read those words, I experienced again the trauma of my own hospitalizations that began in 1962. I shook with the vivid images that replayed in my mind, and my stomach churned with fear. Why had I not heard God speaking? Had I somehow not listened? Most of all, was I in some ways still a young girl, still stuck in a hospital ward?

In order to understand why my head but not my heart believed in God's love for me, that day I was forced to look back to that time with my grown-up mind. I first had to grapple with the question of how at such a young age I could have been put on an airplane by myself and flown far away to a hospital, where all the others and I underwent major surgery. Some had Sunday visitors, but most were like me: alone on my bed all afternoon, bored out of my mind, secretly hoping my mom would surprise me before visiting hours were over. Most never got their wish.

I was afraid to ask why Mom and Dad didn't come, or how come I woke up from anesthesia without so much as a Mylar balloon. I was afraid to say I hurt, was scared, or later, that I was angry for being abandoned. The standards of that Cuban Missile Crisis era did play a role, and Mom wrote letters faithfully. But we never discussed her breaking me out or even smuggling my favorite toy in to help me sleep at night. At the time I felt proud that I could do all it by myself—I was independent to a fault. Yet in the quiet dark I watched snow fall outside the hospital window and prayed I'd make it through another day. I asked God to heal me. Or if God wasn't too busy, would he mind getting me out of there?

As I looked back that day, to my child's mind it appeared I was on my own in the escape department. And it was that sense of aloneness that permeated my days. I came to mistake self-reliance for strength and strove to be as normal as possible in every way. I succeeded in masking my disability so most people didn't notice anything different. But as I tried to please people, I also worked hard to stay beneath God's radar, preventing myself from discovering the truth about God's attitude toward me: that somehow God has loved me and you and each individual ever created from before we came into being. That God knew what names we'd get, before we were proverbial twinkles in our parents' eyes. That God knows our names better than anyone.

And that God was there when I was eight, holding back tears right along with me. I used to think that angels flew over our beds on the girls' ward, and sometimes they stopped to give you a hug. Now I wonder if they dispensed courage and extra amounts of God's love too.

Second, I had to examine my attitudes toward God. This is where I had to face the music. Like so many women, I'm guilty of people-pleasing codependency, and a Christian life full of "shoulds" and "oughts." This is where God's real healing happens for me. If I shed all that stuff about doing good and bad and being grateful, I'll come to a place where God feels electric in the insistence of love. Right and wrong evaporates in love's sizzle. God breathes, "I love you. No matter what." God knows my name, and I'm starting to believe it.

I reached for my old white Bible, now tattered and worn. I wanted to see for myself the verse in Romans where Paul tells us we can never be separated from God's love. It's there, over and over, a message running through Scripture: God has loved and always will love you. You—personally, not just a face in the crowd. Me—disabled and imperfect and slow to understand my worth to God.

The truth of all of this still sometimes eludes me. I see my deep need for healing, emotionally and spiritually. Some days I'm still a little kid, reliving old hurts and missing out on joy. Those times I imagine God as distant and way too famous to stop and shake hands.

But they say God is a persistent lover, not easily rebuffed. Even when you are messed up, God woos you, picking you out from a crowd. God smiles, welcomes you onto the biggest lap in the universe, and tells you you're the most special kid ever.

Believing this heals me every day, and although I do think God can perform earthly healing miracles, I'm not as anxious about physical healing anymore. Sure, it would be nice. But I am far more fearful now of being trapped in anonymity and purposelessness than I ever was of my times in that hospital. I don't know how, but I know that I'm loved, no matter what. Loved by someone who knows my name. Gratitude, I find, doesn't come before healing, but as its direct and wonderful result.

Healing Inspiration

Kristen Johnson Ingram

A Sign of Healing

So they said to him, "What sign are you going to give us then, so that we may see it and believe you? What work are you performing?"

John 6:30

The Church is a sign to the world of what a life of communion is like.

Pope Paul VI

When an ossuary, a stone chest for bones, appeared on the archaeology scene with an inscription that read, "James, son of Joseph, brother of Jesus," Christians held their breath. Did the church, at last, have proof of our Savior's life on earth? Had archaeologists proven the New Testament?

A few weeks after the artifact first appeared in newspapers and magazines such as *Biblical Archaeology*, one group of scholars remained convinced, but new experts said no, the inscription was a fake. I could almost hear the country moan with its disappointment. The debate is still on, but as with many archaeology finds, opinions will always differ.

Everyone longs for something about God that he or she can see and touch, especially in this society in which proof of everything else exists: cable news from across the world, digital photographs, instant replays, on-the-scene reporting, DNA matches that related a man in an English village to a thousand-year-old ancestor from the bog. Telescopes that range across a billion light years to prove the universe is various and beautiful and expanding, fingerprints and retinal scans that confirm anyone's identity: all of those convince us that we can see and hear and prove anything that happens in the world. So why can't we find proof of the central acts of all history, the incarnation, death, and resurrection of our Lord Jesus Christ? Why doesn't God provide us with a visible tool of evangelism, with a sign of healing for a confused and broken world?

The ossuary wasn't the first disappointment. We wanted the Shroud of Turin to be a "photograph" of Jesus before the resurrection, but carbon-14 dating placed its origin in medieval times, and a few people lost their faith after that announcement. When I was in Israel, I visited a church in Cana that claimed to have the very jars in which Jesus turned water to wine—but the Orthodox chapel across the narrow street had jars too, and that church's officials asserted that theirs were the real ones. And churches own enough splinters from the "true cross" to rebuild the World Trade Center. And at least once a year, someone climbs Mount Ararat to find Noah's ark and may claim to have a piece of wood from it—which doesn't stand up to scientific dating.

We even hear claims that another ark, the ark of the covenant, is buried below the Dome of the Rock. No, it's hidden in a church in Ethiopia. No, it's cemented into the wall of a Knights' Templars chapel in England. Or is it in a warehouse, the way we saw it in the movie *Raiders of the Lost Ark?*

The story of the Holy Grail has been the subject of operas, ballets, and folk legends for two thousand years. The communion cup from which Jesus and the disciples drank on the night he was betrayed has become more than a vessel: *grail* means something bigger and more important, perhaps the source of all spiritual energy in the world, and the recent novel *The da Vinci Code* had immense theories about the grail's being hidden in plain sight in the Louvre, proof of God's participation in history. But if I found the grail or the ark or the true cross, what would I do then? Honor it? Worship it? And is that what God commanded us to do with physical objects? I recall something about graven images. . . .

God doesn't offer proof. Jesus, God incarnate, is proof enough; and now God holds out the gift of faith, which is the conviction of things not seen, the assurance of things only hoped for. If you had the grail in your hands and could somehow extract Jesus's DNA from its lip or discover that it was a direct line to God, you wouldn't need faith. You'd have the absolute Sign. Faith is what happens when you hold the grail not in your hands, but in your heart. "Examine yourselves," Paul says, "to see whether you are living in the faith" (2 Cor. 13:5). That means living in the presence of an unseen God, a supreme Being whose beneficence and power we have to take as absolute truth, while having no proof the world would believe.

But we want a sign. And there is a sign: to misquote Pogo, she is us. Women who are alive in the faith, who constantly move closer and closer to God, who pursue the Holy Spirit over the face of mystery and have a prayer life as exciting as dancing, are God's sign of healing for the world. Anyone can recognize a woman of Spirit, a woman whose life revolves around God, because she acts out. Her every move, from shopping for ripe pears to creating a double-entry bookkeeping system, has something godly about it, something spiritual and not only ethical, but good. We are the sign, the evidence of God's passionate concern for our sad, hungry, fractured world.

You are such a woman, or you'd be reading something else. You have already stepped forward, asking to be transformed. Your baptism, your discipleship, and your longing for the face of Christ have brought you into the circle of mystery, where the people of this land and any other can see in you the proof of God, and be healed.

Go ahead.

Don't be scared.

God has invited you to be, like the cross, the sign of his love for the human race.

Take a deep breath.

Now, laugh.

Now, heal.

Kristen Johnson Ingram

What God Says about Healing

A Reflection on Psalm 147

The LORD . . . heals the brokenhearted, and binds up their wounds.

Psalm 147:2–3

As I write this, the police chief in another state is on television. They have found the body of a missing girl, and her parents stand in the background, clinging together as they sob. Their hearts are broken, and only God can heal them.

The trouble is, they don't want their hearts healed. They want their sweet-smiled, light-footed daughter back. The house feels empty now, and even the family dog is restless. He paces around, looking for his ten-year-old companion.

Why didn't God prevent the rape and murder of that innocent girl? Was God with her when a monster of a man attacked and tortured her? Or why didn't God at least let someone find her before she died? After all, verse 6 of Psalm 147 says, "The LORD lifts up the downtrodden; he casts the wicked to the ground," but the wicked man who killed the girl is still at large. So where is the healing?

No matter how many Bible verses we quote, no matter how hard we pray, some people don't get well or survive, and some endure the worst kind of bestial attacks on their way to death. Holding up those verses in the face of tragedy or accident or criminal attack rarely makes the victims—or their families—feel better. They consider God's offer of a healed heart too little and probably too late.

Well, then, no wonder so many couples divorce after their children have died or suffered. How can they love one another after their hearts are split apart? The heart, the spiritual organ of love and delight, can splinter and be useless for love unless they let Christ heal it.

When men tore open the roof of Jesus's house in Capernaum and lowered their paralyzed friend, they expected for him to be healed. Instead, Jesus said, "Son, your sins are forgiven" (Mark 2:5).

Two kinds of outcries went up. The paralytic's friends were disappointed. They wanted physical healing of their friend, not absolution for his sins. The scribes, on the other hand, were enraged because, they said, only God can forgive sins. Meanwhile, the paralyzed man felt new life coursing through his veins. His broken heart was healed and so was his anger at the horse or falling wall or stack of jugs that had fallen on him and injured his spine.

By the time Jesus said, "I say to you, stand up, take your mat, and go to your home," the healing of his heart and mind was complete. The sound of Jesus's voice and the touch of his hand made the sick man able to stand, roll up his litter, and head out. Everybody, including the guys who were lying on the roof, looking down through the hole, exclaimed and applauded. They yelled, "We have never seen anything like this!"

But could any of them testify about what they had actually seen? Had they beheld the forgiveness of sin or cure of paralysis or the mending of a broken heart? Because we're looking at it from two thousand years later, we would probably say all three. And three Greek words in the New Testament describe a remedy for body and mind, and are translated as "heal" and "cure" and "make whole."

Although everyone needs those three kinds of healing, sometimes one at a time and sometimes all three at once, broken hearts are at the core of every healing and every cure. You can't function well when your soul is shattered, can you?

I had a friend whose breast cancer metastasized so that by the end her lungs and liver were involved. But her greatest sorrow wasn't pain or the aftereffects of chemo; what ate her up every day was the break between her and her two grown children. All of us urged her to make peace with them, because they were desperate to be part of their mother's living and dying, but instead she kept a score of their wrongs, and over and over recited to all of us the financial and personal insults they had bestowed. She died alone, unable to let Christ heal her broken heart.

Another acquaintance, Louisa, died this year of a neurological disorder. At first, she felt angry and bitter, but by the time she died, with her family and closest friends gathered around her bed, her heart was so full of joy that she embraced her death as the door to Jesus. Long before the virulent disease claimed her life, she had prayed to be made spiritually whole while her body was wasting away. Each of her loved ones afterward expressed his or her gratitude for Louisa's life, for the way she allowed her soul to be healed, and for the sweet lessons learned from her.

What Psalm 147 says about healing is that no matter what happens to any of us, God is concerned, compassionate, and healing. And the young murdered girl? She is in the arms of Jesus Christ, her earthly life and suffering as nothing compared to the glories she knows today, her broken heart turned to an instrument of praise.

245

Something to Try On

- In the privacy of your bedroom or bathroom, stand in front of a mirror in your underwear. Look at yourself and tell God you're ready to be healed of ailments or attitudes that are troublesome. As God embraces your broken places, embrace yourself as God's creation. Breathe in God's love as you get dressed and face the world.

- Face the music by listening to some of your favorite songs, even if you have to use earphones. Dare to sing along or dance to the beat, thanking God for the healing power of music.

- Choose a loved one or church member who is ill and make a healing sign. Draw a large circle in the middle of a sheet of paper, and in it write the person's name with colorful markers or other decorations. Around the name place Scriptures, affirmations, or pictures that symbolize God's healing this person. Pray for this person as the Holy Spirit prompts.

- Discuss these questions with a trusted friend or in a group setting: What are your feelings about contemporary healings? Are they all supernatural? How do you feel when you pray for healing, should the worst occur? Does death or continued disease mean God is doing nothing?

11

You Walk on the *Hot Coals*

Entering the Flames

Lie down in the Fire
See and taste the Flowing
Godhead through thy being;
Feel the Holy Spirit
Moving and compelling
Thee within the Flowing
Fire and Light of God.

Mechtilde of Magdeburg

Into the Fire

Linda: Fire can germinate a seed. But first, the seed has to fall into the ground and die.

Kris: Oh, man, this is scary. If I let God burn me up, will I be full of fire or just a heap of ashes?

Linda: The only thing that gets burned up is the useless stuff that God won't use.

Kris: I thought the flames were in hell, not in the gateway to God.

Linda: The fires of hell are different flames because the fires of hell have no hope. They destroy, they don't renew.

Kris: So what we're looking for in the fire is an individual Pentecost, a new sense of God's presence. But what about the fire bit? How do I get there, and when do I lie in it?

Linda: And which comes first: grace or healing? I can't help heal the world until I'm healed and I experience grace.

Kris: Yes, I think healing and grace come together. But how will I know when I'm close to the fire? Will God yell, "Jump in!" or will the moment come in a whisper? Wait: I think I hear a still, small voice.

Linda: Part of God's call to "Dare" means there's a possibility of being hurt or disappointed or failing. I always thought that getting closer to God meant getting nicer and nicer and nicer. But I've discovered that it means walking into the fire voluntarily.

Kris: Still taking the whole responsibility on yourself, aren't you? You *must* suffer, and you *must* do all the work yourself.

Linda: You pig.

Kris: I think you don't have to do it all. I think you have to ask God to take you into the fire and walk with you there, as God did with the three young men in Daniel.

On the Lawn
Linda Clare

Refiner's Fire

Trust yourself. Create the kind of self that you will be happy to live with all your life. Make the most of yourself by fanning the tiny, inner sparks of possibility into flames of achievement.

Foster McClellan

Your spa day has taken you through many life-changing places, from the Beauty Salon to the healing Hot Springs. In between you've tuned in to God in the Wind-Chime Atrium, exercised your attitudes in the Workout Area, allowed God's mud pack to polish you, and more. Now you stand on the Lawn at the last spa station, Fire-Walking. You may be thinking, *God's got to be kidding!*

Yet when God asks if you're willing to go wherever he leads you, you likely say yes—that is, until you think about the cost. Then you're not so sure. It's not that you don't want to be used by God; you want this with all your heart. But every time you get closer to God, you smell something burning.

Do you really have to walk across a bed of hot coals to prove your devotion to God?

Whether God calls you into mission work, community service, or any other traditional woman's role, you may start out bravely, and then balk when the going gets rough. Suddenly, God's calling isn't easy and the temperature's rising. If you dare to pursue a nontraditional calling, you may feel the heat even sooner. You long for transformation, but there's a cloud of smoke blocking the way. You look more closely. To your total surprise, you're the one on fire.

You remember something about the Lord purifying us to skim the dross from precious metal. Intense heat is necessary to refine silver and gold, the kind of heat no ordinary human can stand. You barely survived your last sunburn. How can you live through the Refiner's fire?

Well, you can't. God is in the business of making new creatures out of us, not patching up our sorry selves. The old wineskins must go. Sounds simple, and it is. Simple and hard and the most expensive thing you'll ever have.

In order to begin fire-walking, to accept this new creation idea, you'll need to get rid of a few things, such as the notion that you will ever be anything except needy. As C. S. Lewis said, "Grace substitutes a full, childlike and delighted acceptance of our Need, a joy in total dependence. We become 'jolly beggars.'"[1] What better way to begin your new life than to become acquainted with the Comforter? The Holy Spirit waits, ready to escort us through the fire.

Jesus promises us this Comforter in order to transport us to a deeper, more meaningful faith. The Spirit, Jesus says, helps us pray, aids us in our weaknesses, and guides us into all truth. When the apostles received the Holy Spirit, tongues of fire appeared over their heads. The Comforter changed them—the one Jesus said would never leave us.

So you take a step, a careful baby step, onto the Holy Spirit Express. You grab a seat near the aisle in case you need to make a hasty exit. *This is simple*, you think. You've prayed to be anointed with the Spirit and now you're on the bus. No sweat.

The bus pulls away, and it isn't long before you're getter warmer. Warmer. Downright hot. You fan yourself, but you're perspiring heavily. Where's this crazy bus headed, anyway? And where's the nearest stop?

You yell to the driver that you want off the bus. You're trying to get closer to God, not roast in the fires of Hades. The driver turns, smiles at you, and asks if you're thirsty yet.

Of course you're thirsty, you croak. It's as hot as you-know-what in here. You think about jumping out the window, just to escape the flames. Then you remember something Jesus said. "Whoever believes in me, as the Scripture has said, streams of living water will flow from within him" (John 7:38 NIV).

Of course. The Holy Spirit is the living water. You take a long, satisfying drink, maybe douse your smoldering hair. Suddenly the conflagration isn't such a catastrophe.

The flames are getting higher, but you don't get burned. Transformation may consume you, but the living water makes it bearable. By now you know you're not headed for the netherworld, but for a more intimate life with God. You lie down, comforted and secure.

Lying down in the fire is simple but never easy. Walking with God may cost you dearly, because exposing your personal liabilities and weaknesses results in a blaze unlike any other: the Refiner's fire. Each of these inspirations will encourage you to climb aboard the Holy Spirit Express. Relinquish your spirit to the flames. Your transformation may astound you.

Scripture Salon

Kristen Johnson Ingram

A Soul on Fire for God

A Reflection on Deborah in Judges 4–5

And she said, "I will surely go with you; nevertheless, the road on which you are going will not lead to your glory, for the LORD will sell Sisera into the hand of a woman."

Judges 4:9

When the Israelites cried out under the oppression of the Canaanite king, God sent a woman. She led the army of Israel into war; in fact, they say, she stood on the hillside, in armor, and sang during the battle to ensure victory. Her name is Deborah, *D'vrah* in stricter transliteration, and her story is in the fourth and fifth chapters of the book of Judges.

She might have had a husband named Lappidoth, but since his name means "torch," the text may mean she was single and called by the honorary name "Torchbearer." And she was such a torchbearer: her name has been synonymous with women's triumphant joy, with women's leadership, for about three thousand years

As judge over Israel, Deborah was as close to being a governor as the country came at that time. Those of us who sometimes find the Old Testament to be relentlessly patriarchal see her as a fresh face in history: a woman who led God's chosen people. When she handed out judgments, she sat under Deborah's Palm Tree on a Galilean hill we call Mount Tabor, which name is derived from hers. Tabor is a round-shaped mountain in the Jezreel Valley, in lower Galilee, rising 1,750 feet above sea level; its unusual shape, and the fact that it stands alone, attracts attention.

253

Deborah was under that palm the day God gave her a message for the general, Barak. She summoned him and said, "The LORD, the God of Israel, commands you, 'Go, take position at Mount Tabor, bringing ten thousand from the tribe of Naphtali and the tribe of Zebulun.'" God then promised: "I will draw out Sisera, the general of Jabin's army, to meet you by the Wadi Kishon with his chariots and his troops; and I will give him into your hand" (Judg. 4:6–7)

Jabin, king of Hazor, had tormented Israel for twenty years; he had been one of God's instruments, punishing the people for idolatry and other sins, and now their penance was apparently finished. The problem was that Sisera, Jabin's brilliant general, had *nine hundred* of those iron chariots, with enough horses and soldiers to pull and man them.

Barak must have trembled, or at least quailed, at the thought of that immense, ironclad army. What he forgot was that when God orders someone into battle, God wins. So he told Deborah, "I'll go, but only if you go with me."

Think of the world's great generals: Caesar, Hannibal, George Washington, Robert E. Lee, Dwight Eisenhower, Douglas MacArthur. Can you imagine their turning to *any* woman and saying, "I'll go to war only if you ride along with me"?

You can almost see Deborah raise her dark eyebrows and smile. "All right, Barak," she said. "I'll go along. But this won't turn out the way you'd like. You won't vanquish Sisera, a woman will. You won't get honor or glory."

Barak mustered ten thousand men from the tribes of Naphtali and Zebulun, and he marched toward the Kishon River, with Deborah at his side.

When Barak had routed Jabin's army and went in pursuit of Sisera, a woman named Jael went out to meet him, saying, "I will show you the man whom you are seeking." He went to her tent and found Sisera lying dead, with a tent peg in his temple: she had murdered the general, and his fate fell to a woman that day.

According to Judges 4:23–24, "God subdued King Jabin of Canaan before the Israelites. Then the hand of the Israelites bore harder and harder on King Jabin of Canaan, until they destroyed King Jabin of Canaan." And then, Barak and Deborah sang the great hymn that is the fifth chapter of Judges, recounting their own deeds and Jael's; and Deborah calls herself "A mother in Israel" (5:7).

Rabbi Mendel Weinbach, dean of the Ohr Somayach Institution, a Jewish educational foundation, writes on the Internet, "Devorah was not only a prophetess and leader, but a judge of her people as well. When she describes herself, however, she makes no mention of any of these claims to fame. It may be concluded that the title 'Mother in Israel' serves as a combination of all these three attributes. A mother in Israel is a leader of her family who prophetically foresees what is best for each member and judges each of them with the rare blend of wisdom and compassion which Heaven has granted her for fulfilling her role."[2]

A Jewish mother has always kept the faith alive. Judaism is a religion of the home, not the synagogue; Jews are commanded not to attend services every week, but to keep the Sabbath. And the Sabbath is the mother's show. She prepares and plans the meal, serving acceptable foods, including the *challah*, or Sabbath bread, and the wine for the *kiddush* ceremony. The mother gets her family to the table just as the sun sets. She lights the Sabbath candles that have to burn for twenty-four hours, shielding them as she ignites them, to remind herself and her family of a time when Jews had to hide from their enemies. She says the first prayer of the Sabbath, with her hands over her eyes. Only then does her husband repeat the blessings over bread and wine.

A mother in Israel, not necessarily a mother to small children—we know nothing about Deborah's home life—was the one who kept the faith alive on that day at Kedesh.

Deborah didn't set herself up as prophet or judge over Israel; God chose her. Deborah's deeds and her spiritual nature were the foundation of her leadership, but we can't ignore her free spirit and her courage. To march into battle with ten thousand men meant that she accepted God's call and paid little if any attention to a traditional female role. She stood on the hillside and sang, and the battle was the Lord's. And here is part of her song from Judges 5:

My heart goes out to the commanders of Israel
  who offered themselves willingly among the people.
Bless the LORD.

255

Tell of it, you who ride on white donkeys,
    you who sit on rich carpets
    and you who walk by the way.
To the sound of musicians at the watering places,
    there they repeat the triumphs of the LORD,
    the triumphs of his peasantry in Israel.
Then down to the gates marched the people of the LORD.
Awake, awake, Deborah!
    Awake, awake, utter a song!

verses 9–12

Why did God choose Deborah to lead and prophesy and judge her nation, instead of Barak? God's choice of Deborah to lead an army and a nation was God's act, recognized by Eliahu Rabba, a Jewish scholar who wrote an explanatory work on Scripture in the eighth century AD. He said, "And what was the character of Deborah that she deserved to be a judge over Israel and a prophetess over them? I call on the heavens and on the earth to bear witness that whether the person be a non-Jew or a Jew, a man or a woman, a manservant or a woman servant, that God resides with each person according to the merit of his or her deeds."

That ninth-century rabbi repeated almost exactly Paul's words in Galatians 3:28: "There is no longer Jew or Greek, there is no longer slave or free, there is no longer male and female; for all of you are one in Christ Jesus."

Tradition says that Deborah's singing inspired the troops so they could oust Sisera's army. When she sang, they advanced; if she stopped, the Israelites were driven back. Such a voice could come out of only a woman on fire for God.

Linda Clare

A Life Aflame

The kind moment itself is the door that holiness enters through. May it enter us all.

Frederick Buechner

Up to now, you may have thought a deep spiritual life meant denying yourself some earthly comfort. Over history most of the saints of the church fasted and lived in poverty. Maybe you're not Mother Teresa, but you still yearn to know God in a more profound way. Yet when we talk about this spiritual makeover, we often don't know where to begin.

The moment you accepted Christ as your Lord, you began looking for ways to prove it. You stood up in church or knelt at the altar. You went to meetings and services. Most of all, you read, studied, and underlined your Bible in hopes of learning more about God. Off in the distance, a light beckoned, promising a rich life to all who would come. Of course you wanted that rich life, so you ran toward the light. You were on your way to holiness.

Does devotion to God demand that you cover your head with ashes, collect alms, or pray for hours? For some it does. From the Poor Clares (no relation to me) to modern-day missionaries, God has called some Christian women to devote themselves to lives of service and devotion, lives that hunger for more of God.

As for the rest of us, we're eager to find our way to the cool, deep recesses of our selves, where God meets us like a lover on a moonlit night. Nobody there except you and God. A place where your life can blossom and weave itself around God's light. A life aflame.

When you were a child, either literally or as a new convert, you probably measured your spiritual life in terms of public baptism, con-

257

firmation classes, gold foil stars for Bible verses memorized, or tithes in wrinkled collection envelopes. Time passed and you longed to grow up, as the disciple Peter exhorts. He said you wouldn't make it if all you discarded were the obvious things. If you wanted to become a truly devoted Christian, he spelled it out in 1 Peter 2:1–3: put away childish things such as greed, envy, malice, guile, and insincerity. You think you're growing? "Well, let's take a look inside," God says. This was a point not unlike today's airport security, where you and your luggage get x-rayed to see if you're hiding anything.

Then your inner life was laid open before God, and no fair stashing little things in the side pockets. You stood there, fingering your cell phone, shifting your weight from foot to foot while Holy Spirit Security combed through your most private thoughts. The light got brighter; you felt warm. Then you saw where the light emanated. It was a roaring bonfire.

"Oh that," God said when you asked why the fire was there. Then you remembered. You must burn off chaff in order to be whole, die in order to live. A lot of things about Christian maturity sounded like riddles to you. Meanwhile, the blaze consumed everything it touched. You were terrified and yet drawn to the inferno. You shut your eyes and jumped in.

Emotions run high when you make a conscious decision to go in the direction of the flames. You may feel happy, sad, and angry all at once; you may feel like singing or screaming. Your body trembles as you offer it up to God for burning. But you can't back down, not now. No matter how paradoxical or mysterious the growth process, you're changing right in front of your own eyes.

The change isn't as noticeable as water baptism, for this is a baptism of fire. For those of us who dare to pursue the flames of holiness, it matters less whether we cover our heads with ashes than that we joyfully give and receive the nourishment of God's love. As we put away the childish things the Bible warns us of, we replace them with kindness, with caring, with love for one another.

The thirteenth-century Christian Mechtilde of Madgeburg wrote, "To lie down in the fire we drink the wine and blood and tears, the milk and water and honey—all of this richness flows directly and

solely out of whatever depths we have carved out within ourselves."[3]
The more you incinerate the attitudes that keep you centered upon
yourself, the more you make room for a new you, a you that goes far
beyond outward appearances of faith.

Neither is this change necessarily permanent. The Holy Spirit demands we present ourselves *each day* as a living sacrifice. You can't
drink yesterday's living water. Like the human heart, a relationship
with God won't last long without a fresh infusion. God's promises are
new every morning, so in order to remain in the flames you need to
meet God as if for the first time.

A kind word, forgiveness, honesty, hospitality—practice these and
suddenly it becomes easier to smile. Joy no longer plays second fiddle to
self-indulgence and people might say they feel a little warm whenever
you're around. Each day, whether your situation is happy or hopeless,
you can become holy as you dive in. Discover for yourself that the door
to holiness is open to all who dare to enter into a life aflame.

Fire-Walk Inspiration
Vinita Hampton Wright

Lying Down in the Fire

Lately, my greatest fear is to be used up. Maybe it's the shifting hor-
mones of middle age, or maybe it's the accompanying fatigue, but I
fear more and more the loss of energy. I'm aware that I tire quickly
and often—and not just physically. In every way I feel the power
draining from me.

I am being used up, little by little yet faster and faster. I don't like
this. I resent feeling myself slip away.

My first response is to conserve, conserve. Go to bed earlier. Don't commit to so many projects. Say no. Protect yourself. For God's sake, save yourself. After all, who else will look out for your interests?

But all that conservation of energy, time, and passion does little good. Still, I am tired. Still, I am afraid that my very essence is leaving via a hidden leak in the system.

I've had a frightening thought: maybe the whole point of a Christlike life is to be spent completely. Maybe God is the ultimate conservationist, who will not be satisfied until every part of my carcass is put to good use. Maybe I should think of myself as the fallen buffalo at the end of the hunt.

I want to keep myself intact, unhurt, saved away for some future glory. But God wants to use fully every little piece of me. That is the glory, after all, to be consumed.

Let's see, unless a seed falls to the ground and dies, it can't produce anything. Whoever tries to save her life will lose it. Of course, two of my least favorite Bible verses come back to confirm my worst fears.

Theology isn't the only thing I'm up against. There's simple, gradual dilapidation. I am no longer young and energetic enough to compensate for losses. I can no longer outrun my grief or sing loudly enough to drown out my pounding heart. My youth is spent, my reserves depleted. And the good Lord is standing over me, cracking his knuckles, and saying, "Finally, she'll hold still long enough for us to accomplish something."

I've always disliked that horrible test to which God subjected Abraham: "Burn your son as a sacrifice to me." Even though it was called off at the last second, it was a cruel exercise. But now I think it was an image meant to haunt us. Because, ultimately, our purpose is to be consumed. Sooner or later, each of us is asked to lie down on the altar and say yes to the death and the flames.

Sooner or later, we lie down in the fire. We give it all up. We let go of life, relinquish control—or our illusion of control. We leave our treasures in a pile and walk away. We take off our classiest clothes and admit that we are no more than our naked selves. We stop relying on titles, reputations, savings accounts, and connections. We lie our unadorned selves upon the altar and simply wait for what happens next.

What's more extraordinary, we lie down without fear. We lie down in peace. We lie down expecting good things. We lie down trusting God, who holds the torch.

In the early months of my marriage, I occasionally jolted awake in the middle of the night, frightfully aware that I was lying naked in bed next to a man who was also unclothed. It hit me how completely vulnerable I was, that I allowed this man to do all sorts of very personal things to me. He was given the freedom to touch me in any way. He was physically close enough to harm or even kill me. Worse, much worse, he had the power to reject me, to look at my body and laugh or say something demeaning. I had willingly put myself in this situation. So why was I so calm? Where had I found such trust? And where did this desire come from, to be completely overtaken by this man, to be penetrated, locked into embrace?

This was my first lesson in being consumed. I was able to allow it, of course, because I was convinced of my husband's character and felt certain that he would never harm or demean me. And he never has, beyond the sometimes unkind give-and-take of marital dissention (and of the two of us, I am consistently the most unkind).

I understand why the marital act is called *consummation* (although the technical meaning of the word is not connected to *consume*). And I have learned that consummation can hurt a lot. Sometimes it hurts for days, months, years. This intimate connection has cost me many nights' sleep and many days' anxiety because I have taken upon myself my husband's self as well. I really do feel his pain. What worries him worries me. What threatens him threatens me.

There is also the joy of our union, the companionship and joining of gifts and stories, the peaceful days and simple good times. This, too, is part of being consumed. This good part is important to remember when you're lying there waiting for whatever will happen.

I am increasingly convinced that the sexual union is designed to move us toward God. The hunger it creates is much larger than can be fulfilled through the human connection. Yet it teaches us to lie back and say, "I'm yours." It teaches us to sleep peacefully mere inches from danger. The mystics understood this, even those who were physically celibate. The sexual imagery in their writings was not accidental or even subliminal. They knew that God was that close, that dangerous, that personal, that trustworthy, and that passionate. Thus, sex has taught me how to lie down in the fire.

I've learned about the fire through my creative gifts as well. Although I may possess my gifts, those gifts consume me. They infiltrate my whole self, taking over sense and emotion, belief and dream. When I give myself—my energy and attention—to those gifts, I am taken somewhere I don't know in advance, and I discover things I have not yet learned. I am taken, and then I am used. When I try to pull back and be "in control," the creativity is stopped cold. If I relent and give myself over to the flames, then out of those flames emerges the art that God has been stoking inside me for years. The novel is revealed, and both I and the work come out smelling of smoke.

I've decided that one reason I procrastinate as a writer is that I now know what it will cost me. When I sit down to enter that process, I know that ultimately the flames will be there. The terror and grief, the ecstasy and the revelation—all will be there. If I want the story, I have to dive into the heat and the zero visibility.

I can write stories without being consumed. But they are cool and distant and easy to ignore. They don't demand anyone's engagement. They don't bear that scorched smell, or any smell. They are safe, predictable, and easy to digest, and they demand almost nothing. Likewise, they transform nothing.

I avoid many commitments these days. I do so because I understand that it is not possible to give myself to anything without risking my life. I used to believe that I could offer portions of myself, this much passion, that much talent, only so much time. But that kind of giving is artificial and not really giving at all. That's not to say that giving can't be true and also have boundaries. There are nearly always boundaries. But I don't determine the boundaries as much as I would like to believe. The flames follow a path, and I can rarely predict the path. There are always flames somewhere, and I am always in danger of catching fire.

So I lie down in the fire. The heat overwhelms me. Yet I am not destroyed. The only fatalities are my false selves, and they go up like tinder. It is unfortunate that I am so ready to grieve their demise, that

I cling to those flammable selves. The actual me—the soul that is God's—gets refined by the flames. The me who matters gets better the longer it burns. But it's difficult to really understand or embrace that idea. The concept of being consumed yet not destroyed is unnatural to the human view.

And so I watch my fashionable self get turned into ash. Likewise I witness the death of that needy, manipulative self. The self that wields charisma and power curls up and melts like plastic. The self that plays politics is liquidated. The selves that protect the image, project control, and posture for friends and enemies—these burn away. The Vinita who is left when the flames finish is a woman with no leverage, no currency, no alternative world, and no contingency plan. Just Vinita. Just that soul loved by God and longing for God. It is a soul that understands sacrifice to be healthy loss, a soul that does not need to reconstruct history or fabricate a future.

I barely understand what I have written here about lying down in the fire. But I sense that it is a radical, transforming, liberating way to live. When I am willing to be consumed, what is left to fear? When I welcome the departure of false selves, how much easier must it be to love my true self? When my existence does not hang upon happiness and comfort-avoidance of the flames, how much more ready will I be to experience the wild joy of the universe? And when I have stopped striving for self-protection, what adventures will I be free to encounter?

Sometimes now, twelve years into my marriage, I still fear the consuming intimacy of it. Sometimes now, several books into a writing career, I still walk wide circles around my writing chair and laptop. It's always a choice to approach the flames. To submit to the altar, the torch, and the burning away will always be a supreme form of submission to not only a God who loves me but to a life that is truly mine and no one else's. As I lie down in the fire, I am entering some sanctuary of soul that is bright and bold and filled with beauty.

The Burning Anchoress

An elderly Christian anchoress, or woman hermit, lived in the desert and was visited by a younger disciple. After describing her fasts, prayers, and good works, the girl asked the old woman, "What more should I do?"

The old anchoress raised her hands. As she did so fire shot forth from her fingers and speaking through the flames, she said, "Why not become fire all over?"

The younger woman left and immersed herself in prayer, seeking not just the approval of God but the life-giving fire of the Spirit.

The message isn't just for hermits. Any woman can become fire all over, right now.

Fanning the Flame
A Reflection on 2 Timothy 1:6

I remind you to fan into flame the gift of God.
2 Timothy 1:6 NIV

To fan a flame, you first need a fire. This can be of any size from a forest blaze to a flickering candle, but unless you've at least got a fire, or at least a good, strong spark, all fanning will do is move the air . . . which means you have to ignite the spirit within you.

This probably sounds scary. And risky. But John the Baptist warned you: "I baptize you with water for repentance, but one who is more powerful than I is coming after me; I am not worthy to carry his sandals. He will baptize you with the Holy Spirit and fire" (Matt. 3:11). Linda said it in her Fire-Walk Inspiration "A Life Aflame": "Your body trembles as you offer it up to God for burning. But you can't back down, not now."

Christian spirituality isn't passive. You can't lie back and wait for the All to descend, first because the All, or rather the Holy Spirit, has *already* descended, indwells you, and is waiting to be fanned into a roaring, crackling blaze. And not just so you can be a better wife or church member; you fan the flame to become more like God and more with God.

The burning anchoress knew. She invited the fires of God to occupy every cell of her body and soul and spirit, called God to send down something like a seraphim with a hot coal to start things, and then fanned the spark with her breath, her prayers, her inner beauty, and her love for God. With her breath she sang and entertained the angels, in her prayers she blessed the world's population, by her inner beauty she made the earth lovelier, and by her love for God she became fire all over.

Or maybe not. Maybe that was what I'd like for her to have done or wish I could do; maybe she did something entirely different. I don't know any literally burning anchoresses as personal friends, but I'm sure they exist, at least in God's mind.

What I *do* know is how it feels to be on fire for God. And I also know the fanning process: not a formula you can replicate, but a mystery in which to live. First you have to ask, and God will answer, but not necessarily right away. You may need to grow some more before you can leap into the fire. Or you may not really mean it when you ask, or you may put up a condition or two for God to follow: "God," you might say, "I want to be fire all over, but please don't make me [love my next-door neighbor, read the whole Bible, fix breakfast for my husband, speak in tongues, sing in the choir, change a tire on the car]"—you finish it with your own condition. So long as you propose any exception or try to put God on probation, or erect a "no trespassing" area where God can't go, then you're more likely to die of hypothermia than from being burned to death.

And your being burned to death is—I say in hesitation because I can foresee your reaction—what God has in mind. What? *What?* God wants to burn us all alive? Then how can we be witnesses or instruments of peace, if we're charred?

Here's how it works. If you've ever gone camping, you may have an advantage because of your possible experience with Coleman lamps that have not a globe, but a tiny woven sock called a *mantle*. The mantle has to be lighted with a match and then burned completely off in a dull, flickering fire. But if you successfully destroy the "sock," the leftover ash suddenly begins to glow with a brighter light than you could imagine.

The human part of our souls is the mantle that has to be burned off to let our spirits glow. When you just get close enough to God to keep warm and flicker a little, you'll be dull, compared to the conflagration that God has in mind. "You are the light of the world," Jesus told us and reminded us not to hide our light: "No one after lighting a lamp puts it under the bushel basket," he said, "but on the lampstand, and it gives light to all in the house. In the same way, let your light shine before others, so that they may see your good works and give glory to your Father in heaven" (Matt. 5:14–16).

Jesus's words are often used to initiate the offertory in churches. But Jesus wasn't talking about money or offering your gifts or being helpful: he said it in the same context with "Be glad when they persecute you over me." He was talking about risking everything, including your life, to bring light to the world. Which you can do only by having your "mantle" burned off.

So to fan a flame, you have to have a fire. The one that God wants you to become.

Ideas for Reflection & Application

Something to Try On

- Read Daniel 3:20–26, the story of Shadrach, Meshach, and Abednego surviving the furnace. How do you think the story applies to you as a modern Christian? What do you think is meant by the fire in Nebuchadnezzar's furnace? How is the fire of the Holy Spirit different? Are you afraid of God's fire? Why?

- Step out of your comfort zone and into the fire. Extend kindness to a stranger you would normally avoid. Open a door for a disabled person, make eye contact with a homeless person, or donate time, energy, or resources to helping the poor. Even a smile and a "God bless you!" could make a difference in someone's life.

- Make a colored tissue paper collage using "flame" colors. Tear, don't cut, the various pieces and notice how the edges blend with each other to form new shades. Soften your own edges this week by remembering Jesus's commandment to "love one another."

- Resolve to expand yourself spiritually, by practicing the presence, or just "being" with God. Don't allow this expansion to become another "have to" on your list. Take baby steps—a moment here, a smile or quick prayer there. God wants you, not your achievements.

12
You Step Out
Celebrate Transformation

This work is about transformation—from the person we are to the person we really are. In the end, we can't be anyone else.

Marion Rosen

Showing the Transformed Face

Kris: Now we've come to the heart of this matter of transformation. If I really, really show the church and the world who I am, unveil myself, will I be rejected?

Linda: Every time I read or hear the standard Christian opinion that it's "what's on the inside that counts," I wonder the same thing. Because what's on my inside is different from what I know they mean.

Kris: What I want to know is whether I could stand to live with disapproval from everyone but Christ.

Linda: Well, I won't take the chance. I'm a people-pleaser.

Kris: Then where does that leave the unveiled face? Can we unveil a centimeter or so at a time so we won't be so scared?

Linda: It's a matter of trust. The only time I really unveil to God is when nobody else is around.

Kris: I think I show my true colors when I'm least aware of myself. I do only a few things where I can't see myself doing them or talking or even thinking. Only when I'm really absorbed in writing or taking photographs am I completely real.

Linda: I love to sing in the shower, with great acoustics and lots of privacy. That's the real me, because music is the closest I think I get to communicating with God.

Kris: Yeah. When I learned a hard piece on the piano or sang *The Messiah*, I felt that way. I didn't feel conscious of myself—just of God.

Linda: When you have a rare friendship, you can relax and be silly.

Kris: I'm always silly. That's covering my face.

Linda: Well, but you and I can talk about anything or call each other ratpigs without being fearful of rejection.

Kris: But we aren't being a sign to the world that way. Maybe this is what "Blessed are you when men persecute you for my name" is about. I thought that meant getting killed for evangelizing or being a missionary, but maybe it's risking others' approval of you when you say what you think about God.

Linda: Sure is. Say what you really think about God and someone might say you're a heretic, or you don't worship the same God they do.

Kris: We have to start telling the truth to one another, to the world. The God I live with doesn't always conform to what I think God should do.

Linda: But the God I live with always loves. And that's the direction I want to go.

Kris: I don't think we have a choice. The love of Jesus Christ from the cross is so compelling—that love draws us farther and deeper and higher and wider. Toward God.

Stepping Out
Linda Clare

The One Who Waits

If you've read this far, you may have seen yourself or women you recognize somewhere in these pages. Perhaps you're torn between living up to all the "shoulds" and "oughts" of Christian life—with its demands for beauty, flawless relationships, an enhanced spiritual experience—and the longing for a more complete walk with God. The idea of a transformed, more fully realized Christianity appeals to you. Deep inside you sense something waiting, just outside the door of this spa retreat.

That something may take on the same mystery that often invades things we cannot see: the wind, or the farthest reaches of the universe. Even time, known as the fourth dimension, has taken on specific measurements only in the last few centuries. Before clocks or sundials, humans had only *sol* to help them chart their days. And to the ancients, the sun was a mystery indeed.

In the hectic world of today, people say they wish time would stop and allow them to catch their breath. Yet they still want the minutes to fly by when enduring the dentist's drill or a boring sermon. Time management is big business, and it certainly waits for no one.

You may say it's the one thing you're short on this week. Your schedule is so packed with stuff to do, places to go, people to see, that you couldn't possibly spare another minute. You may have decided to pursue God in a fresh way, but what exactly does that mean? You'll try to pencil it in.

Could time be the next step in your journey? Beyond the spa is a place where you and God meet. Alone. No Daytimers, phones, or other distractions. You and the one who made you rest together, chat with each other, breathe in great gulps of God's love. You carve out a small chunk of eternity to reflect, to meditate, to commune.

This time is not about producing. Your prayer list may need a separate session. You're not promising or confessing or bargaining. You're abiding with Jesus, a biblical way of hanging out. And when you're finished in God's day spa, you feel energized, refreshed, more fully you. In the mirror, a fantastic, changed Christian woman stares back. You can't believe your eyes.

You're reaching up toward a balanced view of beauty and material things, even if it hurts a little. You stretch out your arms to touch the lives of others in loving but healthy ways and raise your own self-esteem in the process. You plumb the depths of your own understanding of grace, healing, and spiritual hunger in order to get closer to the God you love and worship. Yet somehow you sense there is still something missing, a mystery that both frightens and tantalizes. It sits in the dark, waiting.

You may try to escape it, terrified and yet drawn to it. If you attempt to spend time alone with God, your mind may wander and you may believe you're not doing it right. If you persist, you may decide to keep coming back for more.

Maybe you walk in your neighborhood or tour a sacred place. Hike in the mountains or stand on the shore of a lake or ocean. Seek a familiar spot in your backyard or perhaps nestle into a favorite chair. Whatever you do, the time you share with Jesus will be between God and you.

Throughout *Revealed* you've met women who've seen the shadow of the mysterious waiting for them, who are compelled to search for the something their hearts tell them is there. Some of their journeys have been difficult or painful. All have been required to open themselves to God in a new way. At the moment of the "big reveal," these women have been amazed to see what God has done.

If you're like any of these women, you know something is waiting for you. You might want to run, and at the same time you may be inexplicably drawn to it, moth to flame. You know you can't ignore it, as much as you may try. Something is out there. How will you access the one who waits?

Kristen Johnson Ingram

Good News for Modern Women

A Reflection on Women in John's Gospel

Jesus goes to a wedding, and late in the day his mother says, "They are out of wine." Jesus cries out, "Oh, lady, why bring me into it? I'm not ready for this yet." But she ignores his protest. "Do whatever he tells you," she instructs the servants, and Jesus does what she asks, turns water into wine. The splendor, the heavenly position of Christ, was manifested because a woman asked for a miracle.

"Give me a drink," he says to an astonished woman at the well, and then he tells her the secrets of heaven. In answer to her questions about Jews drinking Samaritan water, he says that those who drink *living* water will have eternal life and will not thirst anymore. He makes only a brief comment about her living arrangements, to show her who he is. He knows what she has been looking for all these years. Then, like a Zen teacher who dashes tea into his student's face in answer to a question about the weather, Jesus dashes fact into her astounded brain. "I am the Messiah!" he tells her. And he says these words to a woman, words that he hadn't said to anyone, not even his disciples. She leaves her water jar and becomes the first evangelist.

Pharisees drag a woman, guilty of a capital offense, in front of Jesus. "Teacher, we caught her in the act!" they cry.

"Adultery, hmm?" says the young rabbi. He scribbles in the dust a while, listening to the *chunk!* of stones as the crowd bangs them together in their hands. The woman says nothing; her mute plea is eloquent, and nobody makes mention of her partner, a man who also should have been stoned, according to Leviticus 20:10.

Finally Jesus sits back and looks at the men, who are panting for the woman's death.

"All right. You have your rights under the Law of Moses. So kill her." And then he adds, as they get ready to hurl their missiles, "But let the one who hasn't ever committed any sin against that Law begin the stoning." He starts scribbling in the dust again.

In a moment, he looks up and sees that the woman is now alone. "What? Is there nobody here to execute judgment? Neither do I condemn you. Now, don't go back to the same madness that brought you here." In this short incident, Jesus put every woman forever in charge of her own identity. He has told a desperate woman what most of Israel didn't know: that God is love.

Jesus becomes famous throughout his country. They say he heals the lame and makes the blind see. Finally, he sets his face toward Bethany, to raise his friend Lazarus. And to begin the end. Jesus had known for days that Lazarus was sick. He could have journeyed the two miles from Jerusalem to Bethany in less than an hour, but he put off the trip until he knew for sure the man was dead, and that his sisters were mourning. John says that Jesus "loved Martha, and her sister and Lazarus" (John 11:5).

Martha is not one to sit around, as we know. She rushes to Jesus and wails, "If you had been here, Lazarus would be too." Her faith is pure: Jesus hears it. "Your brother will rise again," he says (11:23).

"In the resurrection, yes," murmurs Martha.

"Martha, *I'm* the resurrection," Jesus says, pointing at his chest. "Do you believe that?"

"I believe that you—" She might have stopped a moment before she says, "I believe that you are Christ, the Son of God, the one who is coming into the world." Here is the Good News, the best news, coming from the mouth of a woman.

After raising Lazarus from the dead, Jesus is exhausted. He hides a while in Ephraim, a desert town. But Passover is coming round again, and the chief priests and the Pharisees begin to watch around Jerusalem for the powerful young rabbi.

He will go, of course. But he waits a while in Bethany, with these same friends. Martha serves Lazarus, who was raised from death and who sits at the table with Jesus; and Mary, the quiet one, kneels, as usual, at his feet. She breaks open a container of pure nard and anoints his feet and wipes them with her hair, and the whole house is filled with the fragrance of the ointment.

"Jesus, what is this?" cries Judas, a thief who pretends to piety. "She should have sold the nard and given the money to the poor." It's easy to imagine his black eyes darting around the room, seeking approval for his statement.

"Oh, Judas," Jesus says, "there will always be plenty of poor around for you to help."

The next woman in the drama speaks only a few words. Jesus is betrayed, and John and Peter follow him as he is dragged to the house of the high priest. Peter, his power spent, lurks outside the door, and a serving maid says, "Aren't you one of the man's disciples?" It took a woman to point out Peter's faithlessness. Soon afterward, the cock crows.

Finally, Jesus is on the cross. All his followers have run away, unable to watch the death of God—all, that is, except for four women and John. Jesus looks down and focuses his fading sight on his mother, standing with the beloved disciple.

"Woman," he whispers hoarsely through cracked lips, "here is your son!" (19:26). And each woman in the world, past or present, born or yet unborn, whether she has borne earthly children or not, is immediately linked to Christ's ministry by her own ability to love him. Every woman on earth becomes his mother in that moment.

It's early in the morning when Mary Magdalene goes to the tomb with spices and ointments; the sun is just coming up, and she takes a risk, walking about where Roman soldiers or any other man can assault her. However, she wants to honor Jesus, but the stone is rolled away and the tomb empty, and she runs to find Peter and John.

"He . . . he isn't here!" she pants. "They've taken his body somewhere."

Faced with her news, the disciples rush to the tomb, and John goes inside; then he and Peter leave. But Mary Magdalene is still outside the tomb, weeping. She hasn't read all the Scriptures and doesn't understand the prophecies. She knew Jesus, not the sacred writings.

277

She sees two angels sitting in the tomb. She turns back, and there is the risen Christ.

"Why are you crying?" he says, still obscuring his identity. "For whom are you looking?"

God reveals himself—to a woman.

"Go tell my brothers," he says. This is the first great charge to the church, which at this point consists of one woman. Mary Magdalene had become the first post-resurrection missionary, the first who had enough sight to see the risen Christ, the first to tell the Good News.

New Me, New You

Miracles have a hard time sticking to me. I think it's because I ask a lot of questions. When I was young, my eternal questions were all about me: Why did I feel so unloved? Couldn't Jesus spare a small pony for my birthday? Where would I go if I died?

Even as an adult, I can't take anything at face value. Especially if the subject is God. And I thought by now that I would be more others-oriented, but I find my questions are still mostly about me. Does God love me? Why can't I find my eyeglasses? Where will I go when I die? More and more my questions force me to stare aging and death square in the face—a face that could use some rejuvenation, according to those ads about fighting wrinkles.

Rejuvenation of my body may be a lost cause at this point. No matter what I do, death is inevitable. I know I'm just beginning the journey to AARP, but over and over the aging process points me straight at my faith. The biggest question of all emerges: do I truly believe in the promise of heaven?

I believe in Jesus, but as I have more "senior moments" I don't always remember why. The true meaning of life somehow manages to elude me. I've listened to inspiring lectures and sermons and read books that promised to unlock the mysteries of the ages. I always come away with a renewed sense of purpose. I've finally got it. Yet two hours later, when I scrabble around looking for notes I've taken, those words of wisdom inevitably fall dead upon the page. The miraculous revelation slithers past me. I'm left with the same old questions, such as: what happens when it's all over?

When someone dies, there is usually talk of a "better place" and "eternal peace." I want to believe in the near-death experiences in which the tunnel of light either welcomes me or instructs me to go back and finish some mission on earth. Yet when I underwent neck surgery a few years ago, I was troubled for weeks afterward. Where did I go while under the knife? I felt as if I'd ceased to exist somehow because I didn't have any dreams about looking down on my body or romping through a meadow with my dead grandma. I just passed out and woke up with several hours of my life missing, glad to be alive.

Sixteen years ago I watched my father die. His was a slow death over three days, after kidney disease had taken its toll. At times in the hospital room I prayed for him to be miraculously healed, at others I wanted to end his suffering with a pillow over his face. Most of all I wanted God to show up and do something.

My sister and I darkened the room at the end, and we held his hands and sang softly to him. In his dying gasp I thought he was asking for water, but he was whispering, "Our Father." My sister claims she saw Jesus up in the corner of the hospital room that day, somewhere near the TV. I wish I had been the one to see the miracle, but I didn't. No, Linda the responsible older sister, the questioning one, ran down the hall to fetch my mother so Mom could be at Dad's side. By that time the vision of Christ had long faded.

I wondered if I had somehow missed God that day, if there was something I should have done or not done so I could have seen a vision of Jesus next to the hospital TV. I saw firsthand the process of dying, not as a neat and tidy sound bite but as a tiring marathon that tested my faith. I wanted a miracle, and I wanted it to be supernatural. Like Christian writer Frederick Buechner, secretly I wanted to believe in magic, and alien life, and that in heaven I would reunite with my loved ones. I longed to smell roses and see a Madonna weep. I wanted to hear the laughter of angels, and I wanted to feel assured that I will live after I die. I wanted to stop doubting God, once and for all.

For weeks after Dad died, I dreamed that he sat up suddenly and began to chat as if he weren't dead at all. I found out these types of dreams are common, but I wanted them to be a real contact from beyond, a sign from Dad that he was still with me in some way. I wanted God to lift the ban on communication with the dead just this once, so I could say farewell.

What of my own farewell? I see my reflection in the glass darkly, and the face I must live with each day is giving in to physics. Old people used to frighten me with their rough throat-clearings and odd smells, the papery skin masking a life of sorrow or joy, regret or contentment. Now I look into the eyes of the elderly and see not boredom but cataracts and dementia. The scowl of that gruff old lady at the supermarket comes not from meanness or spite but from encroaching jowls and false teeth. The shuffle of her feet in laughable Velcro joggers is not the gait of the dissolute but comes from arthritis and bad knees. This will be me in a few years, and I dare not forget it.

How do we become transformed? At what place does lofty talk about God find its way into our lives at a meaningful level? Is there a way to become completely renewed in our daily lives?

All I know is that I face myself each day, knitting my life together with small tasks and necessities: I trim my toenails, throw off the covers during hot flashes, feed my trio of pampered cats as they sing for breakfast. It hits me that the heart of my faith lies in each moment that passes, that I am transformed in spirit much the same way as my physical self rebuilds: cell by cell, instructions coded in God's alphabet of DNA, casting off the old and embracing the new.

The self I see in the bathroom mirror can't escape her funny-looking paralyzed arm that won't pull its weight, not after years of therapy and cajoling and embarrassment. On days when I am too pained and weary to see it for what it is I close my eyes, but that shriveled hand, those baby-sized fingers are still there. I feel them. It's hard to remember that God made every crooked little cell. I've spent so long covering up for what I am.

Explanation and disclosure are for sissies, I used to think, and besides they take too much time. So instead of explaining my disability to medical people, I pretend there is nothing wrong. I actually worry sometimes that if I have surgery again someone will not know that they won't find a blood pressure because my left arm's blood vessels are in odd places, that if they poke a needle in my left bicep they might hit bone. I worry about keeping my normal side presented to the world, about showing only my good side in the photo.

The march to death is teaching me that I have no good side at all, that all my compensations for disability hint at a larger, more insidious problem. All attempts to pass myself off as normal will ultimately fail if I am real to those I meet. If I allow myself to be vulnerable and let people see me for who I am, I won't be able to keep the charade going.

At the end of the day or toward the end of my days, Jesus is the only answer to this question of spiritual makeovers. I am restyled, reinvigorated, rejuvenated, but I am one thing more: I am mystery.

As this book has unfolded, I have unfolded too. At the beginning Kris and I talked of paper-doll Christians in a way that suggested we would set those poor shallow women straight. We held a tea for some women we knew, all of whom are intelligent Christian writers themselves. One said she wondered if our paper-doll idea was really about women who longed to be transformed. And so we set off in a different direction, one that wasn't about transforming others. No, this story grew into personal transformation as well.

I got closer to God to ask how women can get real, how their spirituality can be revealed. In the process I got closer to God. My big spiritual reveal happened in ways I never thought possible. The reason for all this is a serendipitous mystery to me. A miracle of mystery that may stick to me after all.

This must be the *why* of my belief, for I can sometimes be too analytical. The core of my belief in Christ comes down to a mystery, a feeling I can't name. I admit that I still fear death and all its aspects, but in some provincial way I cling to the magic tunnel of light, with Jesus beckoning me to join Dad on the other side.

Once when I questioned the existence of an afterlife, Kris told me about Pascal's wager. In the seventeenth century, Blaise Pascal said, "Belief is a wise wager. Granted that faith cannot be proved, what harm will come to you if you gamble on its truth and it proves false? . . . If you gain, you gain all; if you lose, you lose nothing. Wager then, without hesitation, that He exists."[1]

In other words, if I die believing in heaven and there isn't one, I won't know about it. These concepts helped me recommit myself to Jesus and the whole ball of wax. Still, I sometimes feel as if, as Buechner wrote, "the holy name of Jesus is my rabbit's foot, my charm against the evil eye and the dark."[2] I read those words and start to doubt myself again as nothing but a cheap Christian, looking for miracles as a form of entertainment.

And so often my faith is a story of doubt. But as Father Ted Berktold says, "Your story may be one of fear and searching, but so are the stories of the greatest saints." He urges us to tell our friends and family who we really are. "Tell how God has touched your life," he says, "your health, your career, your relationship." Berktold dares me to "let the Word of God in you become flesh, your flesh," and my questions are assuaged.[3]

In the middle of my doubt, the gospel is read and the people whoosh to their feet. I am caught up with them. Tears come and I sense that Jesus inhabits the air I suck in with ragged breaths. The faces of everyone around me shine for an instant, and I have a vision. The sum of belief is the convergence of the earthly makeover and eternal mystery of all I am—aging woman, wife, mother, friend, and Christian. All around me is the miracle that transforms: life itself and me in it.

Heather Harpham Kopp

God's Upraised Hand

Today I read from the prophet Isaiah in the Bible. He was a wild man. All I remember from today's reading was one phrase he kept saying over and over. He would tell them some terrible thing God was going to do to them. Then he'd say, Yet for all this, God's hand is still upraised. His hand is still upraised.

My son who plays football comes up to me almost every day, wanting to measure himself against me. To see if he comes higher on my body. You are still at my eyebrows, I tell him each day. Just like yesterday you are still at my eyebrows.

I told God this morning I didn't want to write today. I think we're moving toward the end of the book, I said. And it needs to be good. I see no point in trying to write it, since I don't feel very holy this morning. I'm not even up to your eyebrows, I said. Not even on tippy-toes.

Yesterday I went to my friend's church and talked to her women's group. It felt like church sometimes feels. They called me one of the "ladies," and they announced after the brunch, and after I spoke, they would offer a craft demonstration. A flower arrangement or a basket or something like that.

I probably didn't talk enough about God. Or about God the way they're used to God's being talked about. I imagined I saw lights in about five sets of eyes, out of thirty. An overweight woman with reddish hair kept crying during the prayer time. By the way several women went over to comfort her automatically, as if they had done it last week, I got the feeling that she always cries at these things. People get impatient with people like the woman with the reddish hair. How long will it take you to get over it? Or to get better?

Trust God, I pictured them saying to her. Trust God. And then I thought of God in the sky with his hand upraised. And I thought, No, watch out! Watch out!

How I loved those women. I really did! How I longed to open up some chamber in their hearts, like a dryer bin, and toss in something that would rattle and clatter until we all woke up again.

When we were young, my mom and stepdad took us to church sometimes. It seemed like nobody in that church knew God at all, but sometimes you could feel him there. His solemn side. And my favorite part, the only part that really moved me as a child, was the doxology.

The organ would start the blaring chord. And the congregation always knew what it meant, what was about to happen. We would all stand up and a shiver would rush down the back of my dress when the voices broke out. Praise God to whom all blessings flow. Praise him all creatures here below.

Everyone sang the last part louder than any other song in the service. Praise him above, ye heavenly host. And the minister would raise his hands, his black gown sleeves hanging down. Praise Father, Son, and Holy Ghost.

Yesterday my youngest son was sitting outside on the curb with his friends. I was on my way for a walk, and I stopped by and said, What are you boys doing? But I asked the question as if I were not one of their mothers and was merely an interested passerby.

We are making weapons! they said, glad for a grown-up to impress. And they held them up for me, their eyes squinting into the sun. Popsicle sticks they had shaved down to sharp points by rubbing them on the sidewalk.

Wow! I said. What are you boys going to use them for? And they said, Oh! We are going to go crow hunting. We are going to kill crows with them. Stab them in the chest! And they raised their hands in a jabbing motion for emphasis.

Oh, really? I said, acting very horrified and impressed. You would really do that?

Oh, yes! they gasped, delighted by my reaction. We would! We would! And I said, Poor birds. Poor little birds! And then I walked away shaking my head over the matter and I could feel their wide smiles behind my back, and I knew they could never.

This morning I noticed the sharpened sticks sitting on the stereo speaker. And I noticed they had no sign of blood on them. Praise him all creatures here below.

I told my friend that I walk with that her son wants to kill birds. I also told her that today God had his hand raised, threatening terrible things. And yet his hand was still upraised. And she said maybe that's because God doesn't really want to let it fall. He hates to.

My friend knows God.

While I was praying this morning, I glanced up to see the pinkest, thinnest cloud I've ever seen. It was almost a film. I could see through it to the dark green outline of the hills. I could even see the blue sky behind it.

It drifted, even as I watched it, holding my breath. And then it thinned and thinned until it was a puff of pink disappearing into the trees.

This is what my life feels like. My son grows up in an instant. A woman still cries and struggles. A boy couldn't kill a bird. A pink cloud passes over. God's hand is still upraised. And I cry, Holy! Holy! God is love! Watch out! Watch out!

Stepping Out Inspiration

Kristen Johnson Ingram

The God Who Knows Your Name

Forty years ago a musical called *Carnival*[4] appeared on Broadway. It starred Anna Maria Alberghetti, a tiny girl with a remarkable big voice. One of the best songs she sang was about her hometown in Mira, where everybody knew her name. "Imagine!" she sang, "can you imagine?"

Everybody knew her name!

I loved the music and played the records over and over, singing with Anna Maria and trying to imagine a town where everyone knew my name, where I would be welcome and received with honor, a place where I'd never be a stranger.

Such a place exists, but it's not a little Italian village. The place where everybody will recognize me is the City of God, a celestial realm where Jesus says I can spend eternity. And because God loves you, saves you, and knows your name, everyone in that city will honor you too and celebrate when you arrive.

I think a name is really important in the eternal scheme. All through the Bible, we read about people naming their children "because." In fact, Adam named his own wife Eve, which in Hebrew means "life," *because* she was the mother of all the living. God replaced the names of Abram and Sarai with Abraham and Sarah *because* they were called to be the parents of all the Hebrew people. When Jacob wrestled with God, he received a new name. Instead of Jacob—which means "supplanter," or even "trickster"—he would from that day be called Israel, *because* it means "struggles (or prevails) with God." Leah named her oldest son Reuben, "See, a son" *because* she believed God saw her unloved condition, and that a son would make Jacob love her. And so on, until Gabriel told Mary she would bear a son and call his name Jesus. Gabriel didn't have to say *because:* everyone already knew that Jesus, Joshua, *Y'shua*, means "Savior."

And in churches that use infant baptism, the priest or pastor, holding the shell with which he or she will scoop and pour water over the child's head in one hand and the baby on the other arm, looks at the parents and says, "Name this child."

I have three first names. I was baptized Dorothy Elizabeth Kristen Johnson; the Dorothy to honor my aunt/godmother, and Elizabeth for my grandmother. I don't answer to either of those, and like most women of my generation, I took my maiden surname for a middle name. So which one of these names does God know me by? I lay awake for a while last night, wondering, and then I decided that I'll know, whatever God calls me, whenever God calls me.

286

I sometimes think of what secret name God has for each of us—a name nobody else can know. The Dineh, or Navajo people, gave a child a name that nobody could hear. People would call a girl Gray Eyes' Daughter, or Sage Picker, or nowadays, by her American name: Sally or Melinda or Jessica. Her true name was ceremonial and spiritual and couldn't be sullied by public use. Some girls of the Dineh once received their secret tribal name at their *kinaalda*, or puberty ceremony.

Secret names occur in many cultures. In some of them, to know and use someone's true name was to exert control over the person, and legends even suggest that the secret name held the power of life and death. Other civilizations believed that everyone had a name known only to God, one he or she might receive in a dream or while running across a meadow or fighting in a war.

What all these ideas, stories, legends, and theories point to is that God knows every woman's name, whether it's the one on her birth certificate or one known to him alone. God writes the names of all who love him in the Book of Life, so I humbly believe my name is there; whether from before the foundation of the world or from the moment the water of baptism flowed over my head, I don't know.

So when I pray, I don't have to introduce myself. I don't have to say, "Excuse me? I'm Kris Ingram, Lord; do you remember me?" I don't have to grovel or prostrate myself or clear my throat to get God's attention; we are already acquainted and God condescends not only to know my name and write it in the Book of Life but to be present to me anytime I look for him. God treats me like a privileged only child.

And longs to treat you the same way.

God knows your name, cherishes you, and hovers over you the way a mother hovers over her little boy as he takes his first steps. The way a honeybee hovers over an orange blossom, perhaps savoring its perfume before sipping its honey. God's love wraps you in a blanket of sheer love, borderless, limitless, eternal love. Because not only does God know your name, God is calling it. God longs for your attention and keeps whispering your name until you fold your hands in prayer or turn your face up toward the heavens to answer him.

Can you imagine that? God knows your name. Listen. Listen. Do you hear?

Stepping Out Poem
Bobbie Christensen

Masks

"How are you?"
"Just fine."
But I ached
and couldn't say so
even though truth is what our lives are all about
and it's what we feel on the inside
when we talk to people on the outside.
Truthfully,
pain tried to reach my eyes,
but I suppressed it, beautifully, with a smile
as I answered the surface question,
"How are you?"

Scripture Salon
Kristen Johnson Ingram

The Unveiled Face

A Reflection on 2 Corinthians 3:18

And we, who with unveiled faces all reflect the Lord's glory, are being transformed into his likeness with ever-increasing glory, which comes from the Lord, who is the Spirit.

2 Corinthians 3:18 NIV

The aeroplane has unveiled for us the true face of the
earth.

Antoine de Saint-Exupery

She lay in state while world dignitaries took turns placing wreaths
beside her bier. He face was swollen in death, but it still shone, and
everybody remembered the light in her eyes, the halo that seemed to
leap all around her. She had reached out to "the poorest of the poor"
and used her Nobel and Templeton Prize moneys to alleviate the suffering of lepers and homeless people who were dying in the streets.
Her Catholic denomination will most certainly saint her, and the
light of her countenance still gleams in the world. Hers was a naked
face, an unveiled face that revealed her pure spirit and gave everyone
who saw her hope.

In the Old Testament, shining faces scared people. Moses had to
veil his countenance because his face glowed with the reflected glory
of God; the Israelites and even his brother, Aaron, were scared by the
sight, so he wore a veil. But about thirteen hundred years later, Paul
boasts of the Christian condition: "And all of us, with unveiled faces,
seeing the glory of the Lord as though reflected in a mirror, are being
transformed into the same image from one degree of glory to another;
for this comes from the Lord, the Spirit." Unlike the Israelites, who
were still new to the idea of a powerful and present deity, Christians
want the world to see glory shining out of their faces.

An unveiled face hides nothing. Without a covering you can ex-
pose a few defects. Being open means you let the rest of humanity see
exactly who you are, inside and out. Almost everyone has something
he or she wants to hide, and often it's the unveiled, vulnerable self,
the one who dwells in a quiet corner of a soul.

Why would a woman hide her own splendor? Sometimes because
society asks her to mask the truth or agree not to discuss what is
unpleasant. In some parts of the country, it's traditional to throw a
coverlet over opinions, perhaps with the smiling dismissal: "Oh, well,
maybe we'd better not talk about that." Though the woman with the
unpopular opinion may be right, and though everybody knows deep
down that she's right, her community may convince her that the truth

is too unpleasant for anyone to look at and that righteousness is scary or immodest.

Another woman may throw her veil not only over herself, but over her family or friends who are addicted or alcoholic or abusive or doing something criminal. Such a woman wears a veil of shame—not for her own sins, but for those of others. And she is convinced they need her help.

Or you could find another hidden behind a veil of perfection. She can quote Scripture like a prophet, her children have amazing manners, and she is the perfect wife, mother, daughter, Sunday school teacher, and cheerleader. The only problem is, she's miserable inside. She may not even know it; she's probably afraid to question God or the Bible or to admit her marriage leaves something to be desired. So she puts on her perfect mask, works like a beaver, and smiles at the world while slowly turning into nobody.

And then there's the woman who has survived sexual abuse, or who is anorexic or bulimic, or whose husband is a batterer: she lives her whole life under a dark tarpaulin, a sweltering veil that won't let her breathe until she throws it off. The one thing she's terrified of doing.

But if any of these women is willing to undergo spiritual transformation, if she will surrender herself to God's love and to the beauty of holiness, she can look in her mirror one day to discover that her skin is made of light, her eyes are like hot coals, and unveiled, beauty and holiness surround her like an aureole.

She will have escaped from the forces that pushed her into conformity. At first, she may only be praying differently, but soon her spiritual life will blaze like a star, gleaming as brightly as the sun; and she throws her veil into a bin with other rubbish. Only one veil is worthy of a godly woman: Christ himself is the screen over the most sacred part of heaven, and he invites us to come through him and into freedom.

Wrap yourself in that screen—come through it, with an ancient English prayer that had its roots in the souls of people who want God to uncover them, want God to see them as they are—the Collect for Purity, taken from *The Book of Common Prayer*: "Almighty God, to whom all hearts are open, all desires known, and from whom no secrets are hid: cleanse the thoughts of our hearts by the inspiration of the Holy Spirit, that we may perfectly love thee and worthily magnify thy holy Name, through Christ our Lord, to whom thee and the Holy Spirit belong all honor and glory. Amen."

Ideas for Reflection & Application

Something to Try On

- Host an impromptu tea party. Ask everyone who attends to dress up in costume or formal wear. Make laughter and fun the order of the day.
- Take a look at your planner. Is there anything unnecessary on your agenda? Places you could cut back? Reorganize your priorities and if necessary, practice saying no.
- Treat yourself to a facial, either in a salon or at home. As you relax under the mask, think about how your attitudes about yourself and others have changed as you've journeyed through *Revealed*. Are you still being "nice" in situations that call for getting real? Are your priorities the same now or different? Does God feel closer? How will you keep your transformation active and growing?

Notes

Chapter 2

1. Ruth Haley Barton, *The Truths That Free Us* (Colorado Springs: Shaw, 2002).

Chapter 3

1. "The Social Psychology of Driving," Trinity College, Department of Social Psychology, San Antonio, TX, 2003.

2. Virginia Ramey Mollencott, Evangelical and Ecumenical Update, Summer 2000. Mollencott is emeritus professor of English at William Paterson University in Wayne, New Jersey, a prolific author, and a much-in-demand speaker.

3. Ibid.

Chapter 4

1. Barton, *Truths*, 102.

2. Amy Dacyczyn, *The Complete Tightwad Gazette* (New York: Random House, 1999).

3. Joyce Landorf, *The Richest Lady in Town* (Grand Rapids: Zondervan, 1973).

4. Charles Swindoll, *Strengthening Your Grip* (Waco: Word, 1972).

Chapter 5

1. Steve Burns, M.D., www.teachhealth.com/dealwith.html.

2. Jose Luis Gonzales-Balado, *Mother Teresa* (New York: Gramercy/Random, 1997).

3. Anne Morrow Lindbergh, *Gift from the Sea* (New York: Pantheon, 1991).

Chapter 6

1. Desmond Tutu, cited in the *Utne Reader*, May/June 1998, 43.

2. Jack N. Sparks, "Epistle of Polycarp to the church at Philippi," *The Apostolic Fathers*, vol. 2 (Nashville: Thomas Nelson, 1978), 125.

3. Elizabeth Hilts, *Getting in Touch with Your Inner Bitch* (Bridgeport, CT: Hysteria, 1993), 21.

4. Henry Cloud and John Townsend, *Boundaries* (Grand Rapids: Zondervan, 1998), 108.

5. H. Norman Wright, *The Power of a Parent's Words* (Ventura, CA: Regal Books, 1991), 96

Chapter 7

1. Lesbia Scott, "I Sing a Song of the Saints of God," 1929.

2. Ibid.

3. Barton, *Truths*, 113.

4. Barbara Johnson, *Fresh Elastic for Stretched Out Moms* (Grand Rapids: Fleming H. Revell, 1986), 46

5. Translated by John Mason Neale, 1853.

Chapter 8

1. Dorothy Blomfield Gurney, "O Perfect Love," composed in 1883.

2. Erich Fromm, *Art of Loving* (New York: Harper & Row, 1957), 37.

3. www.hyperdictionary.com/dictionary/Mandrakes

4. Stanton Peele, *Love and Addiction* (New York: Taplinger, 1975).

5. Ibid.

6. Sheldon Vanauken, *A Severe Mercy* (London: Hodder and Stoughton, Vintage Reprint, 1998).

7. Joan Walsh Anglund, *A Friend Is Someone Who Likes You* (New York: Random House, 1992), 1.

Chapter 9

1. Philip Yancey, *What's So Amazing About Grace?* (Grand Rapids, Zondervan, 1997), 272.

2. James Kilgore, *Try Marriage Before Divorce* (Waco: Word, 1978), 50.

3. Sue Monk Kidd, *When the Heart Waits* (San Francisco: Harper & Row, 1990), 53

4. Ibid.

5. Barton, *Truths*, 33.

6. Evelyn Christenson, *Lord, Change Me!* (Wheaton: Victor Books, 1977), 13.

7. Charles Williams, *Descent into Hell* (New York: Pelligrini and Cudahy, 1949), 211.

Chapter 10

1. Eugenia Price, *No Pat Answers* (Grand Rapids: Zondervan, 1972), 10.

2. Ibid., 12.

3. Mark Mattison, "Women in the Church," www.auburn.edu/~allenkc/openhse/women.html.

4. Reta Halteman Finger, a Mennonite seminary professor and Pauline scholar, wrote a book called *Paul and the Roman House Churches* (Scottdale, PA: Herald Press, 1993). Christian study groups can use the book to simulate the meetings where Phoebe brought the letters, and it allows participants to play the roles of new Christians, Jews, Roman doubters, etc.

Chapter 11

1. C. S. Lewis, *The Four Loves* (New York: Harcourt Brace, 1960), 273.
2. Mendel Weinbach, the Ohr Somayach website, http://ohr.edu/yhiy.php/ohr_so mayach/.
3. Mechtilde of Magdeburg, *Meditations of Mechtilde of Magdeburg* (Brewster, Mass.: Paraclete, 1999).

Chapter 12

1. Blaise Pascal, *Pensées* (New York: E.P. Dutton and Co., 1958), xx.
2. Frederick Buechner, *The Alphabet of Grace* (New York: Harper & Row, 1979), 82.
3. Ted Berktold, sermon, St. Mary's Episcopal Church, Eugene, OR, July 13, 2003.
4. Later, the play became a movie, *Lili*, starring Leslie Caron.

About the Authors

Kristen Johnson Ingram has written and published extensively across a wide range of genres, including short stories, poems, "doctor's office" booklets on health and well-being, devotionals, and about two thousand newspaper and magazine articles on health, travel, folklore, history, religion, interviews, essays, nostalgia, how-to, psychology, domestic violence, and personal growth.

Kristen is the author of twenty nonfiction books, including *Wine at the End of the Feast*; *Beyond Words: 15 Ways of Doing Prayer*; *Devotions for Debtors*; *Devotions for Nibblers*; and the gift book *I'll Ask My Grandmother: She's Very Wise*. She has also published two murder mysteries, *Angel in the Senate* and *Rule of Silence*.

When she isn't writing or teaching writing, Kristen enjoys travel, photography, cooking, and spending time with her husband, Ron, their five grandsons and great-granddaughter, and her eighteen-pound criminal cat, Grendel.

Linda Clare came to freelance writing after a career teaching art in public schools in Arizona. She has published poems, stories, articles, and booklets on subjects ranging from child development to health issues and was nominated for a short story Pushcart Prize in 2004. She is the author of three nonfiction books including *Lost Boys* with Melody Carlson and Heather Harpham Kopp; and teaches novel, essay, and memoir writing at Lane Community College in Eugene, Oregon. She and her husband, Brad, have raised four children, including a set of twins, and currently keep busy with Oliver, Frances, and Xena, Warrior Kitty—three wayward cats that never do what they're told and clamor for tuna at all hours. When she's not writing or teaching, Linda enjoys creating fused glass art and taking walks to keep fit. She is at work on a memoir about her childhood experiences as a polio survivor in 1960s Shriner's hospitals.

About the Contributors

Joyce Carlson has lived off and on in the West African country of Mali for the last twenty years, where she (an anthropologist) and her husband (a linguist) have concentrated on ferreting out the speechways and lifeways of a group of Senufo people who call themselves the Supyire (meaning "the people").

Award-winning author **Melody Carlson** has published more than one hundred books for women, teens, and children, including *Three Days*. She and her husband and Labrador retriever enjoy an active lifestyle of hiking, biking, camping, and skiing in Central Oregon.

Bobbie Christenson lives in Harrisburg, Oregon, with her husband. Their two children are grown, and she is currently a librarian in a public school. She has written poetry for forty-eight years and is currently working on a screenplay.

Andrea Doering is editor-in-chief of Crossings Book Club. She has over ten years of experience in the CBA market, and her selection of books has been instrumental in the growth of America's largest Christian book club, now over 700,000 members. Prior to joining Crossings, Andrea worked for Dr. James Dobson's Focus on the Family ministry. She is author of several children's books and earned her M.A. in English and Creative Writing at the University of Maine.

Lonnie Hull DuPont is a poet living in rural Michigan, where she works as an editor. Her poems are frequently published in journals, anthologies, and periodicals, and in 2002 her poetry was nominated for a Pushcart Prize.

Heather Harpham Kopp is an editor and a best-selling author. Her dozens of books include *Roar! A Christian Family Guide to Narnia* and *The Dieter's Prayer Book*. She enjoys biking, Vanagon camping, and her husband's cooking. Kopp and her writer husband, David, have five adult children and live in Central Oregon.

Marlee LeDai is an author and editorial consultant who lives in the Pacific Northwest. Her latest books are *Go Girl: Finding Adventure Wherever Your Travels Lead* and *Living Spaces: Bringing Style and Spirit into Your Home*. Her life is defined by love of family, women's culture, and travel. She enjoys hiking, snowboarding, and fly fishing as well as writing.

Jo M'Gonigle is a mom, stepmom, grandmom; prefers Ben & Jerry's to the low-carb, nonfat, no sugar variety (as attested to by her cholesterol level); works at the church to serve the Lord and sometimes not; has silk plants mixed in with the real to encourage them to their full potential; can never remember if her husband likes soft-cooked or medium-cooked eggs for breakfast; and thirsts for rainy days on the Oregon coast.

Kathleen Ruckman is a published author of inspirational articles and essays included in national anthologies and Christian periodicals. She is also the author of two creation-based children's picture books. Her oldest son, Mark, was an avid collector of rocks and thunder eggs when he was little, forever asking questions, which inspired Kathleen herself to take a closer look even years later.

Luci Shaw is a poet, author, and co-founder and later president of Harold Shaw Publishers, and has been an adjunct faculty member and Writer in Residence since 1998 at Regent College, Vancouver,

Canada. A charter member of the Chrysostom Society of Writers, she's published eight volumes of poetry, including *Polishing the Petoskey Stone*, *Writing the River*, *The Angles of Light*, and *The Green Earth: Poems of Creation*. She has also edited three poetry anthologies and a festschrift, *The Swiftly Tilting Worlds of Madeleine L'Engle*.

Vinita Hampton Wright has been a book editor for fourteen years. Her fiction includes *Grace at Bender Springs*, *Velma Still Cooks in Leeway*, and *The Winter Seeking*. Her nonfiction includes *Simple Acts of Moving Forward* and *The Soul Tells a Story: Engaging Creativity with Spirituality in the Writing Life*. Wright facilitates creativity workshops across the country. She and her husband, Jim, a photographer, live in Chicago.

Acknowledgments

The idea for this book came out of a discussion at a writers' conference, with some inspiration from Revell editor Jeanette Thomason. We (Linda and Kris) met weekly for more than one year to try on ideas and bounce them off one another. We extended the conversation and invited other well-known Christian writers and poets to speak out in contributed work as well.

But so much more happened as a result of the writing. We gained a heightened awareness of God's presence and felt the need to reach more deeply into our own spiritual lives. We've seen how some of the chapters became very expensive, for they cost us and the contributors something—comfort, privacy, even sleep. Some chapters required many rewritings to make sure the ideas were accessible and contained what we believe God nudged to be written.

Our editor, Holly Halverson, gave this book focus and lent her expert eye to the entire concept. Thanks for everything. And to our readers, we thank God for your willingness to allow God's hand to make over your lives.

Kristen Johnson Ingram and Linda Clare

invite you to this sneak peek of their next book

Making Peace with a Dangerous God

We tiptoe toward God's heart, trembling.

We find God's presence so irresistible we'd go anywhere he is; at moments this pull toward his love overwhelms us. Other times, God is hard to understand, abrasive, even terrifying. We aren't sure what he wants from us, nor can we say for certain what we want from him. Right now Kris wants a bone marrow donor for her oldest grandson, and Linda pleads with God to help one of her children who's emotionally disturbed.

But what's the final goal? For God to fix what we want and provide us a hiding place, or for us to see God face to face?

Rowan Williams, archbishop of Canterbury, says God "always has to be rediscovered. Which means God always has to be heard or seen where there aren't yet words for him."

Journeying toward discovery of the wild, untamed, dangerous God of the cosmos, we have to jettison some of the popular errors we learned, the flimsy theology that surrounded us. We hear and see what we don't yet have words for. We write, struggle for the right phrase, pile books on the floors by our desks, leave trails of paper where we walk. The real project is to know God and translate that knowledge into terms we can grab on to.

There's this puzzle, the enigma of God, the uncovering of a hidden Divinity whose laughter warms us and whose majesty knocks us over backward. God is waiting to be rediscovered.

Join us for the trip of a lifetime, a journey to meet the dangerous God—the God who wants to devour us, who is, as C. S. Lewis said, always good but never safe.

Coming Spring 2006

ISBN 0-8007-3073-9